Mastering openFrameworks: Creative Coding Demystified

A practical guide to creating audiovisual interactive projects with low-level data processing using openFrameworks

Denis Perevalov

[PACKT] open source*
PUBLISHING   community experience distilled

BIRMINGHAM - MUMBAI

Mastering openFrameworks:
Creative Coding Demystified

First published: September 2013

Production Reference: 1160913

Published by Packt Publishing Ltd.
Livery Place
35 Livery Street
Birmingham B3 2PB, UK.

ISBN 978-1-84951-804-8

www.packtpub.com

Cover Image by Asher Wishkerman (wishkerman@hotmail.com)

Credits

Author

Denis Perevalov

Reviewers

Mathias Paumgarten

Tim Pulver

Acquisition Editor

Nikhil Karkal

Lead Technical Editor

Sweny M. Sukumaran

Technical Editors

Sharvari Baet

Aparna Kumari

Hardik B. Soni

Copy Editors

Aditya Nair

Brandt D'Mello

Gladson Monteiro

Adithi Shetty

Project Coordinators

Shiksha Chaturvedi

Hardik Patel

Proofreader

Mario Cecere

Indexer

Priya Subramani

Production Coordinator

Arvindkumar Gupta

Cover Work

Arvindkumar Gupta

Foreword

Confucius said, "Choose a job you love, and you will never have to work a day in your life". Probably this piece of wisdom is meant right for you. Maybe you have already found your vocation. Maybe you are just looking for it. Anyway there's something that made you take this book. If so, let me tell you a little story.

My name is Igor Tatarnikov, also known as Sodazot. I'm an artist, although not by my education, but rather by my way of life. I keep on looking for a new and interesting occupation to take up. I've had different hobbies. I've tried a lot of jobs.

Three years ago I didn't even think about the interactive video, although my major occupation at that time was making video clips. I used to employ the stop-motion technique combined with computer animation. I also did some filming. By the by I grew more and more interested in the live VJ performances and generative video. I began experimenting with different techniques and posted my clips on the Internet.

At the same time there appeared the first available depth camera - Microsoft Kinect on offer. After it, things went crazy. Hundreds of video clips with reviews and tests of this camera's possibilities appeared every day on the Net. I took an interest in it all and kept track of the news. Watching the possibilities displayed I got a lot of new creative ideas. And finally my friends presented me the gadget. Of course I was happy, but at first I lost my head and didn't know what to do with it.

Also, it was not long since one person had written me an e-mail asking for permission to use my experimental video clip in his lecture for the students. I gladly agreed and since then we've been communicating by e-mail. It happened that this man lived in Ekaterinburg and we were thousands of kilometers apart.

As we communicated, we found a lot of common interests and decided to do something together. My head was boiling with ideas. I drew lots of sketches, shared them all with my friend, and he knew how to put them to life using the openFrameworks toolkit. We took counsel and the discussions brought us even more new ideas.

So we created our first commercial project for a special event at one of the Moscow cinemas. It was a funny video installation, where the picture responded to the visitor's movements. Coming up to the screen, a visitor saw himself as a funny character. The visitors of the event liked it very much and our big customers were happy — they played before the screen of the installation like children. We enjoyed the result of the work and it inspired us to create something new.

We've been working together for two years since and we've made several interesting and successful projects, using openFrameworks as our main tool. This is how our visual laboratory Kuflex was created. Our projects now grow more complicated and interesting, and our team became more and more numerous. We also work with musicians, artists, dancers, architects, and we have recently created a project with a real symphony orchestra.

If you still haven't guessed, I'll tell you that the friend with whom everything started is the author of this book Denis Perevalov.

The content of the book is based on our experience of creating interactive installations and performances. It teaches you the openFrameworks' multimedia capabilities and the principles of their usage for building interactive projects, which work with video, 3D graphics, sound, and cameras. The core of the book consists of the real working examples of projects for openFrameworks. Some of them are based on our works, the others were designed exclusively for this book. Besides, across the text you will find hints that will help you avoid many pitfalls in the practical use of openFrameworks.

Study openFrameworks, invent, and create your own projects and soon you'll realize that you can implement practically everything you can imagine using it.

Igor (Sodazot) Tatarnikov,
Artist

About the Author

Denis Perevalov is a computer vision research scientist. He works at the Institute of Mathematics and Mechanics of the Ural Branch of the Russian Academy of Sciences (Ekaterinburg, Russia). He is the co-author of two Russian patents on robotics computer vision systems and an US patent on voxel graphics. Since 2010 he has taught openFrameworks in the Ural Federal University. From 2011 he has been developing software for art and commercial interactive installations at `kuflex.com` using openFrameworks. He is the co-founder of interactive technologies laboratory `expo32.ru` (opened in 2012).

Acknowledgement

I would like to thank my family—wife Svetlana and son Timofey for their patience and suggestions. And many thanks to my parents and grandparents for great pirozhki, which was a necessary part of the book-writing process.

My creative coding experience and the desire to write the book appeared, thankfully, to artist Igor Sodazot, who invented and designed most of the interactive installations, which I program for him using openFrameworks. He is the coauthor of most of the book's examples and its video/audio contents.

Thanks to my scientific supervisor Victor Borisovich Kostousov for expending so many efforts to shape my scientific style of thinking and writing.

I would like to thank my colleagues working at interactive media art, experimental music, and dance fields—Prof. Yoichi Nagashima, Tatyana Komarova, Ekaterina Zharinova, and my first curator Ksenia Fedorova, for their teaching and influence.

And big thanks to my friends and scientific colleagues for supporting me and helping me with ideas: Nikolay Mikhalev, Sergey Samuraev, Kirill Kostousov, Fedor Kornilov, Elizaveta Sayfutdinova, and Prof. Pavel Konstantinovich Kuznetzov.

This book would be impossible without hard work on proof-reading by Angelina Poptzova, and technical reviewing by Mathias Paumgarten and Tim Pulver.

Thanks to Packt Publishing, who made this book possible.

Thanks to the openFrameworks' creators and openFrameworks community for developing this amazing toolkit.

All the book's examples were developed together with Igor Sodazot, except the *Dancing cloud example*, which is based on the idea of *nCode* installation by Andrey Krel, Igor Sodazot, Denis Perevalov, and Pavel Tikhonenko (2011, Moscow).

About the Reviewers

Mathias Paumgarten is a creative developer from Austria. He is currently living and working in Santa Monica, California.

Starting with a background in Flash development, Mathias found his passion for code-driven animation at a very young age. Over the years while working for and at several agencies he has broadened his skillset by leaving the web platform and working on installations using low-level languages such as C/C++.

After graduating with a Bachelor's degree at the University of Applied Sciences, Salzburg, Austria, he decided to leave Austria while focusing on modern web technologies such as HTML5 and JavaScript, currently working as a frontend JavaScript developer.

Mathias has worked for several renowned agencies such as B-Reel, Soap Creative, and Firstborn working on projects for Sony, Fox Entertainment, Pepsi Co., and many more.

After receiving recognitions such as FWA and other awards, Mathias has also contributed to publications such as HTML5 Games Most Wanted.

Tim Pulver is an interaction design student from Potsdam, Germany. As a teenager he was fascinated by the demo scene and how people were able to transform code into something beautiful. He now uses Processing, openFrameworks, and Arduino to create interactive installations, data-visualizations, and user-interface prototypes.

One of his recent projects is interactive fulldome data visualization, where users can playfully explore global crop production.

In another project, Tim wrote a program that translated an image of an eye based on its structure into unique jewelry, which was printed out using a 3D printer.

He likes the idea of sharing and free culture. In 2011, he founded the electronic music netlabel Yarn Audio, which supports sharing and remixing of released music. All the cover artwork for this netlabel has been generated using custom made tools, too. You can contact him at `http://www.timpulver.de`.

I would like to thank my family for their support and Hanna Schatz, Paul Vollmer, Kim Albrecht, Fabian Althaus, and Martin von Lupin for great collaboration.

www.PacktPub.com

Support files, eBooks, discount offers and more

You might want to visit www.PacktPub.com for support files and downloads related to your book.

Did you know that Packt offers eBook versions of every book published, with PDF and ePub files available? You can upgrade to the eBook version at www.PacktPub.com and as a print book customer, you are entitled to a discount on the eBook copy. Get in touch with us at service@packtpub.com for more details.

At www.PacktPub.com, you can also read a collection of free technical articles, sign up for a range of free newsletters and receive exclusive discounts and offers on Packt books and eBooks.

http://PacktLib.PacktPub.com

Do you need instant solutions to your IT questions? PacktLib is Packt's online digital book library. Here, you can access, read and search across Packt's entire library of books.

Why Subscribe?
- Fully searchable across every book published by Packt
- Copy and paste, print and bookmark content
- On demand and accessible via web browser

Free Access for Packt account holders

If you have an account with Packt at www.PacktPub.com, you can use this to access PacktLib today and view nine entirely free books. Simply use your login credentials for immediate access.

Table of Contents

Preface

openFrameworks is a simple and powerful C++ toolkit designed to develop real-time projects with focus on generating and processing graphics and sound. Nowadays, this is a popular platform for experiments in generative and sound art and creating interactive installations and audiovisual performances.

Mastering openFrameworks: Creative Coding Demystified covers programming openFrameworks 0.8.0 for Windows, Mac OS X, and Linux. It provides a complete introduction to openFrameworks, including installation, core capabilities, and addons. Advanced topics like shaders, computer vision, and depth cameras are also covered.

You will learn everything you need to know to create your own projects, ranging from simple generative art experiments to big interactive systems consisting of a number of computers, depth cameras, and projectors.

This book focuses on low-level data processing, which allows you to create really unique and cutting-edge works.

What this book covers

7 *Chapter 1, openFrameworks Basics,* covers installing openFrameworks, the structure of openFrameworks projects, and creating the pendulum-simulation project.

3 2 *Chapter 2, Drawing in 2D,* explains the basics of two-dimensional graphics, including drawing geometric primitives, working with colors and drawing in the offscreen buffer. It also contains a generative art example of using numerical instability for drawing.

59 *Chapter 3, Building a Simple Particle System,* teaches the basics of particle system modeling and drawing. By the end of this chapter, you will build a fully featured project that can be used as a sketch for further experiments with particles.

83 *Chapter 4, Images and Textures,* covers the principles of working with images, including loading images from file; rendering it on the screen with different sizes, color, and transparency; creating new images; and modifying existing images. It also touches the basics of image warping and video mapping.

113 *Chapter 5, Working with Videos,* covers basic and advanced topics on playing, layering, and processing videos, including playing video files, processing live video grabbed from a camera, and working with image sequences. This chapter contains an implementation of the slit-scan effect and a simple video synthesizer, which uses a screen-to-camera feedback loop to create vivid effects on prerecorded videos.

145 *Chapter 6, Working with Sounds,* explains how to play sound samples, synthesize new sounds, and get sounds from the microphone. It includes the project wherein we generate music using bouncing-ball simulation, the PWM synthesizer, and the image-to-sound transcoding. Finally, it teaches us how to use spectrum analysis for creating an audio-reactive visual project.

183 *Chapter 7, Drawing in 3D,* covers representing, modifying, and drawing 3D objects. It includes examples of drawing a sphere-shaped cloud of triangles, an oscillating surface, and a twisting 3D knot.

211 *Chapter 8, Using Shaders,* explains how to use fragment, vertex, and geometry shaders for creating 2D video effects and 3D object deformations.

239 *Chapter 9, Computer Vision with OpenCV,* teaches the basics of computer vision using the OpenCV library. It explains how to perform filtering and correct perspective distortions in images and how to look for motion areas and detect bright objects in the videos. It includes an advanced example of using optical flow for video morphing.

281 *Chapter 10, Using Depth Cameras,* covers using depth cameras in openFrameworks projects using the ofxOpenNI addon. It includes an example of the projector-camera interactive system, which lets us draw abstract images on the wall. The example can be used as a sketch for creating interactive walls, tables, and floors.

301 *Chapter 11, Networking,* covers how to use OSC and TCP protocols in your openFrameworks projects for creating distributed projects that run on several computers. It includes an image-streaming example.

311 *Appendix A, Working with Addons,* teaches the basic principles of addons, explains how to link addons to your projects, and discusses some of the most useful addons.

321 *Appendix B, Perlin Noise,* explains the principles of using Perlin noise, which is employed in many of the examples in the book.

What you need for this book

For working with this book's examples and creating your openFrameworks projects, you need a computer with the Windows, Mac OS X, or Linux operating system.

You will also need to install some development environment (Visual Studio C++ Express, Xcode, or Code::Blocks) and openFrameworks itself. In the first chapter of the book, you will find detailed instructions for installation. All required software are free.

Some examples can require additional equipment:

- *The video synthesizer example* section in *Chapter 5, Working with Videos*, and the *The streaming images example* section in *Chapter 11, Networking*, need a webcam for grabbing live video. If you are using a laptop, it most probably has a built-in webcam.

- *The loop sampler example* section in *Chapter 6, Working with Sounds*, needs a microphone. If you are using a laptop, it most probably has a built-in microphone.

- *The furry carpet example* section in *Chapter 8, Using Shaders*, uses a geometry shader, and therefore needs a modern video card.

- The *Creating interactive surface* section in *Chapter 10, Using Depth Cameras*, needs a depth camera like Microsoft Kinect, Asus Xtion, or PrimeSense Carmine. Having a projector would be ideal, but is not compulsory.

Who this book is for

If you are a visual artist, designer, or programmer interested in creative coding with openFrameworks, this book is for you. Basic knowledge of programming, such as C++, Java, Python, or ActionScript, would be helpful.

Conventions

In this book, you will find a number of styles of text that distinguish between different kinds of information. Here are some examples of these styles, and an explanation of their meaning.

Code words in text, database table names, folder names, filenames, file extensions, pathnames, dummy URLs, user input, and Twitter handles are shown as follows: "Now you can call `setNormals( mesh )` and the normals will be computed."

A block of code is set as follows:

```
for ( int i=0; i<16; i++ ) {
    table[i] = ofRandom( 0, 255 );
}
```

When we wish to draw your attention to a particular part of a code block, the relevant lines or items are set in bold:

```
for ( int i=0; i<16; i++ ) {
    table[i] = ofRandom( 0, 255 );
}
```

Any command-line input or output is written as follows:

```
ping 192.168.0.3
```

New terms and **important words** are shown in bold. Words that you see on the screen, in menus or dialog boxes for example, appear in the text like this: "Go to http://www.codeblocks.org, click on the **Downloads** menu item, and click on **Download the binary release**."

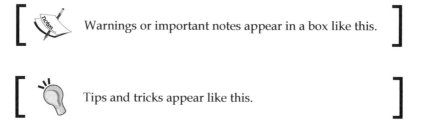

Warnings or important notes appear in a box like this.

Tips and tricks appear like this.

Reader feedback

Feedback from our readers is always welcome. Let us know what you think about this book—what you liked or may have disliked. Reader feedback is important for us to develop titles that you really get the most out of.

To send us general feedback, simply send an e-mail to feedback@packtpub.com, and mention the book title via the subject of your message.

If there is a topic that you have expertise in and you are interested in either writing or contributing to a book, see our author guide on www.packtpub.com/authors.

Customer support

Now that you are the proud owner of a Packt book, we have a number of things to help you to get the most from your purchase.

Downloading the example code

You can download the example code files for all Packt books you have purchased from your account at http://www.packtpub.com. If you purchased this book elsewhere, you can visit http://www.packtpub.com/support and register to have the files e-mailed directly to you.

Downloading the color graphics PDF

For downloading the colored graphics of this book visit: http://www.packtpub.com/sites/default/files/downloads/8048OS_ColoredImages.pdf

Errata

Although we have taken every care to ensure the accuracy of our content, mistakes do happen. If you find a mistake in one of our books—maybe a mistake in the text or the code—we would be grateful if you would report this to us. By doing so, you can save other readers from frustration and help us improve subsequent versions of this book. If you find any errata, please report them by visiting http://www.packtpub.com/submit-errata, selecting your book, clicking on the **errata submission form** link, and entering the details of your errata. Once your errata are verified, your submission will be accepted and the errata will be uploaded on our website, or added to any list of existing errata, under the Errata section of that title. Any existing errata can be viewed by selecting your title from http://www.packtpub.com/support.

Piracy

Piracy of copyright material on the Internet is an ongoing problem across all media. At Packt, we take the protection of our copyright and licenses very seriously. If you come across any illegal copies of our works, in any form, on the Internet, please provide us with the location address or website name immediately so that we can pursue a remedy.

Please contact us at copyright@packtpub.com with a link to the suspected pirated material.

We appreciate your help in protecting our authors, and our ability to bring you valuable content.

Questions

You can contact us at questions@packtpub.com if you are having a problem with any aspect of the book, and we will do our best to address it.

1
openFrameworks Basics

In this chapter you will get acquainted with openFrameworks, learn its specifics and cases when you should use it. Also you will study how to install openFrameworks, run its examples, and make your first openFrameworks project:

- Installing openFrameworks and running your first example
- File structure of a project
- Code structure of a project
- Creating a first project – the Pendulum example
- Running the book's examples

About openFrameworks

openFrameworks is an open source C++ toolkit for creative coding. It was initially released by *Zachary Lieberman* in 2005. Today openFrameworks is one of the main creative coding platforms, which is actively developed by *Zachary Lieberman*, *Theodore Watson*, and *Arturo Castro* with help from the openFrameworks community.

 The current openFrameworks' version is 0.8.0.

The toolkit is indebted to two significant precursors: the Processing development environment, created by *Casey Reas*, *Ben Fry*, and the Processing community; and the ACU Toolkit, a privately distributed C++ library developed by *Ben Fry* and others in the MIT Media Lab's Aesthetics and Computation Group.

openFrameworks' website is `http://openframeworks.cc`. It contains latest downloads, documentation, tutorials, and forums.

The main purpose of openFrameworks is to provide users with an easy access to multimedia, computer vision, networking, and other capabilities in C++ by gluing many open libraries into one package. Namely, it acts as a wrapper for libraries such as OpenGL, FreeImage, and OpenCV. The term wrapper means that openFrameworks provides you with new functions and classes, and gives hints on a project structure, but does not limit you. Namely, you can still use all of the C++ capabilities, and directly call functions from all of the linked libraries without using the wrapper's classes.

openFrameworks is cross-platform compatible with Windows, Mac OS X, Linux, iOS, and Android as the supported platforms. It means that if you develop a project for one of the platforms, you can copy the source files and compile the project for any other platform from the list. In the book we will cover developing a project for Windows, Mac OS X, and Linux only. Though many of the examples considered will work on mobile platforms too.

There are many great projects made with openFrameworks. Here are a few "classical" ones:

- *Funky Forest* by *Emily Gobeille* and *Theodore Watson*, *2007* – the interactive forest installation
- *Body Paint* by *Mehmet Akten*, *2009* – drawing on the wall by moving the user's body
- *Hand from Above* by *Chris O'Shea*, *2009* – outdoor installation working on a big billboard and interacting with pedestrians

Use cases

openFrameworks has the following architectural specifics:

- Its core is based around multimedia, including 2D and 3D graphics, images, video, and sound. So openFrameworks is especially appropriate for developing multimedia projects working in real-time environments.
- It works using C++ language, which implies that the code is compiled into native machine instructions and hence works very fast. So it lets you create computing-intensive, ground-breaking projects, using the top capabilities of modern computing technologies.

Such specifics determine cases when you should and should not use openFrameworks for a project development.

You definitely can employ openFrameworks when:

- You need to make a creative coding project, such as an interactive audio-visual installation or performance, which works with multimedia in a nontrivial and custom way. Namely, such a project would render a custom particle system, apply effects such as video morphing and slit-scan, or even perform data transcoding.

- You need to create a project, which performs intensive data analysis, for example, analyzing data from depth cameras.

Maybe you should not use openFrameworks when:

- The project is centered on working with visual controls such as buttons, checkboxes, lists, and sliders. In this case the better option is in using developing platforms like QT, Cocoa, or .Net.

openFrameworks contains a number of classes implementing visual controls like buttons and sliders, which are great for creating simple graphical user interfaces. But currently visual interface is not the main focus of the openFrameworks' evolution.

- The project does not use multimedia or intensive computations a lot. For example, if you just want to send simple commands to a robot, it is definitely simpler to use Processing.

Though openFrameworks is an open source project, currently you can use it for developing commercial projects (see details in the openFrameworks license at http://www.openframeworks.cc/about/license.html). To protect the project's content, to add licensing, and to create an installer, you should use special additional software. Note that all of this software is included in iOS and Android development kits, so commercial developing for mobile platforms is quite easy.

Installing openFrameworks and running your first example

Now we will consider how to install openFrameworks in Windows, Mac OS X, and Linux, and execute one of the openFrameworks' examples.

Historically (and currently) openFrameworks works best in Mac OS X. So when we use openFrameworks in interactive performances, we often do it in Mac OS X. Because performance is a short event (5 to 30 minutes), it is highly critical the software works as maximally fast and stable as it can.

For interactive installations, which are exhibited for a longer time (hours to months), and rare interruption in work is not so critical, we use any OS, depending on the available hardware.

The installation files and setup guides for all supported operating systems are located at http://www.openframeworks.cc/download/. Let's consider them in detail.

Installing on Windows

Within Windows 7 and 8 there are two choices of programming environments: Microsoft Visual Studio and Code::Blocks. Microsoft Visual Studio is one of the most popular environments in the world. It is very mature and stable. Many libraries (included and not included in openFrameworks) are adopted for Visual Studio. So if you are a novice in C++ programming, but you know that you need to link additional libraries in your project, Visual Studio is the best option for you.

Code::Blocks is a more lightweight environment and some developers prefer to use it. If you are a novice and just want to play with openFrameworks in simple projects, you should probably to do it with Code::Blocks.

Microsoft Visual Studio

The current version of Microsoft Visual Studio is 2012. In general Microsoft Visual Studio 2012 is a commercial software. But it has a lightweight free version, Microsoft Visual Studio Express, which is full enough for developing projects with openFrameworks.

The installation steps are as follows:

1. Install Microsoft Visual Studio Express 2012 for Windows Desktop. Navigate to `http://microsoft.com`, enter `Visual Studio Express 2012 for Windows Desktop download` in the search line, and press *Enter* to start searching. Click the **Download** button. When downloading page opens, press the **Install now** button. Then you will go through the process of installation. When installation is finished, run Visual Studio and register it (registration is free).

2. Download the openFrameworks' archive. Go to `http://www.openframeworks.cc/download/` and download the version for Visual Studio. The downloaded ZIP file should be named like `of_v0.8.0_vs_release.zip`. Unzip the downloaded file; it will be a folder containing openFrameworks. Move the folder to any location on your computer, for example, `C:\openFrameworks`.

3. Let's compile and run some example to verify openFrameworks is working correctly. Navigate to the `examples/3d/pointCloudExample` openFrameworks folder and open `pointCloudExample.sln` in Visual Studio.

4. Press *F7* to compile the project.

5. Press *F5* to run the project.

6. You will see an application window with a boy's face made from 3D points as shown in the following screenshot:

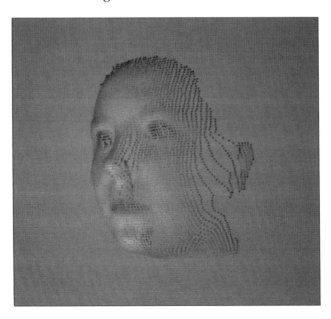

7. Press the left mouse button and move the mouse to rotate the face, or press the right mouse button and move the mouse to scale the face.

To understand the code of the example you need to learn how to work with images and 3D graphics, see *Chapter 4, Images and Textures*, and *Chapter 7, Drawing in 3D*. For creating your own point cloud, for example, from your own face, you need to learn how to work with depth cameras, see *Chapter 10, Using Depth Cameras*. Also check out the description of the project's files in the *File structure of a project* section.

8. Also, note the second window associated with the running application. It is colored in black and possibly contains some text. This is a console window, where openFrameworks writes various information, warnings, and errors. When you have some problems, check the contents of this window.

9. Now press *Esc* for closing the application.

You have successfully run the openFrameworks example and now can develop your own projects.

If you try to run a project made with Visual Studio on some other computer, it will probably not start, and show an error message. The possible reason is that you need to install Visual Studio redistributables. To download it, go to http://microsoft.com, enter Visual C++ Redistributable for Visual Studio in the search line, and press *Enter* to start searching. Click on the first search result and download the installation file.

Before installing the redistributables, try to run your project. Maybe it will work.

Code::Blocks (Windows)

Code::Blocks is an open source development environment for Windows. The current version is 12.11. The installation steps are as follows:

1. Install Code::Blocks. Go to http://www.codeblocks.org, click on the **Downloads** menu item, and click on **Download the binary release**. Then select the file to download, which includes **mingw**. For example, codeblocks-12.11mingw-setup.exe.

2. Install additions for Code::Blocks, which are needed for openFrameworks working. Go to `http://www.openframeworks.cc/setup/codeblocks/` and see instructions in the **Add files to MinGW** section.

3. Download the openFrameworks archive. Go to `http://www.openframeworks.cc/download/` and download openFrameworks for Code::Blocks (Windows). The downloaded ZIP file should be named like `of_v0.8.0_win_cb_release`. Unzip the downloaded file; it will be a folder containing openFrameworks. Move the folder to any location on your computer, for example, `C:\openFrameworks`.

4. Let's compile and run an example to verify openFrameworks is working correctly. Navigate to the `examples/3d/pointCloudExample` openFrameworks folder and open `pointCloudExample.workspace` in Code::Blocks.

5. The first time you open Code::Blocks it will ask you which compiler you want to use. Be sure **GNU GCC Compiler** is selected and continue.

6. Press the **Build** button and then the **Run** button:

7. Follow the steps 6, 7, 8, and 9 from the *Microsoft Visual Studio* section.

Installing on Mac OS with Xcode

We will be using Mac OS X 10.8.4 and Xcode 4.6.3. The installation steps are as follows:

1. Install Xcode by downloading it from the Mac App Store.

2. Download the openFrameworks archive. Go to `http://www.openframeworks.cc/download/` and download openFrameworks for Xcode. The downloaded ZIP file should be named like `of_v0.8.0_osx_release`. Unzip the downloaded file; it will be a folder containing openFrameworks. Move the folder to any location on your computer, for example, on the desktop.

3. Let's compile and run some examples to verify openFrameworks is working correctly. Navigate to the `examples/3d/pointCloudExample` openFrameworks folder and open `pointCloudExample.xcodeproj` in Xcode.

4. The project in Xcode contains several schemes for building openFrameworks and the example itself. For compiling your project, you need to select the example's scheme. Check it out. If the current scheme is openFrameworks, you will see the following button:

5. Click on it on the left-hand side and select the example project, `pointCloudExample`:

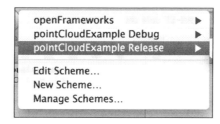

6. Press *Command + B* to compile the project.

7. Press the **Run** button.

8. Follow the steps 6, 8, and 9 from the *Microsoft Visual Studio* section. (Considering step 7, describing console window, the separate console window does not appear in Mac OS X, and all such information is printed in the Xcode console.)

Downloading the color graphics PDF

For downloading the colored graphics of this book visit:
`http://www.packtpub.com/sites/default/files/downloads/8040OS_ColoredImages.pdf`

Installing on Linux with Code::Blocks

This section will guide you in installing openFrameworks for Code::Block on the Ubuntu version of Linux. The current version is 12.11.

You can install openFrameworks not only on Ubuntu, but also on Debian and Fedora versions of Linux. See installation guides at `http://www.openframeworks.cc/setup/linux-codeblocks/`.

Also, you can use Eclipse development environment instead of Code::Blocks. See `http://www.openframeworks.cc/setup/linux-eclipse/`.

The installation steps are as follows:

1. Install Code::Blocks. In the main menu in Ubuntu, click on the **Dash** home icon, search for **Ubuntu Software Center**, and open it by selecting the **Ubuntu Software Center** icon. Search for Code Blocks here. The Code::Blocks program should be the first item listed. Click on the **Install** button and follow the instructions.

2. Download the openFrameworks archive. Go to `http://www.openframeworks.cc/download/` and download openFrameworks for Code::Blocks (Linux), for a 32- or 64-bit operating system. The downloaded ZIP file should be named like `of_v0.8.0_linux_release.tar` or `of_v0.8.0_linux64_release.tar`. Unzip the downloaded file; it will be a folder containing openFrameworks. Move the folder to any location on your computer.

3. Now you should install openFrameworks by running some scripts from Terminal. Please refer to `http://www.openframeworks.cc/setup/linux-codeblocks/` for detailed instructions.

4. Follow the steps 4, 5, 6, and 7 from the *Code::Blocks (Windows)* section for installation steps on running an openFrameworks example.

openFrameworks' folders

Till now we have installed openFrameworks and checked its working. Let's explore the contents of its folder. It consists of a number of folders, including addons, apps, examples, libs, projectGenerator, and text files such as license.md and readme.txt.

 It is a good idea to read the license file license.md carefully before using openFrameworks.

Let's consider some of the most important folders in detail.

The examples folder

This folder contains simple examples covering almost all the aspects of openFrameworks, sorted by the following topics:

- 3d: This folder demonstrates the basics of 3D graphics and 3D math (see *Chapter 7, Drawing in 3D*, for more information on the topic)

- addons: This folder contains examples of using various addons, which are extensions of openFrameworks' core (see *Appendix A, Working with Addons*, for more information on the topic)

- communication: This folder contains examples of communicating with peripherals using serial port (most often via USB), for example, for connecting with Arduino

- empty: This folder contains emptyExample, the simplest project for openFrameworks, which we will use as a starting point for developing most of the examples across the book

- events: This folder demonstrates built-in openFrameworks' event system usage, like key pressing and timing, and also working with custom event objects

- gl: This folder contains advanced examples on 2D and 3D graphics, including FBO, VBO, and shaders (see *Chapter 2, Drawing in 2D*, *Chapter 7, Drawing in 3D*, and *Chapter 8, Using Shaders*, for detailed information on these topics)

- graphics: This folder demonstrates basic 2D graphics capabilities and working with images (see *Chapter 2, Drawing in 2D*, and *Chapter 4, Images and Textures*, for more information on these topics)

- gui: This folder exposes how to add graphical user interface, containing buttons, sliders, and checkboxes to an openFrameworks project

- `math`: This folder has examples on working with Perlin noise, simple particle system, and also with vector mathematics (see *Appendix B, Perlin noise*, and *Chapter 3, Building a Simple Particle System*, for more information on these topics)

- `sound`: This folder contains examples that demonstrate how to play, generate at low-level, and record sounds (see *Chapter 6, Working with Sounds*, for more information on the topic)

- `utils`: This folder demonstrates working with small but important topics such as converting values between different types (for example, converting int to string), working with directories, and using threads

- `video`: This folder demonstrates how to play videos, process video frames, and grab live video from camera (see *Chapter 5, Working with Videos*, for more information on the topic)

Though most of the topics will be covered in this book, we highly recommend that you run and see as many examples of the code as you can. It is very helpful for dipping into the openFrameworks world.

The apps folder

This is a folder, in which all your projects should live. More specifically, you should place the projects inside some subfolder of the `apps` folder. By now this folder contains the `myApps` folder, and you can use it for your projects. Also you can create new folders, like `Performances2014`, and place corresponding projects there.

Note, if you will try to compile a project placed outside a subfolder of the `apps` folder, the compiler can give an error that it can not find the openFrameworks library.

The addons folder

This folder contains addons. These are the extensions of the basic openFrameworks capabilities. When you need to add some extension to openFrameworks, you will install it into this folder. We discuss the addons in detail in *Appendix A, Working with Addons*.

File structure of a project

All openFrameworks projects have a similar structure of folders and files. Let's consider this in detail by looking at the openFrameworks' `pointCloudExample` project.

Open the `examples/3d/pointCloudExample` folder. It consists of the following files and folders:

- The `bin` folder contains an executable file of the project (maybe also a number of libraries in the `.dll` files will be there—it depends on your operating system). If you compile the project, as it is described in the *Installing openFrameworks and running your first example* section, most probably you will find there is an executable file named `pointCloudExample_debug`.

  The `_debug` suffix means that the project was compiled in the **Debug** mode of compilation. This mode lets you debug the project by using breakpoints and other debugging tools.

   Breakpoint is a debugging tool, which pauses execution of the project in a specified line of code and lets you inspect the current values of the project's variables.

  Projects compiled in the **Debug** mode can work very slowly. So when your project is working properly, always compile it in the **Release** mode of the compilation. Many examples in the book should be compiled in the **Release** mode for good performance. In this case, the executable file will be called without the `_debug` suffix, such as `pointCloudExample`.

- Also, inside the `bin` folder you will find the `data` subfolder. This is a folder where all your contents should be located: images, videos, sounds, XML, and text files. openFrameworks projects use this folder as a default place for loading and saving the data.

  In the considered project, this folder contains one image file named `linzer.png`.

   This image consists of pixels, which hold red, green, blue, and alpha color components (`red`, `green`, `blue`, `alpha`). Each image's pixel (x, y) is transformed into a 3D point (x, y, z) with color (r, g, b, a), so that the point's third coordinate z is calculated from the `alpha` value. As a result we obtain the resultant 3D point cloud, which is drawn on the screen. (See *Chapter 4, Images and Textures*, for details on getting the pixels' colors from the images.)

- The `src` folder contains C++ source codes for your project. Often, source codes are represented in just three files: `main.cpp`, `testApp.h`, and `testApp.cpp`. We will consider these files a bit later, in the *Code structure of a project* section. Note that this folder can contain other `.h` and `.cpp` files of your project.

Also the project's folder contains a special project file for your development environment. It has extension `.sln` (Visual Studio), `.xcodeproj` (Xcode), or `.workspace` (Code::Blocks). This is the file which you should open in your development environment in order to edit, compile, and run the project. (In the considered example it has the name `pointCloudExample.sln`, `pointCloudExample.xcodeproj`, or `pointCloudExample.workspace`.)

Additionally, the project's folder can contain some other files, for example, the current project settings (the set of files depend on the development environment).

Code structure of a project

Source codes of an openFrameworks' project are placed in the project's `src` folder and consist of at least three files: `main.cpp`, `testApp.h`, and `testApp.cpp`.

> Remember the following convention: if some function or class name begins with `of`, it means that it belongs to openFrameworks. Examples are `ofPoint`, `ofImage`, and `ofSetColor()`. (If some name begins with `ofx`, it means that it is part of some openFrameworks addon, for example, `ofxXmlSettings`.)

main.cpp

In C++ language specification each project must have a `.cpp` file with the defined `main()` function. This function is an entry point for an operating system to start the application. In openFrameworks, the `main()` function is contained in the `main.cpp` file. The most important line of the function is the following:

```
ofSetupOpenGL( &window, 1024, 768, OF_WINDOW );
```

This `ofSetupOpenGL()` function calling instructs openFrameworks that you need to create a window for visual output with the width 1024 and height 768 pixels. The last parameter `OF_WINDOW` means that you need to create a window, which the user can move and resize on the desktop screen. If you specify the last parameters as `OF_FULLSCREEN`, the project will run at full screen—such a mode is important for many projects.

For example, if you need to show your project on the full screen with dimensions 1920 x 1024 pixels, you can do it by replacing the `ofSetupOpenGL()` call with the following line:

```
ofSetupOpenGL( &window, 1920, 1024, OF_FULLSCREEN );
```

Normally you need not change the `main.cpp` file at all, because the settings of screen size can be done in the `testApp.cpp` text, which we consider now.

> Be careful! Inside the `main()` function most of the openFrameworks objects such as `ofImage` do not work properly, because paths and other variables are not set yet. So, indeed, in most cases you should keep `main.cpp` untouched and do all you need in `testApp.cpp`.

testApp.h

This file begins with `#pragma once`. This is a compiler directive, which should be present at the beginning of all the `.h` files. The next line is `#include "ofMain.h"`. It includes openFrameworks' core classes and functions. After this, the code contains declaration of the `testApp` class, which is inherited from the openFrameworks' `ofBaseApp` class:

```
#pragma once

#include "ofMain.h"

class testApp : public ofBaseApp{
public:
   //openFrameworks' standard functions declarations
   void setup();
   void update();
```

```
    void draw();

    //...

    //Declarations of custom objects for the project
    ofEasyCam cam;
    ofMesh mesh;
    ofImage img;
};
```

The testApp class contains a number of functions, setup(), update(), draw(), and some others. These are the functions required for your project to work. They are defined in the ofBaseApp class and called by openFrameworks. (The linking of the testApp class to the openFrameworks engine is done within the main() function. Its last line creates an object of this class and links it to the window, controlled by openFrameworks.) We will describe the meaning of the functions in the next section.

In the end of the class definition you will see declarations of the cam, mesh, and img objects. These are custom objects defined just in this example. In your own projects, you should add declarations of your objects here too.

For simplicity you can declare objects right in the testApp.cpp file, but be careful, objects of some classes like ofEasyCam, ofThread, and ofxTCPServer will not work properly and can cause the application to crash if defined as static variables not belonging to the testApp class. The reason is that openFrameworks performs some actions before the testApp class' object is created, and such classes rely on this. Note that in some examples of the book we sometimes use such declarations for simple types (float, int, ofPoint, ofImage, and others).

Let's sum up: when creating your own project you should keep declarations of the setup(), update(), draw() functions, and others untouched, and also add your objects' and functions' declarations, which are needed for your project.

testApp.cpp

The testApp.cpp file contains definitions of all functions, declared in testApp.h. Let's explain the standard functions of the testApp class.

The most important functions are `setup()`, `update()`, and `draw()`. `setup()` is called first, and then `update()` and `draw()` are called in an infinite cycle, until the user presses the *Esc* key to close the project:

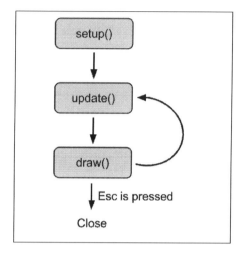

 Besides pressing *Esc*, to finish the projects' execution, the user can just close the projects' window.

If you need the project to terminate itself, call the `OF_EXIT_APP( val )` function with some integer value `val`.

Let's consider these functions in detail.

setup()

The `setup()` function is called by openFrameworks just once, at the start of the project. This is the best place for setting screen parameters such as refresh rate, load images and videos, and start processes like camera grabbing.

The typical functions for controlling screen parameters are the following:

- `ofSetFrameRate( rate )`: This parameter sets the frame rate of screen refresh equal to the value `rate` of type `int`. Also, it controls the rate of calling `update()` and `draw()`. The typical value is 60, which corresponds to the frame rate of most TVs and projectors. The default value is zero, which means that the frame rate is as large as possible (in some cases it is unwanted).

- ofSetVerticalSync(v): This parameter enables or disables synchronization of screen refresh with the video card's physical refresh, with v of type bool. Enabling this mode improves the quality of a fast-moving object's rendering, but slightly decreases the performance. By default the synchronization is enabled.

- ofSetFullscreen(v): This parameter enables or disables full screen mode, with v of type bool.

- ofSetWindowShape(w, h): This parameter sets the size of the output window so that the drawing area will have size width w and height h pixels.

Note that you can call these functions from other functions of the testApp class too.

update()

This function is called by openFrameworks right after the setup() call. This is the place where all computations should be performed, like changing positions of objects, analyzing data from cameras, and network exchange.

 Also, drawing into offscreen buffers (FBOs) can be done here.

draw()

This function is called by openFrameworks after update(). All drawing functions should be placed here. After draw(), openFrameworks again calls update(), so we obtain a cycle of the update() and draw() methods.

The typical drawing functions are as follows:

- ofSetBackground(r, g, b), where r, g, and b are integer values from 0 to 255, specifying red, green, and blue components of screen background

- ofSetColor(r, g, b) sets the drawing color

- ofLine(x1, y1, x2, y2) draws a line segment connecting points (x1, y1) and (x2, y2)

Other functions

The testApp.cpp file contains definitions of other functions, declared in testApp.h. These are event-driven functions; openFrameworks calls them when some event occurs, like mouse moving or keyboard pressing. Some of the most important functions are the following:

- The keyPressed(key) and keyReleased(key) functions are called by openFrameworks when some key is pressed or released. Here key is an int value, which can be compared with char values like 'a', and with constants denoting special keys like OF_KEY_RETURN for the *Return* (*Enter*) key, OF_KEY_LEFT for the left cursor key, and so on. See the full list of special keys constants in the libs/openFrameworks/utils/ofConstants.h file.

- The mouseMoved(x, y) function is called when the mouse is moved over the project's window without pressing any keys. Here x and y are the mouse pointer coordinates in pixels, with the center of the coordinates in the top-left corner of the window.

- The mouseReleased(x, y, button), mouseDragged(x, y, button), and mousePressed(x, y, button) functions are called when a mouse button is pressed, when the mouse is moving, and when the mouse button is released, respectively. Here button equals to 0, 1, and 2 for left, center, and right mouse buttons respectively.

- The windowResized(w, h) function is called when the size of the window is changed by the user or by calling the ofSetWindowShape() function. Here w and h are equal to the current width and height of the window.

Now we will discuss the ways for creating a new openFrameworks project.

Creating a new project

For developing your projects you have two possibilities: start it from an existing example or create it using the Project Generator wizard. Let's discuss both in detail.

Creating a project from an existing example

The easiest way to start your own project is to just copy some existing examples (or your own project) into the apps/myApps folder, or any other subfolder of the apps folder. Then rename the folder as you want (for example, to myInteractiveWall), and open the project using your developing environment. Now you can change the code, and run the project.

This way, almost all the examples in the book are made from the emptyExample project, located in the examples/empty folder.

Such an approach is indeed very easy. Also, it is especially useful for working with some complicated addons such as ofxOpenNI (see *Chapter 10, Using Depth Cameras*, for more information on this addon). Namely, you can have difficulties with linking such addons by yourself or with projectGenerator. In this case, just start your project from the existing working addon's example.

Creating a project using Project Generator

You can create a new project using the Project Generator wizard, located in the projectGenerator folder. It lets you specify the project's name, its folder, and the list of addons needed in the project.

Such a way is simple too, and it is especially useful when you start a new project, which needs to use many addons. Manual linking of addons can take much time, and Project Generator does it automatically for you. For further details see the *Using Project Generator* section in *Appendix A, Working with Addons*.

In our opinion, using Project Generator just for creating projects with proper names is not so important, because you can rename the project by yourself using the development environment. So, we use this wizard just for linking addons to new projects.

Now we are ready to create our first project with openFrameworks.

Creating your first project – the Pendulum example

Let's create an openFrameworks project, which draws a moving pendulum in 2D, consisting of a ball dangled on a rubber segment. The example is based on the emptyExample project in openFrameworks. Perform the following steps to create the project:

1. Copy the emptyExample project's folder into the folder intended for holding your applications (like apps/myApps), and rename it to Pendulum.

2. Go inside the Pendulum folder and open this project in your development environment (emptyExample.sln for Visual Studio, emptyExample.xcodeproj for Xcode, or emptyExample.workspace for Code::Blocks).

3. Open the file testApp.h in the development environment, and in the testApp class declaration add the declarations for the pendulum's center of suspension and the ball's position and velocity:

```
ofPoint pos0;          //Center of suspension
ofPoint pos;           //Ball's position
ofPoint velocity;      //Ball's velocity
```

Here ofPoint is the openFrameworks' class for holding point coordinates, it has x and y members (we will study it in *Chapter 2, Drawing in 2D*).

4. Open the file testApp.cpp, and fill the body of the testApp::setup() function definition:

```
void testApp::setup(){
  //Set screen frame rate
  ofSetFrameRate( 60 );

  //Set initial values
  pos0 = ofPoint( 512, 300 );
  pos = ofPoint( 600, 200 );
  velocity = ofPoint( 100, 0 );
}
```

In this function we set the frame rate to 60 frames per second, and we also set initial values for all three points.

5. Now fill the body of the testApp::update() function definition:

```
void testApp::update(){
  //Constants
  float dt = 1.0 / 60.0;          //Time step
  float mass = 0.1;               //Mass of a ball
  float rubberLen = 200.0;        //Segment's length
  float k = 0.5;                  //Segment's stiffness
  ofPoint g( 0.0, 9.8 );          //Gravity force

  //Compute Hooke's force
  ofPoint delta = pos - pos0;
  float len = delta.length();     //Vector's length
  float hookeValue = k * (len - rubberLen);
  delta.normalize();              //Normalize vector's length
  ofPoint hookeForce = delta * (-hookeValue);

  //Update velocity and pos
```

```
    ofPoint force = hookeForce + g;    //Resulted force
    ofPoint a = force / mass;          //Second Newton's law
    velocity += a * dt;                //Euler method
    pos += velocity * dt;              //Euler method
}
```

This function updates `velocity` and `pos`, using Newton's second law and the Euler method. For such a purpose, we compute the force acting on a ball as a sum of Hooke's force between the ball, suspension point, and gravity force.

> The details on the Euler method can be seen in the *Defining the particle functions* section in *Chapter 3, Building a Simple Particle System*. The information on the Newton's second law, Hooke's force, and gravity force can be seen at the following links:
>
> * http://en.wikipedia.org/wiki/Newton's_laws_of_motion
> * http://en.wikipedia.org/wiki/Hooke's_law
> * http://en.wikipedia.org/wiki/Gravitational_field

6. Finally, fill the body of the `testApp::draw()` function definition:

```
void testApp::draw(){
    //Set white background
    ofBackground( 255, 255, 255 );

    //Draw rubber as a blue line
    ofSetColor( 0, 0, 255 );                    //Set blue color
    ofLine( pos0.x, pos0.y, pos.x, pos.y );    //Draw line

    //Draw ball as a red circle
    ofSetColor( 255, 0, 0 );                    //Set red color
    ofFill();                                   //Enable filling
    ofCircle( pos.x, pos.y, 20 );               //Draw circle
}
```

Here we set a white background, draw a rubber as a blue line from `pos0` to `pos`, and also draw a ball as a red circle. Note that we use the `ofFill()` function, which enables openFrameworks' mode to draw filled primitives (circles, rectangles, and triangles). See more details on these drawing functions in *Chapter 2, Drawing in 2D*.

7. Run the project. You will see the animation of a moving ball:

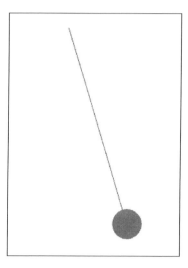

Play with numerical values in the setup() and update() functions and see how it affects the dynamics of the pendulum.

Running the book's examples

We just saw the first of the book's examples. You will see there are many other examples in the book. Some examples require additional content files, and also the code of some of the examples is given in shortened form. So for efficient work with the book, please download the book's example source codes and its content files from the **Support** tab of the book's page available at the following link:

http://www.packtpub.com/mastering-openframeworks-creative-coding-demystified/book

Note all the example projects are presented just as source files (.h and .cpp). The content files such as images, videos, and sounds are located in separate folders. For running an example, you need to create a new openFrameworks project, copy the .h and .cpp source files of the downloaded example to the src folder of this project (with replacing files), and copy the needed content files into the bin/data folder of the project.

We will always specify which project should be taken as a base for the example project, and which content files are required for running the example. Also, for convenience, we will place the name of the folder with the example's codes in an information box, like this:

 This is example `01-Basics/01-Pendulum`.

Basic utility functions

The last section of the chapter mentions some utility functions, which will be used in examples across the book, or just can be useful in your projects.

- `ofMap( v, v0, v1, out0, out1 )`: This function performs linear interpolation of a float value v from the segment `[v0, v1]` to the segment `[out0, out1]`. Note, it does not control boundaries of v, and just uses the formula *(v-v0)/(v1-v0)*(out1-out0) + out0*. For controlling boundaries, call this function with the last optional parameter set to `true`: `ofMap( v, v0, v1, out0, out1, true )`. Then the result will be clamped to `[out0, out1]`.

- `ofClamp( v, v0, v1 )`: This function clamps the float value v to the segment `[v0, v1]` that is returns `min( max( v, v0 ), v1 )`.

- `ofRandom( a, b )`: This function generates a pseudo-random number in the segment `[a, b]`. (Actually, it returns a value always less than that of b).

- `ofNoise ( x )`, `ofNoise( x, y )`, `ofNoise( x, y, z )`, and `ofNoise( x, y, z, w )`: These functions return Perlin noise value, see the details in *Appendix B, Perlin Noise*.

- `ofToString( v )`: This function converts the `int` or `float` value v into string-returning value

- `ofToInt( s )` and `ofToFloat( s )`: These functions convert the string s into `int` or `float` returning values respectively.

- `ofGetWidth()` and `ofGetHeight()`: These functions return the current width and height of the project's screen, in pixels.

- `ofGetElapsedTimef()`: This function returns the value of seconds lapsed from the project's start. This is a `float` value, measured with millisecond accuracy. For example, returned value 123.4 means 123 seconds and 400 milliseconds.

- `ofShowCursor()` and `ofHideCursor()`: These functions show and hide the mouse cursor.

For printing information into a console window, you can use the standard `cout` stream. For example, for printing time from the project's start, use the following code:

```
cout << "Time: " << ofGetElapsedTimef() << endl;
```

Here, `endl` is a standard constant, which means starting a new line in the console.

Summary

In this chapter we learned what is openFrameworks and when it should be used, how to install it, and run its examples. Also, we explored the project's folder and code structure, and finally made the first project with pendulum simulation.

In the next chapter we learn how to work with 2D graphics using openFrameworks.

2
Drawing in 2D

Drawing is one of the main capabilities of openFrameworks. Here, we consider the basics of 2D graphics, including drawing geometric primitives, working with colors, and drawing in an offscreen buffer. In this chapter we will cover:

- Geometric primitives
- Using ofPoint
- Coordinate system transformations
- Colors
- Using FBO for offscreen drawings
- Playing with numerical instability
- Screen grabbing

Drawing basics

The screens of modern computers consist of a number of small squares, called **pixels** (**picture elements**). Each pixel can light in one color. You create pictures on the screen by changing the colors of the pixels.

Graphics based on pixels is called raster graphics. Another kind of graphics is vector graphics, which is based on primitives such as lines and circles. Today, most computer screens are arrays of pixels and represent raster graphics. But images based on vector graphics (vector images) are still used in computer graphics (for details, see the *Images basics* section in *Chapter 4, Images and Textures*). Vector images are drawn on raster screens using the rasterization procedure.

The openFrameworks project can draw on the whole screen (when it is in fullscreen mode) or only in a window (when fullscreen mode is disabled). See how to set screen modes in the *main.cpp* and *setup()* sections in *Chapter 1, openFrameworks Basics*. For simplicity, we will call the area where openFrameworks can draw, the **screen**. The current width and height of the screen in pixels may be obtained using the ofGetWidth() and ofGetHeight() functions.

For pointing the pixels, openFrameworks uses the screen's coordinate system. This coordinate system has its origin on the top-left corner of the screen. The measurement unit is a pixel. So, each pixel on the screen with width w and height h pixels can be pointed by its coordinates (x, y), where x and y are integer values lying in the range 0 to w-1 and from 0 to h-1 respectively.

In this chapter, we will deal with two-dimensional (2D) graphics, which is a number of methods and algorithms for drawing objects on the screen by specifying the two coordinates (x, y) in pixels.

The other kind of graphics is three-dimensional (3D) graphics, which represents objects in 3D space using three coordinates (x, y, z) and performs rendering on the screen using some kind of projection of space (3D) to the screen (2D). For details on 3D graphics, go through *Chapter 7, Drawing in 3D*.

The background color of the screen

The drawing on the screen in openFrameworks should be performed in the testApp::draw() function (see the *testApp.cpp* section in *Chapter 1, openFrameworks Basics*). Before this function is called by openFrameworks, the entire screen is filled with a fixed color, which is set by the function ofSetBackground(r, g, b). Here r, g, and b are integer values corresponding to red, green, and blue components of the background color in the range 0 to 255. Note that each of the ofSetBackground() function call fills the screen with the specified color immediately.

You can make a gradient background using the ofBackgroundGradient() function. See its description in the *The triangles cloud example* section in *Chapter 7, Drawing in 3D*.

You can set the background color just once in the testApp::setup() function, but we often call ofSetBackground() in the beginning of the testApp::draw() function to not mix up the setup stage and the drawing stage.

Pulsating background example

You can think of `ofSetBackground()` as an opportunity to make the simplest drawings, as if the screen consists of one big pixel. Consider an example where the background color slowly changes from black to white and back using a sine wave.

 This is example `02-2D/01-PulsatingBackground`.

The project is based on the openFrameworks `emptyExample` example. Copy the folder with the example and rename it. Then fill the body of the `testApp::draw()` function with the following code:

```
float time = ofGetElapsedTimef();   //Get time in seconds

//Get periodic value in [-1,1], with wavelength equal to 1 second
float value = sin( time * M_TWO_PI );

//Map value from [-1,1] to [0,255]
float v = ofMap( value, -1, 1, 0, 255 );

ofBackground( v, v, v );            //Set background color
```

This code gets the time lapsed from the start of the project using the `ofGetElapsedTimef()` function, and uses this value for computing `value = sin( time * M_TWO_PI )`. Here, `M_TWO_PI` is an openFrameworks constant equal to 2π; that is, approximately 6.283185. So, `time * M_TWO_PI` increases by 2π per second. The value 2π is equal to the period of the sine wave function, `sin()`. So, the argument of `sin(...)` will go through its wavelength in one second, hence `value = sin(...)` will run from -1 to 1 and back. Finally, we map the value to v, which changes in range from 0 to 255 using the `ofMap()` function, and set the background to a color with red, green, and blue components equal to v.

 See the descriptions of the `ofGetElapsedTimef()` and `ofMap()` functions in the *Basic utility functions* section in *Chapter 1, openFrameworks Basics*.

Run the project; you will see how the screen color pulsates by smoothly changing its color from black to white and back.

Replace the last line, which sets the background color to
ofBackground(v, 0, 0);, and the color will pulsate from
black to red.

Replace the argument of the sin(...) function to the formula
time * M_TWO_PI * 2 and the speed of the pulsating increases
by two times.

We will return to background in the *Drawing with an uncleared background* section.
Now we will consider how to draw geometric primitives.

Geometric primitives

In this chapter we will deal with 2D graphics. 2D graphics can be created in the
following ways:

- Drawing geometric primitives such as lines, circles, and other curves and
  shapes like triangles and rectangles. This is the most natural way of creating
  graphics by programming. Generative art and creative coding projects are often
  based on this graphics method. We will consider this in the rest of the chapter.

- Drawing images lets you add more realism to the graphics, and this is
  considered in *Chapter 4, Images and Textures*.

- Setting the contents of the screen directly, pixel-by-pixel, is the most
  powerful way of generating graphics. But it is harder to use for simple things
  like drawing curves. So, such method is normally used together with both
  of the previous methods. A somewhat fast technique for drawing a screen
  pixel-by-pixel consists of filling an array with pixels colors, loading it in
  an image, and drawing the image on the screen (see its description in the
  Creating images section in *Chapter 4, Images and Textures*). The fastest, but a
  little bit harder technique, is using fragment shaders (see its explanation in
  the *A simple fragment shader example* section in *Chapter 8, Using Shaders*).

openFrameworks has the following functions for drawing primitives:

- ofLine(x1, y1, x2, y2): This function draws a line segment connecting
  points (x1, y1) and (x2, y2)

- ofRect(x, y, w, h): This function draws a rectangle with the top-left
  corner (x, y), width w, and height h

- ofTriangle(x1, y1, x2, y2, x3, y3): This function draws a triangle
  with vertices (x1, y1), (x2, y2), and (x3, y3)

- ofCircle(x, y, r): This function draws a circle with center (x, y) and
  radius r

openFrameworks has no special function for changing the color of a separate pixel. To do so, you can draw the pixel (x, y) as a rectangle with width and height equal to 1 pixel; that is, `ofRect( x, y, 1, 1 )`. This is a very slow method, but we sometimes use it for educational and debugging purposes.

All the coordinates in these functions are `float` type. Although the coordinates (x, y) of a particular pixel on the screen are integer values, openFrameworks uses float numbers for drawing geometric primitives. This is because a video card can draw objects with the `float` coordinates using modeling, as if the line goes between pixels. So the resultant picture of drawing with float coordinates is smoother than with integer coordinates.

Using these functions, it is possible to create simple drawings.

The simplest example of a flower

Let's consider the example that draws a circle, line, and two triangles, which forms the simplest kind of flower.

 This is example `02-2D/02-FlowerSimplest`.

This example project is based on the openFrameworks `emptyExample` project. Fill the body of the `testApp::draw()` function with the following code:

```
ofBackground( 255, 255, 255 );              //Set white background
ofSetColor( 0, 0, 0 );                      //Set black color

ofCircle( 300, 100,  40 );                  //Blossom
ofLine( 300, 100,  300, 400 );              //Stem
ofTriangle( 300, 270,  300, 300,  200, 220 );   //Left leaf
ofTriangle( 300, 270,  300, 300,  400, 220 );   //Right leaf
```

On running this code, you will see the following picture of the "flower":

Controlling the drawing of primitives

There are a number of functions for controlling the parameters for drawing primitives.

- ofSetColor(r, g, b): This function sets the color of drawing primitives, where r, g, and b are integer values corresponding to red, green, and blue components of the color in the range 0 to 255. After calling ofSetColor(), all the primitives will be drawn using this color until another ofSetColor() calling. We will discuss colors in more detail in the *Colors* section.

- ofFill() and ofNoFill(): These functions enable and disable filling shapes like circles, rectangles, and triangles. After calling ofFill() or ofNoFill(), all the primitives will be drawn filled or unfilled until the next function is called. By default, the shapes are rendered filled with color. Add the line ofNoFill(); before ofCircle(...); in the previous example and you will see all the shapes unfilled, as follows:

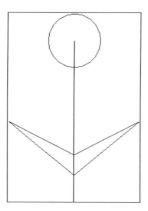

- ofSetLineWidth(lineWidth): This function sets the width of the rendered lines to the lineWidth value, which has type float. The default value is 1.0, and calling this function with larger values will result in thick lines. It only affects drawing unfilled shapes. The line thickness is changed up to some limit depending on the video card. Normally, this limit is not less than 8.0.

 Add the line ofSetLineWidth(7); before the line drawing in the previous example, and you will see the flower with a thick vertical line, whereas all the filled shapes will remain unchanged. Note that we use the value 7; this is an odd number, so it gives symmetrical line thickening.

Note that this method for obtaining thick lines is simple but not perfect, because adjacent lines are drawn quite crudely. For obtaining smooth thick lines, you should draw these as filled shapes.

- `ofSetCircleResolution( res )`: This function sets the circle resolution; that is, the number of line segments used for drawing circles to `res`. The default value is `20`, but with such settings only small circles look good. For bigger circles, it is recommended to increase the circle resolution; for example, to `40` or `60`. Add the line `ofSetCircleResolution( 40 );` before `ofCircle(...);` in the previous example and you will see a smoother circle. Note that a large `res` value can decrease the performance of the project, so if you need to draw many small circles, consider using smaller `res` values.

- `ofEnableSmoothing()` and `ofDisableSmoothing()`: These functions enable and disable line smoothing. Such settings can be controlled by your video card. In our example, calling these functions will not have any effect.

Performance considerations

The functions discussed work well for drawings containing not more than a 1000 primitives. When you draw more primitives, the project's performance can decrease (it depends on your video card). The reason is that each command such as `ofSetColor()` or `ofLine()` is sent to drawing separately, which takes time. So, for drawing 10,000, 100,000, or even 1 million primitives, you should use advanced methods, which draw many primitives at once. In openFrameworks, you can use the `ofMesh` and `ofVboMesh` classes for this (for details, see the *Using ofMesh* section in *Chapter 7, Drawing in 3D*).

Using ofPoint

Maybe you noted a problem when considering the preceding flower example: drawing primitives by specifying the coordinates of all the vertices is a little cumbersome. There are too many numbers in the code, so it is hard to understand the relation between primitives. To solve this problem, we will learn about using the `ofPoint` class and then apply it for drawing primitives using control points.

`ofPoint` is a class that represents the coordinates of a 2D point. It has two main fields: `x` and `y`, which are `float` type.

Actually, `ofPoint` has the third field `z`, so `ofPoint` can be used for representing 3D points too (we use this capability in *Chapter 7, Drawing in 3D*). If you do not specify `z`, it sets to zero by default, so in this case you can think of `ofPoint` as a 2D point indeed.

Operations with points

To represent some point, just declare an object of the `ofPoint` class.

```
ofPoint p;
```

To initialize the point, set its coordinates.

```
p.x = 100.0;
p.y = 200.0;
```

Or, alternatively, use the constructor.

```
p = ofPoint( 100.0, 200.0 );
```

You can operate with points just as you do with numbers. If you have a point `q`, the following operations are valid:

- `p + q` or `p - q` provides points with coordinates (`p.x + q.x`, `p.y + q.y`) or (`p.x - q.x`, `p.y - q.y`)

- `p * k` or `p / k`, where k is the `float` value, provides the points (`p.x * k`, `p.y * k`) or (`p.x / k`, `p.y / k`)

- `p += q` or `p -= q` adds or subtracts q from p

There are a number of useful functions for simplifying 2D vector mathematics, as follows:

- `p.length()`: This function returns the length of the vector p, which is equal to `sqrt( p.x * p.x + p.y * p.y )`.

- `p.normalize()`: This function normalizes the point so it has the unit length `p = p / p.length()`. Also, this function handles the case correctly when `p.length()` is equal to zero.

See the full list of functions for `ofPoint` in the `libs/openFrameworks/math/ofVec3f.h` file. Actually, `ofPoint` is just another name for the `ofVec3f` class, representing 3D vectors and corresponding functions.

All functions' drawing primitives have overloaded versions working with `ofPoint`:

- `ofLine( p1, p2 )` draws a line segment connecting the points p1 and p2
- `ofRect( p, w, h )` draws a rectangle with top-left corner p, width w, and height h
- `ofTriangle( p1, p2, p3 )` draws a triangle with the vertices p1, p2, and p3
- `ofCircle( p, r )` draws a circle with center p and radius r

Using control points example

We are ready to solve the problem stated in the beginning of the *Using ofPoint* section. To avoid using many numbers in drawing code, we can declare a number of points and use them as vertices for primitive drawing. In computer graphics, such points are called **control points**.

Let's specify the following control points for the flower in our simplest flower example:

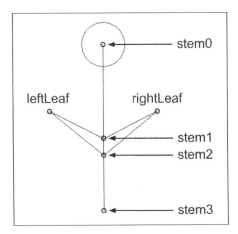

Now we implement this in the code.

This is example `02-2D/03-FlowerControlPoints`.

Add the following declaration of control points in the `testApp` class declaration in the `testApp.h` file:

```
ofPoint stem0, stem1, stem2, stem3, leftLeaf, rightLeaf;
```

Then set values for points in the `testApp::update()` function as follows:

```
stem0 = ofPoint( 300, 100 );
stem1 = ofPoint( 300, 270 );
stem2 = ofPoint( 300, 300 );
stem3 = ofPoint( 300, 400 );
leftLeaf = ofPoint( 200, 220 );
rightLeaf = ofPoint( 400, 220 );
```

Finally, use these control points for drawing the flower in the `testApp::draw()` function:

```
ofBackground( 255, 255, 255 );          //Set white background
ofSetColor( 0, 0, 0 );                  //Set black color

ofCircle( stem0, 40 );                  //Blossom
ofLine( stem0, stem3 );                 //Stem
ofTriangle( stem1, stem2, leftLeaf );   //Left leaf
ofTriangle( stem1, stem2, rightLeaf );  //Right leaf
```

You will observe that when drawing with control points the code is much easier to understand.

Furthermore, there is one more advantage of using control points: we can easily change control points' positions and hence obtain animated drawings. See the full example code in `02-2D/03-FlowerControlPoints`. In addition to the already explained code, it contains a code for shifting the `leftLeaf` and `rightLeaf` points depending on time. So, when you run the code, you will see the flower with moving leaves.

Coordinate system transformations

Sometimes we need to translate, rotate, and resize drawings. For example, arcade games are based on the characters moving across the screen.

When we perform drawing using control points, the straightforward solution for translating, rotating, and resizing graphics is in applying desired transformations to control points using corresponding mathematical formulas. Such idea works, but sometimes leads to complicated formulas in the code (especially when we need to rotate graphics). The more elegant solution is in using coordinate system transformations. This is a method of temporarily changing the coordinate system during drawing, which lets you translate, rotate, and resize drawings without changing the drawing algorithm.

The current coordinate system is represented in openFrameworks with a matrix. All coordinate system transformations are made by changing this matrix in some way. When openFrameworks draws something using the changed coordinate system, it performs exactly the same number of computations as with the original matrix. It means that you can apply as many coordinate system transformations as you want without any decrease in the performance of the drawing.

Coordinate system transformations are managed in openFrameworks with the following functions:

- `ofPushMatrix()`: This function pushes the current coordinate system in a matrix stack. This stack is a special container that holds the coordinate system matrices. It gives you the ability to restore coordinate system transformations when you do not need them.

- `ofPopMatrix()`: This function pops the last added coordinate system from a matrix stack and uses it as the current coordinate system. You should take care to see that the number of `ofPopMatrix()` calls don't exceed the number of `ofPushMatrix()` calls.

Though the coordinate system is restored before `testApp::draw()` is called, we recommend that the number of `ofPushMatrix()` and `ofPopMatrix()` callings in your project should be exactly the same. It will simplify the project's debugging and further development.

- `ofTranslate( x, y )` or `ofTranslate( p )`: This function moves the current coordinate system at the vector (x, y) or, equivalently, at the vector p. If x and y are equal to zero, the coordinate system remains unchanged.

- `ofScale( scaleX, scaleY )`: This function scales the current coordinate system at `scaleX` in the x axis and at `scaleY` in the y axis. If both parameters are equal to `1.0`, the coordinate system remains unchanged. The value `-1.0` means inverting the coordinate axis in the opposite direction.

- `ofRotate( angle )`: This function rotates the current coordinate system around its origin at `angle` degrees clockwise. If the `angle` value is equal to `0`, or k * `360` with k as an integer, the coordinate system remains unchanged.

All transformations can be applied in any sequence; for example, translating, scaling, rotating, translating again, and so on.

The typical usage of these functions is the following:

1. Store the current transformation matrix using `ofPushMatrix()`.

2. Change the coordinate system by calling any of these functions: `ofTranslate()`, `ofScale()`, or `ofRotate()`.

3. Draw something.

4. Restore the original transformation matrix using `ofPopMatrix()`.

 Step 3 can include steps 1 to 4 again.

For example, for moving the origin of the coordinate system to the center of the screen, use the following code in `testApp::draw()`:

```
ofPushMatrix();
ofTranslate( ofGetWidth() / 2, ofGetHeight() / 2 );
//Draw something
ofPopMatrix();
```

If you replace the `//Draw something` comment to `ofCircle( 0, 0, 100 );`, you will see the circle in the center of the screen.

 This transformation significantly simplifies coding the drawings that should be located at the center of the screen.

Now let's use coordinate system transformation for adding triangular petals to the flower.

 For further exploring coordinate system transformations, see the example in the *Rotating images* section in *Chapter 4, Images and Textures*.

Flower with petals example

In this example, we draw petals to the flower from the `02-2D/03-FlowerControlPoints` example, described in the *Using control points example* section.

 This is example `02-2D/04-FlowerWithPetals`.

We want to draw unfilled shapes here, so add the following lines at the beginning of `testApp::draw()`:

```
ofNoFill();          //Draw shapes unfilled
```

Now add the following code to the end of `testApp::draw()` for drawing the petals:

```
ofPushMatrix();      //Store the coordinate system

//Translate the coordinate system center to stem0
ofTranslate( stem0 );

//Rotate the coordinate system depending on the time
float angle = ofGetElapsedTimef() * 30;
ofRotate( angle );

int petals = 15;   //Number of petals
for (int i=0; i<petals; i++) {
  //Rotate the coordinate system
  ofRotate( 360.0 / petals );

  //Draw petal as a triangle
  ofPoint p1( 0, 20 );
  ofPoint p2( 80, 0 );
  ofTriangle( p1, -p1, p2 );
}

//Restore the coordinate system
ofPopMatrix();
```

This code moves the coordinate system origin to the point `stem0` (the blossom's center) and rotates it depending on the current time. Then it rotates the coordinate system on a fixed angle and draws a triangle `petals` times. As a result, we obtain a number of triangles that slowly rotate around the point `stem0`.

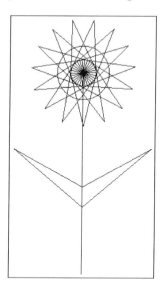

Colors

Up until now we have worked with colors using the functions `ofSetColor( r, g, b )` and `ofBackground( r, g, b )`. By calling these functions, we specify the color of the current drawing and background as r, g, and b values, corresponding to red, green, and blue components, where r, g and b are integer values lying in the range 0 to 255.

 When you need to specify gray colors, you can use overloaded versions of these functions with just one argument: `ofSetColor( gray )` and `ofBackground( gray )`, where gray is in the range 0 to 255.

These functions are simple, but not enough. Sometimes, you need to pass the color as a single parameter in a function, and also do color modifications like changing the brightness. To solve this problem, openFrameworks has the class `ofColor`. It lets us operate with colors as we do with single entities and modify these.

ofColor is a class representing a color. It has four float fields: r, g, b, and a. Here r, g, and b are red, green, and blue components of a color, and a is the alpha component, which means the opacity of a color. The alpha component is related to transparency, which is discussed in detail in the *Transparency* section in *Chapter 4, Images and Textures*.

In this chapter we will not consider the alpha component. By default, its value is equal to 255, which means truly opaque color, so all colors considered in this chapter are opaque.

> The ofSetColor(), ofBackground(), and ofColor() functions include the alpha component as an optional last argument, so you can specify it when needed.

Operations with colors

To represent some color, just declare an object of the ofColor class.

```
ofColor color;
```

To initialize the color, set its components.

```
color.r = 0.0;
color.g = 128.0;
color.b = 255.0;
```

Or, equivalently, use the constructor.

```
color = ofColor( 0.0, 128.0, 255.0 );
```

You can use color as an argument in the functions ofSetColor() and ofBackground(). For example, ofSetColor(color) and ofBackground(color).

openFrameworks has a number of predefined colors, including white, gray, black, red, green, blue, cyan, magenta, and yellow. See the full list of colors in the libs/openFrameworks/types/ofColors.h file. To use the predefined colors, add the ofColor:: prefix before these names. For example, ofSetColor(ofColor::yellow) sets the current drawing color to yellow.

You can modify the color using the following functions:

- `setHue( hue )`, `setSaturation( saturation )`, and `setBrightness( brightness )`: These functions change the hue, saturation, and brightness of the color to specified values. All the arguments are float values in the range 0 to 255.

- `setHsb( hue, saturation, brightness )`: This function creates a color by specifying its hue, saturation, and brightness values, where arguments are float values in the range 0 to 255.

- `getHue()` and `getSaturation()`: These functions return the hue and saturation values of the color.

- `getBrightness()`: This function returns the brightest color component.

- `getLightness()`: This function returns the average of the color components.

- `invert()`: This function inverts color components; that is, the `r`, `g`, and `b` fields of the color become `255-r`, `255-g`, and `255-b` respectively.

Let's consider an example that demonstrates color modifications.

Color modifications example

In this example, we will modify the red color by changing its brightness, saturation, and hue through the whole range and draw three resultant stripes.

This is example `02-2D/05-Colors`.

This example project is based on the openFrameworks `emptyExample` project. Fill the body of the `testApp::draw()` function with the following code:

```
ofBackground( 255, 255, 255 );     //Set white background

//Changing brightness
for ( int i=0; i<256; i++ ) {
  ofColor color = ofColor::red;  //Get red color
  color.setBrightness( i );      //Modify brightness
  ofSetColor( color );
  ofLine( i, 0, i, 50 );
}

//Changing saturation
for ( int i=0; i<256; i++ ) {
  ofColor color = ofColor::red;  //Get red color
```

```
    color.setSaturation( i );      //Modify saturation
    ofSetColor( color );
    ofLine( i, 80, i, 130 );
}

//Changing hue
for ( int i=0; i<256; i++ ) {
    ofColor color = ofColor::red;   //Get red color
    color.setHue( i );              //Modify hue
    ofSetColor( color );
    ofLine( i, 160, i, 210 );
}
```

Run the project and you will see three stripes consisting of the red color with changed brightness, saturation, and hue.

As you can see, changing brightness, saturation, and hue is similar to the color-corrections methods used in photo editors like Adobe Photoshop and Gimp. From a designer's point of view, this is a more powerful method for controlling colors as compared to directly specifying the red, green, and blue color components.

 See an example of using the described color modification method end of the *Defining the particle functions* section in *Chapter 3, Building a Simple Particle System*.

Now we will consider how to perform drawings with uncleared background, which can be useful in many creative coding projects related to 2D graphics.

Drawing with an uncleared background

By default, the screen is cleared each time before `testApp:draw()` is called, so you need to draw all the contents of the screen inside `testApp::draw()` again and again. It is appropriate in most cases, but sometimes we want the screen to accumulate our drawings. In openFrameworks, you can do this by disabling screen clearing using the `ofSetBackgroundAuto( false )` function. All successive drawings will accumulate on the screen. (In this case you should call `ofBackground()` rarely, only for clearing the current screen).

This method is very simple to use, but is not flexible enough for serious projects. Also, currently it has some issues:

- In Mac OS X, the screen can jitter.
- In Windows, screen grabbing does not work (more details on screen grabbing can be seen in the *Screen grabbing* section later in this chapter)

 See an example of using this method in the *The bouncing ball example* section in *Chapter 6, Working with Sounds.*

So, when you need to accumulate drawings, we recommend you to use the FBO buffer, which we will explain now.

Using FBO for offscreen drawings

FBO in computer graphics stands for **frame buffer object**. This is an offscreen raster buffer where openFrameworks can draw just like on the screen. You can draw something in this buffer, and then draw the buffer contents on the screen. The picture in the buffer is not cleared with each `testApp::draw()` calling, so you can use FBO for accumulated drawings.

In openFrameworks, FBO is represented by the class `ofFBO`.

The typical scheme of its usage is the following:

1. Declare an `ofFbo` object, `fbo`, in the `testApp` class declaration.

   ```
   ofFbo fbo;
   ```

2. Initialize `fbo` with some size in the `testApp::setup()` function.

   ```
   int w = ofGetWidth();
   int h = ofGetHeight();
   fbo.allocate( w, h );
   ```

3. Draw something in `fbo`. You can do it not only in `testApp::draw()` but also in `testApp::setup()` and `testApp::update()`. To begin drawing, call `fbo.begin()`. After this, all drawing commands, such as `ofBackground()` and `ofLine()`, will draw to `fbo`. To finish drawing, call `fbo.end()`. For example, to fill `fbo` with white color, use the following code:

```
fbo.begin();
ofBackground( 255, 255, 255 );
fbo.end();
```

4. Draw `fbo` on the screen using the `fbo.draw( x, y )` or `fbo.draw( x, y, w, h )` functions. Here, x and y are the top-left corner, and w and h are the optional width and height of the rendered `fbo` image on the screen. The drawing should be done in the `testApp::draw()` function. The example of the corresponding code is the following:

```
ofSetColor( 255, 255, 255 );
fbo.draw( 0, 0 );
```

> The `ofFbo` class has drawing behavior similar to the image class `ofImage`. So, the `ofSetColor( 255, 255, 255 );` line is needed here to draw `fbo` without color modulation (see details in the *Color modulation* section in *Chapter 4, Images and Textures*).

You can use many FBO objects and even draw one inside another. For example, if you have `ofFbo fbo2`, you can draw `fbo` inside `fbo2` as follows:

```
fbo2.begin();
ofSetColor( 255, 255, 255 );
fbo.draw( 0, 0 );
fbo2.end();
```

> Be careful: if you call `fbo.begin()`, you should always call `fbo.end()`; do it before drawing FBO's contents anywhere.

The following tips will be helpful for advanced `ofFbo` usage:

- `fbo` has texture of the type `ofTexture`, which holds its current picture. The texture can be accessed using `fbo.getTextureReference()`. See the *Using ofTexture for memory optimization* section in *Chapter 4, Images and Textures*, for details on operations with textures.

- The settings of your video card, such as like antialiasing smoothing, does not affect FBO, so it may happen that your smooth drawing on screen becomes aliased when you perform this drawing using `fbo`. One possible solution for smooth graphics is using `fbo` that is double the size of the screen and shrinking `fbo` to screen size during drawing.

- When you perform semi-transparent drawing to `fbo` (with alpha-blending enabled), most probably you should disable alpha-blending when drawing `fbo` itself on the screen. In the opposite case, transparent pixels of `fbo` will be blended in the screen one more time, so the resultant picture will be overblended. See the *Transparency* section in *Chapter 4, Images and Textures*, for details on blending.

- By default, `fbo` holds color components of its pixels as unsigned char values. When more accuracy is needed, you can use float-valued `fbo` by allocating it with the optional last parameter `GL_RGB32F_ARB`.

  ```
  fbo.allocate( w, h, GL_RGB32F_ARB );
  ```

  See an example of using this method in the *Implementing a particle in the project* section in *Chapter 3, Building a Simple Particle System*.

Let's consider an example of using the `ofFbo` object for accumulated drawing.

Spirals example

Consider a drawing algorithm consisting of the following steps:

1. Set `a = 0` and `b = 0`.
2. Set the `pos` point's position to the screen center.
3. Set `a += b`.
4. Set `b += 0.5`.
5. Move the `pos` point a step of fixed length in the direction defined by the angle `a` measured in degrees.
6. Each 100 steps change the drawing color to a new color, generated randomly.
7. Draw a line between the last and current positions of `pos`.
8. Go to step 3.

This algorithm is a kind of generative art algorithm—it is short and can generate interesting and unexpected drawings.

The result of the algorithm will be a picture with the the colored trajectory of pos moving on the screen. The b value grows linearly, hence the a value grows parabolically. The value of a is an angle that defines the step pos will move. It is not easy to predict the behavior of steps when the angle changes parabolically, hence it is hard to imagine how the resultant curve will look. So let's implement the algorithm and see it.

We will use the ofFbo fbo object for holding the generated picture.

 This is example 02-2D/06-Spirals.

The example is based on the emptyExample project in openFrameworks. In the testApp class declaration of the testApp.h file, add declarations for a, b, pos, fbo, and some additional variables. Also, we declare the function draw1(), which draws one line segment by performing steps 3 to 7 of the drawing algorithm.

```
double a, b;              //Angle and its increment
ofPoint pos, lastPos;     //Current and last drawing position
ofColor color;            //Drawing color
int colorStep;            //Counter for color changing
ofFbo fbo;                //Drawing buffer
void draw1();             //Draw one line segment
```

Note that a and b are declared as double. The reason is that a grows fast, so the accuracy of float is not enough for stable computations. However, we will play with the float case too, in the *Playing with numerical instability* section.

The testApp::setup() function initializes the fbo buffer, fills it with a white color, and sets initial values to all variables.

```
void testApp::setup(){
  ofSetFrameRate( 60 );  //Set screen frame rate

  //Allocate drawing buffer
  fbo.allocate( ofGetWidth(), ofGetHeight() );

  //Fill buffer with white color
  fbo.begin();
  ofBackground( 255, 255, 255 );
  fbo.end();

  //Initialize variables
  a = 0;
```

```
    b = 0;
    pos = ofPoint( ofGetWidth() / 2, ofGetHeight() / 2 );
                                            //Screen center
    colorStep = 0;
}
```

The `testApp::update()` function draws line segments in `fbo` by calling the `draw1()` function. Note that we perform 200 drawings at once for obtaining the resultant curve quickly.

```
void testApp::update(){
  fbo.begin();        //Begin draw to buffer
  for ( int i=0; i<200; i++ ) {
    draw1();
  }
  fbo.end();          //End draw to buffer
}
```

The `testApp::draw()` function just draws `fbo` on the screen.

```
void testApp::draw(){
  ofBackground( 255, 255, 255 );  //Set white background

  //Draw buffer
  ofSetColor( 255, 255, 255 );
  fbo.draw( 0, 0 );
}
```

Note that calling `ofBackground()` is not necessary here because `fbo` fills the whole screen, but we have done so uniformly with other projects.

Finally, we should add a definition for the `draw1()` function.

```
void testApp::draw1(){
  //Change a
  a += b * DEG_TO_RAD;
  //a holds values in radians, b holds values in degrees,
  //so when changing a we multiply b to DEG_TO_RAD constant

  //Change b
  b = b + 0.5;

  //Shift pos in direction defined by angle a
  lastPos = pos;      //Store last pos value
  ofPoint d = ofPoint( cos( a ), sin( a ) );
  float len = 20;
```

```
    pos += d * len;

    //Change color each 100 steps
    if ( colorStep % 100 == 0 ) {
      //Generate random color
      color = ofColor( ofRandom( 0, 255 ),
                       ofRandom( 0, 255 ),
                       ofRandom( 0, 255 ) );
    }
    colorStep++;

    //Draw line segment
    ofSetColor( color );
    ofLine( lastPos, pos );
  }
```

In the original algorithm, described at the beginning of the section, a and b are measured in degrees. In the openFrameworks implementation, we decide to hold b in degrees and a in radians. The reason for this will be explained later, in the *Playing with numerical instability* section. So, in the code, we convert degrees to radians using multiplication to the DEG_TO_RAD constant, which is defined in openFrameworks and is equal to π/180 degrees.

```
    a += b * DEG_TO_RAD;
```

Run the project; you will see a curve with two spiral ends constantly changing their color:

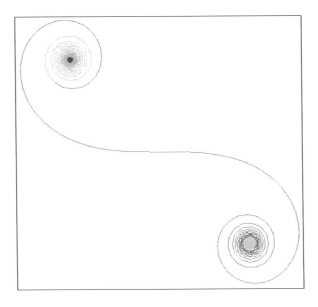

This particular behavior of the curve is determined by the parameter `0.5` in the following line:

```
b = b + 0.5;
```

The parameter defines the speed of increasing b. Change this parameter to `5.4` and `5.5` and you will see curves with 4 and 12 spirals, as shown here:

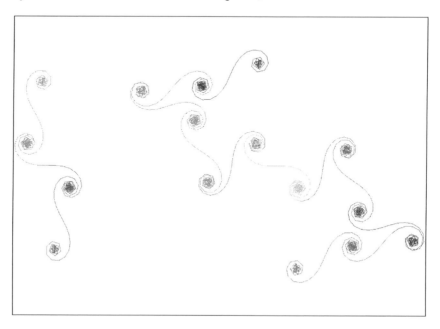

Try your own values of the parameter. If the resultant curve is too large and does not fit the screen, you can control its scale by changing the `len` value in the following line:

```
float len = 20;
```

For example, if you set `len` to `10`, the resultant curve shrinks twice.

Playing with numerical instability

In the openFrameworks code, we declare a and b as `double` values. The double type has much more accuracy when representing numbers than `float`, and it is essential in this example because a grows fast.

But what will happen if we declare a and b as `float`? Do it! Replace the line `double a, b;` with `float a, b;` and run the project. You will see that the resultant curve will be equal to the curve from the `double` case just in the first second of the running time. Then, the centers of the spirals begin to move.

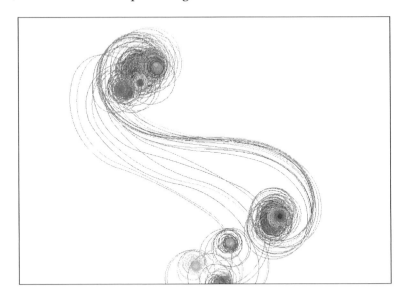

Gradually, the two-spiral structure will be ruined and the curve will demonstrate unexpected behavior, drawing circles of different sizes.

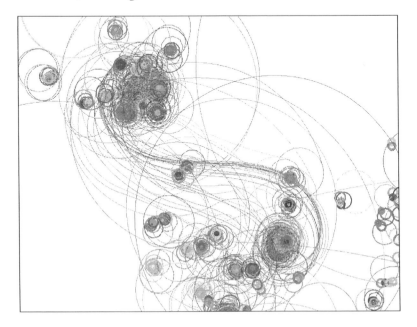

The reason for such instability is that the values of a are computed with numerical inaccuracy.

Note that the exploited instability effect can depend on the floating-point arithmetics of your CPU, so your resultant pictures can differ from the presented screenshots.

> In many serious tasks such as physical simulation or optimal planning, we need to have the exact result, so such computing instability is unallowable. But from the creative coding and generative art field point of view, such instability lets you create interesting visual or audio effects. So such instability is often permitted and desirable. For more details on the mathematics of such processes, read about the **deterministic chaos** theory.

Now change the parameter 0.5 in the line b = b + 0.5; to 17, and you will see a big variety of shapes, including triangles, squares, heptagons, and stars. Then try the values 4, 21, and your own. You will see a large number of similar but different pictures generated by this simple drawing algorithm.

Finally, note that the main computing lines of the algorithm are the following:

```
a += b * DEG_TO_RAD;
//...
b = b + 0.5;
//...
ofPoint d = ofPoint( cos( a ), sin( a ) );
```

These are very sensitive to any changes. If you change it somehow, the resultant curves will be different (in the float case). In this sense, such creative coding can be considered art because it depends heavily on the smallest code nuances, which often cannot be predicted.

Screen grabbing

Sometimes it is desirable to save the picture drawn by your project in the file. You can do it using tools of your operating system, but it's more comfortable to do it right in your project. So let's see how to save the contents of your project screen to an image file.

For such purposes, we need to use the ofImage class for working with images. Though the class is considered in *Chapter 4, Images and Textures*, for screen grabbing, it is just enough to understand that the ofImage object holds an image.

The following code saves the current screen to file on the pressing of the Space bar. It should be added to the `testApp::keyPressed()` function as follows:

```
//Grab the screen image to file
if ( key == ' ' ) {
  ofImage image;  //Declare image object

  //Grab contents of the screen
  image.grabScreen( 0, 0, ofGetWidth(), ofGetHeight() );

  image.saveImage( "screen.png" );  //Save image to file
}
```

The parameters of the `image.grabScreen()` function specify the rectangle of the grabbing. In our case, it is the whole screen of the project.

This code is implemented in the `02-2D/06-Spirals` example. Run it and press the Space bar; the contents of the screen will be saved to the `bin/data/screen.png` file in your project's folder.

The PNG files are small and have high quality, so we often use these for screen grabbing. But, writing to a PNG file takes some time because the image has to be compressed. It takes up to several seconds, depending on the CPU and image size. So if you need to save images fast, use the BMP file format.

```
image.saveImage( "screen.bmp" );
```

Additional topics

In this chapter, we have considered some of the basic topics of 2D drawing. For reading further on openFrameworks 2D capabilities, we suggest the following topics:

- Drawing text using the function `ofDrawBitmapString()` or the class `ofTrueTypeFont`. See the openFrameworks example `examples/graphics/fontShapesExample`.

- Drawing filled shapes using the functions `ofBeginShape()`, `ofVertex()`, and `ofEndShape()`. See the openFrameworks example `examples/graphics/polygonExample`.

- Creating PDF files with openFrameworks drawings. Such files will contain vector graphics suitable for high-quality printing purposes. See the openFrameworks example `examples/graphics/pdfExample`.

For deeper exploration of the world of 2D graphics, we suggest the following topics:

- Using Perlin noise for simulating life-like motion of objects. See *Appendix B, Perlin Noise*.

- Using the algorithmic method of recursion for drawing branched structures like trees.

If you are interested in playing with generative art, explore the huge base of Processing sketches at openprocessing.org. Processing is a free Java-based language and development environment for creative coding. It is very similar to openFrameworks (in a way, openFrameworks was created as the C++ version of Processing). Most of the Processing examples deal with 2D graphics, are generative art projects, and can be easily ported to openFrameworks.

Summary

In this chapter we learned how to draw geometrical primitives using control points, perform transformations of the coordinate system, and work with colors. Also, we studied how to accumulate drawings in the offscreen buffer and considered the generative art example of using it. Finally, we learned how to save the current screen image to the file.

In the next chapter we will continue learning 2D graphics and will consider one powerful method of generating fascinating animations and drawings – particle systems.

3
Building a Simple Particle System

Particle systems are used in computer graphics for drawing fuzzy-shaped objects such as fire, clouds, and trails of dust. The basic idea for such systems is drawing a large number of small, moving particles and controlling their motion.

Here we consider the basic principles of modeling and drawing particle systems and demonstrating them by building a simple 2D particle system. In this chapter, we will cover the following topics:

- The basics of particle systems
- A single particle
- An emitter
- The attraction, repulsion, and spinning forces
- Graphical user interface

By the end of this chapter, you will have a fully-featured project for experimenting with the particle system.

 This is the only chapter where we create custom C++ classes.

The basics of particle systems

Objects such as clouds and fire have no distinct shape, so it is hard to draw them using polygons. The novel method for drawing such objects was proposed by *William T. Reeves* in his article, *Particle Systems — a Technique for Modeling a Class of Fuzzy Objects* (ACM Transactions on Graphics, April 1983). The idea is in using **particle systems**, which are controllable sets of particles — small independently moving objects, considered as elementary components of the rendered object.

Today, particle systems play an important role in 2D and 3D computer graphics as a tool for photorealistic rendering of real-world fuzzy objects. Also, they are widely used for experimental and creative coding graphics.

Particles are independent objects that move according to some rules such as gravity, force, and friction. Each particle has a number of attributes such as position, velocity, lifetime, size, and color that changes with time.

The most important property of each particle system is an **interaction type** between the particles. It determines the kinds of objects and behaviors, which can be represented by the particle system, and designates methods of its physical modeling.

Interaction types

The frequently used interaction types are as follows:

- **No interaction between particles**: In this case, each particle can have a limited or an infinite *lifetime*. New particles can be generated from some point or region called **emitter**. Also, points can attract to or repel from some points or regions. This interaction type is appropriate for modeling sparse objects such as clouds, fire, traits, and also fireworks. Actually, this type was considered by *William Reeves* in his article and is considered later in this chapter.

  You can play with a particle system consisting of a fixed number of particles with infinite lifetime in the openFrameworks example, `examples/math/particlesExample`. Use keys *1*, *2*, *3*, and *4* for switching between several modes of the project; in these modes, particles will attract or repel from the mouse position, get attracted to some random points on the screen, or just fall like snowflakes.

- **Particles attract to and repel from other particles**: In this case, the attraction and repulsion forces between two particles usually depend on the distance between them. For example, particles that are far attract, and particles that are closer repel. Such particle systems are used for modeling micro or macro physical systems such as molecules or galaxies and also for modeling the flocks.

Number of particles' pairs grow in a square law of particles' number. For example, if we have a particle system with 10,000 particles, there are *10,000 × 9,999 / 2 ~ 50* millions of particles' pairs. So performing direct calculations of all possible pairs' interactions is very inefficient, and methods such as geometric hashing are always used for computations' speedup.

- Particles interact in a complex way, indirectly, through some underlying nonstationary field. In this case, the field affects the particles' velocity, and (in some models) particles can affect the field itself. The most widely known example of such an interaction is fluid mechanics, modeled by the Navier–Stokes equations. Fluid mechanics is quite complex to implement and consumes a lot of computational resources, but it exhibits behaviors (that are impossible in simpler interaction types), such as vortices and turbulence. Particle systems using this interaction are widely used in 2D and 3D graphics for photorealistic modeling of smoke, water, and many other objects, and, of course, for experimental graphics.

In openFrameworks, there exists an excellent implementation of fluid mechanics in an addon, `ofxMSAFluid`, by *Memo Akten*. You can download it from `ofxaddons.com`. See *Appendix A*, *Working with Addons*, for details on addons.

Particle systems are quite huge objects, so computing and rendering them can be a challenging task. In the next two subsections, we will consider various methods for doing it.

Computing particles' physics

Usually, each particle in a particle system is constantly moving. Hence, before each rendering step, we need to recompute the position, velocity, size, color, and other attributes using the chosen physical modeling method. The algorithmic complexity of such recomputing linearly depends on the number of particles.

For achieving high-quality graphics, particle systems should consist of thousands and even millions of particles. So computing particles' physics is often a resource-consuming task that affects the structure of the whole project. There are several schemas of organizing such computing. They are as follows:

- **Single core computing**: This performs all the computing in the `testApp::update()` function. This is the simplest method, which uses a single CPU's core. It lets us operate in openFrameworks with 10,000 to 40,000 particles at 60 FPS. This method is used in projects where the number of particles is in the specified range. Also, it is often used for prototyping a project.

- **Multiple core computing**: This divides a particle system into several smaller subsystems and processes each of them in a separate thread. The operating system automatically distributes the threads' execution among all the available CPU's cores. This is the simplest way for revealing the power of all your CPUs' cores and to speedup the calculations. For doing this in openFrameworks, use the `ofThread` class (see its usage in openFrameworks' example, `examples/utils/threadExample`).

  The speedup in this case highly depends on a number of available cores and the speed of a separate core. A typical PC has 4 to 16 cores working at 2 to 3 GHz, and the Intel Xeon Phi coprocessor has 60 cores working at 1 GHz. So, in principle, it is possible to compute a million particles in real time.

Until now we have considered CPU-based methods. All other methods are GPU-based and let us operate easily with 100,000 to 1,000,000 particles (depending on the video card). Let us see these methods:

- **Using vertex shaders**: We use this to set the initial positions of particles in the `ofMesh` object and then apply the vertex shader for changing its position in time. This method is simple and works fast but is limited. It creates non-interactive particles that fly just by predefined trajectories (specified by the vertex shader). See *Chapter 7, Drawing in 3D*, and *Chapter 8, Using Shaders*, for details on the `ofMesh` class and shaders.

It is possible to create interactive particles that change trajectories depending on the changing control parameters (such as the attractor position). To do it, you need to use a vertex shader with OpenGL's **Transform Feedback** feature.

- **Using fragment shaders**: This is used to represent each particle by a pixel in texture. For example, four color components (red, green, blue, and alpha) can hold the x and y coordinates of position and velocity of a particle. We then use a fragment shader for the corresponding processing pixels of the texture using the **Ping-Pong FBO** method. This method is quite simple, works fast, and can be used for computing particles without interaction and for moving particles in the fluid mechanics model (without computing the field). If you need to use more parameters for representing a particular particle, just use several textures. Each texture gives four additional float parameters.

  Such a method is implemented in the openFrameworks' example, `examples/gl/gpuParticleSystemExample`.

- **Using compute shaders**: Compute shaders are used for universal computations, and they let you perform advanced particles' modeling. See a demonstration of this technology at *Stan Epp's* video at `youtube.com/watch?v=jwCAsyiYimY`. The description of this video contains a link to the project's source codes.

- **Using other GPU technologies**: Most advanced GPU-based technologies are OpenCL and NVIDIA CUDA. You can use them for performing the most complicated computations. Note, if you are a novice in these technologies, adopting them in the openFrameworks project can require some effort from you.

Rendering particles

Visually, a particle system is a large number of small homogeneous objects called particles, which are drawn using different color and size but have quite a simple shape. There are several ways to render a particle system on the screen:

- **Drawing each particle as a primitive (circle, triangle, or star)**: We do this by using functions such as `ofCircle()` or `ofTriangle()`. This way is the simplest, but works slowly, because each drawing command is sent separately in the video card. This method performs well only when the number of particles is small (from 1,000 to 10,000, depends on a video card).

- **Drawing each particle as a sprite**: Here we use one image or array of images having the type ofImage or ofTexture (see *Chapter 4, Images and Textures*). They represent all possible particles' shapes. We draw each particle using the image.draw(x, y, w, h) function. This method is as slow as the previous one, but the resulting picture can be more expressive because it lets you create complex and blurred shapes. Also it is possible to use image sequences for creating animated particles such as flying moths (see the *Using image sequence* section in *Chapter 5, Working with Videos*).

- **Drawing each particle as a sprite**: We do this using ofMesh or ofVboMesh (See details on using ofMesh and ofVboMesh in the *Using ofMesh* section in *Chapter 7, Drawing in 3D*). Compared to the previous methods, this method works much faster because all the drawing commands are stored in a single array and are sent to the video card at once. Using this method, you can draw 10,000 to 1,000,000 particles (depends on the video card).

  In this method, you need to tile all the desired particles' images in one "big" image, and then use the mesh object for representing all the particles as quads with specified texture coordinates. Note, in this method, you need to specify four quad corners for each particle, which is a CPU-consuming task.

All the preceding methods can be used with CPU-based computing methods (single-core computing and multiple-core computing). Now we will consider the two most powerful methods that can be used successfully used with all the described methods of computing:

- **Using point sprites**: Point sprites is a method of drawing images by specifying only their center. Compared with using quads (described in previous item), it is a simple and also an efficient method but is limited by its expressive capabilities, for example, you cannot use different images for particles and rotate them. Though, you can change the size and color of the particles, which is enough in many projects.

  See openFrameworks' example, examples/gl/pointsAsTextures, where this method is used for drawing particles with different sizes. (For changing sizes, it uses a vertex shader; see details about shaders in *Chapter 8, Using Shaders*).

- **Using a geometry shader**: This method is as fast as point sprites but is free of its limitations—you can draw particles using different sprites and rotate them. In this method, you represent each particle as a vertex and specify its needed attributes such as the drawing position, index of using sprite, color, angle and size and then pass it in the geometry shader. (You can pass a particle's velocity too for affecting the shape of the particle on the screen.)

  The shader translates each particle in a quad that is rendered on the screen.

Note that a geometry shader can also draw particles not as sprites but as shapes consisting of a number of lines (for example, stars) and constantly change their shape for obtaining vivid particles. See an example of using the geometry shader in the *The furry carpet example* section in *Chapter 8, Using Shaders*.

Creating a particle system – summary

Let's sum up all the described categories of interaction, modeling, and drawing. To make a project which draws a particle system, you need to specify its properties:

- **Particles interaction type**: This property checks whether the particles are independent (fire and clouds), interact with each other (flocks), or interact via some underlying field (liquid).

- **Visualization**: This property lets you define how a particle will be drawn—as a geometrical shape or a sprite—and how the particle's view should change during its lifetime (shape, color, size, and so on).

- **A desired order of the particles' number**: This property lets you set a desired order of the particles' number as 1,000 to 10,000, 10,000 to 100,000, 100,000 to 1,000,000, or more.

Having prepared this list, you should choose appropriate methods for physics computing and visualization:

- 1,000 to 10,000 particles with simple physics can be calculated using a single CPU core and rendered with simple methods (using `ofCircle()`, `ofTriangle()`, or `image.draw()`)

- 10,000 to 100,000 can be calculated with CPU too (using single or several cores) and rendered using `ofMesh`

- For 100,000 to 1,000,000 particles and (or) complex physics, you definitely should use the GPU methods for computing and rendering

 If your particle system is big and complex, before implementing it, we strongly suggest creating its prototype with several thousands of particles for debugging basic physics by using a single CPU and simple drawing.

In the rest of the chapter, we will implement a simple but fully-featured particle system consisting of several thousands of particles. These particles will be independent, and we will compute them using a single CPU's core and draw them as circles.

The aim of this project is in exploring the beauty of patterns, generated by a particle system, having a circular symmetry. The style of particles' behavior and a set of control parameters is taken from our Kuflex's project, **Abstract Wall** (see kuflex.com for details about this project).

Let's begin with modeling and drawing just one particle.

A single particle

In this section, we will create a project that will model and draw one particle. It will be represented by our custom C++ class, Particle.

The best C++ programming style suggests declaring and implementing each new class in separate .h and .cpp files (in our case, it should be Particles.h and Particles.cpp) because it improves readability and reusability of the code. But for simplicity, we will declare and implement all the classes of the example only in testApp.h and testApp.cpp files respectively.

 This is example 03-Particles/01-SingleParticle.

The example is based on the emptyExample project in openFrameworks. In the testApp.h file, after the #include "ofMain.h" line, add the following declaration of a Particle class:

```
class Particle {
public:
  Particle();              //Class constructor
  void setup();            //Start particle
  void update( float dt ); //Recalculate physics
  void draw();             //Draw particle

  ofPoint pos;             //Position
  ofPoint vel;             //Velocity
  float time;              //Time of living
  float lifeTime;          //Allowed lifetime
  bool live;               //Is particle live
};
```

The notable thing here is that the update() function has a parameter dt. This is a **time step**, that is, the time in seconds between the current and the previous callings of this function. This parameter will be used for physics computing.

The particle holds the following attributes: position (pos), velocity (vel), and time from when it's born (time). Other attributes—color and size—will be calculated based on the time value. The lifeTime is a constant value, meaning the maximal time of living for the particle; when time is greater than lifeTime, the particle dies, that is, it becomes inactive. The live value holds the current state of a particle's activity—is it live (true) or not (false)? An inactive (dead) particle is not updated and not being drawn.

Before implementing methods of this class, we need to represent the control parameters for particles that fly. Each parameter should be accessible by all the particles, and also can be changed in the testApp class. The simplest way to achieve this is by using a **global variable**. Also, it is better not to use many global variables, and hence we combine all the parameters in a separate class and declare just one global variable.

Control parameters

Let's discuss the control parameters we should use. We want our particle to be born inside a circular area; it means we have circular **emitter**, with the center eCenter and a radius eRad. A particle will start moving with its initial random velocity limited by some value (velRad):

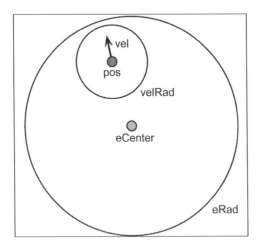

A particle has a limited lifetime (`lifeTime`). Also, we want to have a possibility to rotate its velocity vector with a constant speed (`rotate`).

As a result, we obtain the following control parameters' class declaration, which you should add in the `testApp.h` file:

```
class Params {
public:
  void setup();
  ofPoint eCenter;     //Emitter center
  float eRad;          //Emitter radius
  float velRad;        //Initial velocity limit
  float lifeTime;      //Lifetime in seconds

  float rotate;     //Direction rotation speed in angles per second
};

extern Params param;   //Declaration of a global variable
```

The last line declares `param` as a global variable using the `extern` C++ keyword. It means that `param` is accessible in each C++ file, which includes the `testApp.h` file. Though in our example, it is not necessary (we will use `param` just in the `testApp.cpp` file); this method of defining global variables can be useful if you extend this project further.

Note, the `extern Params param;` line is just a declaration but not a definition of `param`. For successful compiling, we must add the `Params param;` line in the `testApp.cpp` file. Also, we should define the `Params::setup()` function, which sets the initial values for control parameters:

```
Params param;          //Definition of global variable

void Params::setup() {
  eCenter = ofPoint( ofGetWidth() / 2, ofGetHeight() / 2 );
  eRad = 50;
  velRad = 200;
  lifeTime = 1.0;

  rotate = 90;
}
```

Now, we are ready to define all the functions for the `Particle` class.

Defining the particle functions

In the `testApp.cpp` file, add the constructor of the `Particle` class:

```
Particle::Particle() {
  live = false;
}
```

It has no parameters, so this is a **default constructor** of the `Particle` class. In C++, such constructors are called automatically when an object of a corresponding class is created. In our case, the constructor just sets the `live` value to `false`. It means that all created particles will be inactive by default. To make them start flying, we need to directly call their `setup()` function.

Before defining the `Particle::setup()` function, we insert an additional function `randomPointInCircle()` definition, which returns a random vector lying in a circle with center (0, 0) and radius `maxRad`:

```
ofPoint randomPointInCircle( float maxRad ){
  ofPoint pnt;
  float rad = ofRandom( 0, maxRad );
  float angle = ofRandom( 0, M_TWO_PI );
  pnt.x = cos( angle ) * rad;
  pnt.y = sin( angle ) * rad;
  return pnt;
}
```

We will use this function for initializing a particle's position and velocity. Though the `randomPointInCircle( maxRad )` function returns a random vector inside a circle, the resultant **probability distribution** is not uniform (when `maxRad` is greater than zero). For our example, such nonuniformity is not important but is interesting.

Now we define the `Particle::setup()` function. It initializes all the parameters and sets the value of `live` to `true` so the particle becomes active and begins to fly:

```
void Particle::setup() {
  pos = param.eCenter + randomPointInCircle( param.eRad );
  vel = randomPointInCircle( param.velRad );
  time = 0;
  lifeTime = param.lifeTime;
  live = true;
}
```

This function uses all the control parameters held in a `param` object, except the `velRotate` value. This value will be used in the `Particle::update()` function, so a user can change this parameter dynamically and it will affect the particle system.

Next, the `Particle::update()` function's code checks whether the particle is active and then rotates the velocity vector, updates the position, and checks the particle's lifetime. The input parameter `dt` is a time step:

```
void Particle::update( float dt ){
  if ( live ) {
      //Rotate vel
      vel.rotate( 0, 0, param.rotate * dt );

      //Update pos
      pos += vel * dt;      //Euler method

      //Update time and check if particle should die
      time += dt;
      if ( time >= lifeTime ) {
          live = false;    //Particle is now considered as died
      }
  }
}
```

The first notable thing here is how we rotate the `vel` vector using the `vel.rotate()` function. This function performs rotation of `vel`, considered as a vector in 3D space, by specifying three parameters as rotation angles in x, y, and z axes respectively. So, in the code, we rotate in the z axis only; therefore, `vel` rotates just in the xy plane. This is exactly what we need.

The second thing to mention is the use of the Euler method for updating the position using velocity.

The **Euler method** is a popular method used for an approximate integration. It states that for the given continuous functions, $f(t)$ and $g(t)$, if $f(t)$ is equal to $g'(t)$, and $f(t0)$ is given, we can use the following formula for an approximate computing of $f(t0 + dt)$:

$$f(t0 + dt) = f(t0) + g(t0) \cdot dt$$

In our case, velocity is derivative of position. Following the Euler method, if we know the current position pos of a particle, after dt seconds, it will be equal to the sum of pos and vel multiplied by dt ((pos + vel) * dt). We don't care about the previous pos values, so just replace the pos value with a new one as follows:

```
pos += vel * dt;
```

See more information on the Euler method at en.wikipedia.org/wiki/Euler_method. There is another popular integration method, which is more accurate than the Euler method and often used for particles' physics computing. It is called the **Verlet integration**; see en.wikipedia.org/wiki/Verlet_integration for further details.

Finally, we define the body of the drawing function `Particle::draw()`. This function checks whether the particle is active and then computes the size and color of a particle in dependence of `time`. During its lifetime, the size increases from 1 to 3 and then decreases back, and the color hue is constantly changing. The particle is rendered as a circle:

```
void Particle::draw(){
    if ( live ) {
        //Compute size
        float size = ofMap(
            fabs(time - lifeTime/2), 0, lifeTime/2, 3, 1 );

        //Compute color
        ofColor color = ofColor::red;
        float hue = ofMap( time, 0, lifeTime, 128, 255 );
        color.setHue( hue );
        ofSetColor( color );

        ofCircle( pos, size );  //Draw particle
    }
}
```

We specify the `Particle` and `Params` classes and now use them in the project.

Implementing a particle in the project

Let's implement one particle object in the project's testApp class. Also, we will add a possibility for particles to leave trails that will slowly disappear. We will implement it using the offscreen buffer FBO (see the *Using FBO for offscreen drawing* section in *Chapter 2, Drawing in 2D*).

In the testApp.h file, in the testApp class declaration, add the following declarations:

```
Particle p;            //Particle
ofFbo fbo;             //Offscreen buffer for trails
float history;         //Control parameter for trails
float time0;           //Time value for computing dt
```

The history variable will take values in the range [0, 1]. It controls the decaying time of the trails. Value 0.0 means that trails disappear immediately (so there are no trails), and value 1.0 means that trails are infinite. The dependence between history and trails' length is nonlinear; trails are slightly visible when history is about 0.5, and trails become long only when history is more than 0.8.

In the testApp.cpp file, fill the body of the testApp::setup() function with the following code, which sets up buffer and parameters:

```
void testApp::setup(){
  ofSetFrameRate( 60 );      //Set screen frame rate

  //Allocate drawing buffer
  int w = ofGetWidth();
  int h = ofGetHeight();
  fbo.allocate( w, h, GL_RGB32F_ARB );

  //Fill buffer with white color
  fbo.begin();
  ofBackground(255, 255, 255);
  fbo.end();

  //Set up parameters
  param.setup();             //Global parameters
  history = 0.995;

  time0 = ofGetElapsedTimef();
}
```

The notable part here is the last parameter of the fbo.allocate() function calling, namely, GL_RGB32F_ARB.

The code to call `fbo.allocate()` with the last optional argument `GL_RGB32F_ARB` is as follows:

```
fbo.allocate( w, h, GL_RGB32F_ARB );
```

The preceding line of code means that `fbo` will hold the pixel color components as the `float` values. This is a much more accurate representation of colors than what we find in the default mode (in which pixels' components are the `unsigned char` values). It is unimportant when we use `fbo` just for accumulating drawings. But when we are gradually erasing the buffer's content, the accuracy of the `unsigned char` values is insufficient and leads to visual artifacts.

Note, the float `fbo` occupies four times more video memory. Also, it may not work on old or integrated video cards. In case of problems, you can allocate `fbo` using the ordinary method `fbo.allocate( w, h )`, though, the picture with trails will not be so clean and perfect.

The `testApp::update()` function computes `dt`, activates a particle if it is not alive, and updates the particle state:

```
void testApp::update(){
    //Compute dt
    float time = ofGetElapsedTimef();
    float dt = ofClamp( time - time0, 0, 0.1 );
    time0 = time;

    //If the particle is not active - activate it
    if ( !p.live ) {
        p.setup();
    }

    //Update the particle
    p.update( dt );
}
```

The `dt` is a time step value that is computed as a time difference between the current time and time of previous calling of the `update()` function. We use the `ofClamp()` function for limiting its value by `0.1`. The reason for this is that sometimes `time - time0` can be a large value. (For example, if the user drags the window or hides the application's window, `update()` callings can be paused—it depends on the operating system.) So if we don't limit this, formulas in the Euler method will work in an unstable way, and the model will literally explode.

The `testApp::draw()` function performs drawing in the `fbo` buffer and then draws it on the screen:

```
void testApp::draw(){
  ofBackground( 255, 255, 255 );  //Set white background

  //1. Drawing to buffer
  fbo.begin();

  //Draw semi-transparent white rectangle
  //to slightly clearing a buffer (depends on history value)

  ofEnableAlphaBlending();        //Enable transparency

  float alpha = (1-history) * 255;
  ofSetColor( 255, 255, 255, alpha );
  ofFill();
  ofRect( 0, 0, ofGetWidth(), ofGetHeight() );

  ofDisableAlphaBlending();       //Disable transparency

  //Draw the particle
  ofFill();
  p.draw();

  fbo.end();

  //2. Draw buffer on the screen
  ofSetColor( 255, 255, 255 );
  fbo.draw( 0, 0 );
}
```

Note that drawing in buffer consists of two steps: slightly erasing the current buffer's content (level of erasing depends on the `history` value) and drawing the particle. Erasing is performed by drawing a semitransparent white rectangle in the buffer. For achieving it, we enable working with transparency by calling the `ofEnableAlphaBlending()` function, and after that we disable it by calling `ofDisableAlphaBlending()`. See details on working with transparency in the *Transparency* section in *Chapter 4, Images and Textures*.

Run the project. It will activate the single particle; this particle will fly and get deactivated when its `lifeTime` exceeds `param.lifeTime`, which is 1.0 seconds. So each second particle will be activated in a random place with random velocity. The buffer keeps the trails, so you will see a picture as shown in the following screenshot:

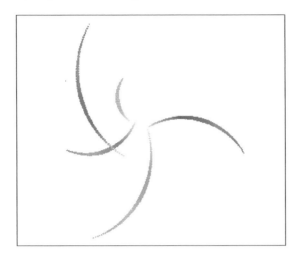

Notice that the old trails gradually disappear. Also, notice that the particle's trajectories are curvilinear because its velocity vector rotates (due to the `rotate` parameter), and the particle changes its color from aqua to red. You can play with the control parameters and see how it affects the particle's behavior.

Now, let's add to the project the capability to working with many particles.

An emitter

In this section, we add to the project the **emitter**, which will create particles at a specified rate.

 An example of this is `03-Particles/02-ParticlesEmitter`.

The example is based on the `03-Particles/01-SingleParticle` project, implemented in the previous section. We implement the emitter right inside the `testApp` class. In the class declaration, replace the following line with declaration of a single particle `Particle p;` with an array of particles:

```
vector<Particle> p;    //Particles
```

We will delete inactive particles from any parts of the p array. So for computational efficiency, it is preferable to use the deque class instead of vector. But for simplicity, in this example, we use vector. It works fast enough for our purposes in the example.

See usage of deque in the *Radial slit-scan example* section in *Chapter 5, Working with Videos*.

Next, add the declaration of the parameter bornRate and the supplementary variable bornCount:

```
float bornRate;      //Particles born rate per second
float bornCount;     //Integrated number of particles to born
```

The bornRate parameter sets the number of particles that should be born in one second. If its value is small, the particles should not be born with each testApp::update() calling, so we need a method of detecting when we should emit new particles. Such a method is using the float variable bornCount, which accumulates the number of particles that would be born. When it becomes greater than 1.0, we emit the int(bornCount) particles.

To initialize the values bornRate and bornCount, add the following lines to the testApp::setup() function:

```
bornRate = 1000;
bornCount = 0;
```

The main part of the modification needed for the emitter implementation is in the testApp::update() function. It's the beginning that computes dt that remains untouched from the previous project. Then it deletes the inactive particles from the p array, gives birth to new particles depending on the bornRate value parameter, and finally updates all the particles:

```
void testApp::update(){
  //Compute dt
  float time = ofGetElapsedTimef();
  float dt = ofClamp( time - time0, 0, 0.1 );
  time0 = time;

  //Delete inactive particles
  int i=0;
  while (i < p.size()) {
      if ( !p[i].live ) {
          p.erase( p.begin() + i );
      }
```

```
        else {
            i++;
        }
    }


    //Born new particles
    bornCount += dt * bornRate;        //Update bornCount value
    if ( bornCount >= 1 ) {            //It's time to born particle(s)
        int bornN = int( bornCount );//How many born
        bornCount -= bornN;            //Correct bornCount value
        for (int i=0; i<bornN; i++) {
            Particle newP;
            newP.setup();              //Start a new particle
            p.push_back( newP );       //Add this particle to array
        }
    }


    //Update the particles
    for (int i=0; i<p.size(); i++) {
        p[i].update( dt );
    }
}
```

Finally, in `testApp::draw()`, you will find the ensuing lines:

```
//Draw the particle
ofFill();
p.draw();
```

Replace the preceding lines with the following lines:

```
//Draw the particles
ofFill();
for (int i=0; i<p.size(); i++) {
  p[i].draw();
}
```

The project is ready.

 We suggest compiling and running the project in the **Release** mode of your development environment for better performance.

Run it, and you will see a beautiful and vivid picture made by many particles flying in curvilinear trajectories and leaving the trails, as shown in the following screenshot:

Now we add a couple of new control parameters for extending the behavior of the particle system.

The attraction, repulsion, and spinning forces

Let's extend our particle's model with three new control parameters—attraction/repulsion, spinning forces inside the emitter (the `force` and `spinning` parameters), and friction that freezes the motion (the `friction` parameter).

 An example of this is `03-Particles/03-ParticlesForces`.

The example is based on the `03-Particles/02-ParticlesEmitter` project, implemented in the previous section. Add a declaration of the new parameters to the `Params` class declaration:

```
float force;      //Attraction/repulsion force inside emitter
float spinning;   //Spinning force inside emitter
float friction;   //Friction, in the range [0, 1]
```

Then add their initialization in `Params::setup()`:

```
force = 0;
spinning = 0;
friction = 0;
```

Finally, implement these parameters by inserting the following code in the `Particle::update()` function after the `vel.rotate(...)` line:

```
ofPoint acc;            //Acceleration
ofPoint delta = pos - param.eCenter;
float len = delta.length();
if ( ofInRange( len, 0, param.eRad ) ) {
  delta.normalize();

  //Attraction/repulsion force
  acc += delta * param.force;

  //Spinning force
  acc.x += -delta.y * param.spinning;
  acc.y += delta.x * param.spinning;
}
vel += acc * dt;                //Euler method
vel *= ( 1 - param.friction );  //Friction
```

If you run the project and notice nothing changing in the picture, it's because all the new parameters are initialized with zeros. Now try the following sets of parameters:

- The first set is as follows:
  - In `Params::setup()`, add the following:
    ```
    eRad = 100;
    velRad = 0;
    lifeTime = 2.0;
    rotate = 0;
    force = 1000;
    spinning = 1000;
    friction = 0.05;
    ```

○ In `testApp::setup()`, add the following:

```
history = 0.9;
bornRate = 1500;
```

- The second set is as follows:

  ○ In `Params::setup()`, add the following:

  ```
  eRad = 300;
  velRad = 0;
  lifeTime = 3.0;
  rotate = 500;
  force = -1000;
  spinning = 1000;
  friction = 0.05;
  ```

  ○ In `testApp::setup()`, add the following:

  ```
  history = 0.9;
  bornRate = 2500;
  ```

By running the project with these parameters, you obtain the following pictures respectively, as shown in the following screenshot:

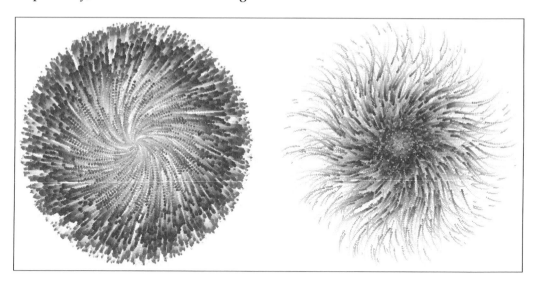

Graphical user interface

When you play with our particle system, soon you find that adjusting parameters by changing their values right in the code is very uncomfortable. The solution for this is adding the **Graphical User Interface (GUI)** to the project that shows sliders for changing the parameters using the mouse, as shown in the screenshot:

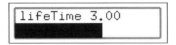

We have implemented a similar GUI in the example project `03-Particles/04-Particles`. There are two new classes: `Slider` for a single slider and `Interface` for managing all the sliders.

While running the project, you can adjust all the control parameters using the mouse. Also, you can load and save parameters' settings (**presets**) using keys *1, 2, … 9*, and *Shift + 1, Shift + 2, … Shift + 9*. See the example's code for more details.

Finally, you can add to the project the capability to receive **OSC** network messages and control it from tablets such as iPad and VJ programs such as VDMX and Max/MSP. For details, see the *Using OSC protocol* section in *Chapter 11, Networking*.

> In this example, we implemented simplest GUI for demonstrating how to create custom GUIs in our projects. But, openFrameworks has a variety of ready-to-use GUI classes, which implement sliders, buttons, and checkboxes. Their values can be saved and loaded from XML files and controlled by OSC network messages. See the examples of using these classes in openFrameworks' folder `examples/gui`.

Additional topics

In the chapter, we covered just a part of particle systems' ideas and methods. For further exploration of this field, we would suggest the following topics:

- See the great introduction on particle systems' physics (for **Processing** language) in *The Nature of Code, Daniel Shiffman*, at `natureofcode.com/book/chapter-4-particle-systems/`

- Look at the **Box2D** physics library, which can be used for modeling elastic bounces between particles. Actually, this is a universal and an extremely popular 2D physics library, which can be useful in various projects even not related to particles. To use the library in openFrameworks, you can use the **ofxBox2d** addon by *Vanderlin* available at `ofxaddons.com`.

- Play with the **marching cubes** algorithm, which provides the other way for rendering particles, not as sprites but as polygonal volumes in 3D space. Such a method of particles' visualization is called **metaballs**, and it can be a fruitful source of interesting visual effects. (See the *Additional topics* section in *Chapter 7, Drawing in 3D*, for more information).

Summary

In this chapter, we covered the particle systems, a fruitful tool for generating stunning and vivid graphics. We built a project which draws a simple particle system. It can be used as a sketch for your further experiments with particles.

In the next chapter, we begin to consider multimedia capabilities of openFrameworks, and start with working with images.

4
Images and Textures

It is often insufficient to create rich visualizations using only basic geometric primitives. Images are the building blocks that help in adding decoration, style, and even photorealism to an interactive scene. In this chapter we will cover the basic operations that we can perform on images:

- Loading and drawing an image
- Rotating images
- Color modulation
- Transparency
- Creating and modifying images
- Using of Texture for memory optimization
- Image warping and video mapping

Raster and vector images

In computer graphics and computer vision, an image is a two-dimensional picture that is used for a wide range of purposes. There are two classes – **raster** and **vector** images.

Raster images are rectangular arrays of picture elements (called **pixels**) and they are natural for representing photos from digital cameras. Modern computer screens are physical arrays of pixels, hence the screens are natural devices for displaying raster images.

Vector images consist of a number of graphical primitives such as lines, circles, and curves, and they are natural for representing precise drawings such as cartoons and graphs. Vector images can be scaled up without any loss of quality and increase in the size of memory, hence they are used for parametrical drawings.

openFrameworks works with both raster and vector images. In this chapter, we will deal with raster images only. For working with vector images, the `examples/addons/svgExample` example.

Let's consider the two basic operations with an image – loading an image from a file and drawing it on the screen.

Loading and drawing an image

For loading and drawing an image, you need to declare the image object, load the image from a file, and add a drawing function call in the `testApp::draw()` function. Perform the following steps:

1. Declare the image as an `ofImage` object:

   ```
   ofImage image;
   ```

   The best way is to declare images in the `testApp` class declaration in the `testApp.h` file. For simplicity, sometimes we will declare them right on top of the `testApp.cpp` file.

2. Load an image from a file using the `loadImage` function:

   ```
   image.loadImage( fileName );
   ```

   Here, `fileName` is a string value specifying the filename; for example, `sunflower.png`. Normally, images should be located in the `bin/data` folder of your application. If you want to use an image from another folder, it is possible to use absolute paths; for example, `image.loadImage( "C:\\myimage.png" )` in Windows.

3. Draw the image using the `image.draw( x, y )` function inside the `testApp::draw()` function. Here, x and y are float values specifying the top-left corner of the image on the screen.

Let's implement these steps in a project. It just draws a single image on the screen. The project is based on openFrameworks' `emptyExample` example. Copy the folder with the example and rename it. Then place the image `sunflower.png` into the `bin/data` folder of the project. Now, replace the beginning of the `testApp.cpp` file with the following code:

```
#include "testApp.h"

ofImage image;        //Declare image object

void testApp::setup(){
  //Load image file
```

```
    image.loadImage("sunflower.png");
}

void testApp::update(){
}

void testApp::draw(){
    //Set up gray background
    ofBackground(128, 128, 128);

    //Draw image with top left corner x=100, y=50 pixels
    image.draw( 100, 50 );
}
```

 This is example 04-Images/01-ImageDraw.

Run the project; you will see the image shown in the following screenshot on the screen:

As you can see, we used an image in PNG file format. Besides, openFrameworks allows us to load and save images in JPG, BMP, and TIFF file formats. Among these, PNG is the most usable because it keeps the high quality of the original image, can maintain transparency, has small file size, and decodes very fast. JPG is good for smooth and realistic images such as photos. This format can reduce visible image quality, and does not work with transparency, but has smaller file size in case of real-life photos. BMP and TIFF store images in uncompressed form. They are good for holding and processing images without losing quality. They are rarely used in interactive applications because their file sizes are too large and image loading from such files is slow.

You can not only load images but also save them to PNG, JPG, BMP, or TIFF files. For such purposes, use the `image.saveImage()` method. See the following example:

```
image.saveImage( "test.png" );
```

It is possible to move, scale, and stretch images on the screen using the overloaded version of the `draw()` method: `image.draw( x, y, w, h )`. It draws the `image` object, additionally specifying the width `w` and the height `h` in pixels.

Also, there are overloaded versions of the `image.draw()` method which allows us to simplify the code:

- `image.draw( p )` – draws image using point p of type `ofPoint`
- `image.draw( rect )` – draws image using rectangle `rect` of type `ofRectangle`

For retrieving the original image size in pixels, you can use its width and height fields, `image.width` and `image.height`, having type `int`. The following are examples of using these:

- Drawing an image that is 50 percent of its size with top-left corner at (0, 0):
  ```
  image.draw( 0, 0, image.width*0.5, image.height*0.5 );
  ```

- Drawing an image with width equal to `300` pixels and proportional height:
  ```
  image.draw( 0, 0, 300, 300.0*image.height/image.width );
  ```

- Drawing an image with arbitrary proportions; for example, width `100` and height `200`:
  ```
  image.draw( 0, 0, 100, 200 );
  ```

- Images can be flipped using a negative value for width or height. For example, for vertical flipping use the following code:
  ```
  image.draw( 0, image.height, image.width, -image.height);
  ```

Instead of writing big formulas inside the arguments of the `image.draw( x, y, w, h )` method, you can use the `ofTranslate( x, y )` and `ofScale( scaleX, scaleY )` methods for translating and scaling the coordinate system, which is used for drawing everything on the screen. (See the *Coordinate system transformations* section in *Chapter 2, Drawing in 2D* for details.) You can call `ofTranslate()` and `ofScale()` in the required succession to obtain the desired transformations. If you are not very familiar with coordinate transformations, it will seem harder. But, trust me, it makes your code cleaner and easy to read and maintain. Also, see the next section for details.

Rotating images

The `image.draw()` method does not have parameters to rotate images on arbitrary angles. To achieve this effect, we need to work with coordinate system transformations, which are described in detail in the *Coordinate system transformations* section in *Chapter 2, Drawing in 2D*.

We need to carry out the following steps for drawing a rotated image:

1. Store the current transformation matrix using `ofPushMatrix()`.
2. Change the matrix by applying rotation transformation using `ofRotate()`.
3. Draw the image using `image.draw()`.
4. Restore the original transformation matrix using `ofPopMatrix()`.

The following code illustrates these steps. It draws the image rotated at 10 degrees around the current center of coordinates, which is (0, 0).

```
void testApp::draw(){
  ofPushMatrix();           //Store the transformation matrix
  ofRotate( 10.0 );         //Applying rotation on 10 degrees
  image.draw( 0, 0 );       //Draw image
  ofPopMatrix();            //Restore the transformation
}
```

Sometimes, we will want to rotate an image around its center instead of the top-left corner. To achieve this, we need to translate the center of coordinates to the desired center of rotation, rotate the coordinate system, and finally draw an image translated in such a way that the center of the image is located in the coordinate center. The following code demonstrates this by drawing an image that slowly rotates over time:

```
void testApp::draw(){
  ofPushMatrix ();

  //Shift center of coordinate system ( 0,0 ) to the desired
  //point, which will be rotation center
  ofTranslate( 500, 400 );

  //Rotate coordinate system, 10 degrees per second
  ofRotate( 10.0 * ofGetElapsedTimef() );

  //Draw image in a way that its center on the screen coincide
  //with ( 0,0 )
  image.draw( -image.width/2, -image.height/2 );

  ofPopMatrix();
}
```

Also, there is a more elegant way to draw an image centered at a particular point. Instead of using image.draw(-image.width/2, -image.height/2), we can change the **anchor point** of the image; that is, a point used as the origin while drawing an image. It can be done by calling the following function:

```
image.setAnchorPercent( 0.5, 0.5 );
```

The preceding method sets the anchor point to 50 percent; that is, 50 percent of image size, which is the center of the image. Then call the image.draw(0, 0) method, which will draw the image, centered at (0, 0). To reset the anchor to its default state, call image.setAnchorPercent(0, 0) or image.resetAnchor().

You can also set an anchor point by specifying it in pixel coordinates (x, y) using the image.setAnchorPoint(x, y) function.

Using ofTranslate(), ofScale(), and ofRotate() is a good way of experimenting with parametric drawing. Here is an example of creating a collage of images:

 This is example 04-Images/02-ImageSpiral.

```
void testApp::draw(){
    //Set up white background
    ofBackground( 255, 255, 255 );

    for (int i=0; i<20; i++) {
        ofPushMatrix();

        //Translate system coordinates to screen center
        ofTranslate( ofGetWidth() / 2, ofGetHeight() / 2 );

        //Rotate coordinate system on i * 15 degrees
        ofRotate( i * 15 );

        //Go right on 50 * i * 10 pixels
        //in rotated coordinate system
        ofTranslate( 50 + i * 10, 0 );

        //Scale coordinate system for decreasing drawing
        //image size
        float scl = 1.0 - i * 0.8 / 20.0;
        ofScale( scl, scl );
        //scl decreases with i, so the images
```

```
        //became gradually smaller

        //Draw image
        image.draw( -100, -100, 200, 200 );

        ofPopMatrix();
    }
}
```

Run the project; you will see a spiral made of images, as shown in the following screenshot:

Color modulation

There is a nice way to change the overall color of a drawing image by multiplying ("modulating") the color components of each pixel by some fixed number. It is realized by using the `ofSetColor()` function. Namely, calling `ofSetColor( r, g, b )` or `ofSetColor( r, g, b, a )` before `image.draw()` implies that the red, green, blue, and alpha components of each image's pixel will be multiplied by $r' = r / 255.0$, $g' = g / 255.0$, $b' = b / 255.0$, and $a' = a / 255.0$ respectively.

Note that the parameters r, g, b, and a in `ofSetColor` lie in the 0 to 255 range, so r', g', b', a' lie in the range $[0..1]$. So, by using such a modulation, you can decrease or retain the color components of pixels but you cannot increase them.

For arbitrary manipulations with color components while drawing images, use the fragment shader (see *Chapter 8, Using Shaders*). Also, you can change all the pixels of the image itself. This method is good and appropriate but works slowly when it changes the image. For details, see the *Creating and modifying images* section.

The following are some examples:

- Drawing an image with unchanged colors:

  ```
  ofSetColor( 255, 255, 255 );
  image.draw( 0, 0, 200, 100 );
  ```

- Drawing an image with half-value of colors:

  ```
  ofSetColor( 128, 128, 128);
  image.draw( 250, 0, 200, 100 );
  ```

- Drawing only a red channel of an image:

  ```
  ofSetColor( 255, 0, 0 );
  image.draw( 150, 0, 200, 100 );
  ```

You will see the images shown in the following screenshot:

You can note that the result of the color modulation resembles a tonal correction in a photo editor such as Adobe Photoshop or Gimp.

Remember, calling `ofSetColor()` affects all the images being drawn after the call. So, if you need to draw images without modulation, it is a good idea to call `ofSetColor( 255, 255, 255 )` before drawing your images.

You can see that in these examples we didn't demonstrate the usage of the alpha channel. This is a very important matter of transparency, and we will discuss it in detail now.

Transparency

Using the methods described in the earlier sections, we can construct overlapped collages of images, changing their size, orientation, and color. Until now, such collages were made of images, which look like colored rectangles. But we often want to have collages made of non-rectangular images, as shown in the following screenshot:

In the preceding screenshot, the collage is made of a number of sunflower images, having not a rectangular but quite a difficult curvilinear shape. Modeling such shapes directly is a difficult and memory-consuming task. A more elegant solution, used in raster graphics, is using the alpha channel. In this technique, we still use rectangular images but consider the pixels as having not only color components but also an additional alpha component that controls the pixel's opacity. The minimum alpha value (0) means that the pixel is absolutely transparent; that is, invisible to the user. And the maximum alpha value (255) means that the pixel is opaque. You can prepare an image with transparent pixels using your preferred image editor, such as Adobe Photoshop or Gimp. In the editor, remove the background pixels with the **Magic Wand** tool or the **Eraser** tool and save the file in the PNG format. While saving, select the 24- or 32-bit PNG format, but not an 8-bit PNG format because it has a limited palette and isn't good for our purposes.

 Note that JPG files do not maintain transparency.

The result of deleting the background is shown in the following screenshot:

There are not only the absolute transparent and opaque pixels (alpha 0 and 255) but also everything in between (alpha values from 1 to 254). How to deal with such pixels? The process of overlapping colors with transparency is called **blending**. By default, blending a new color (r, g, b, a) over the old color (R, G, B, A) of the screen pixel is performed using the following formulas:

- $R' = (1-a/255) \cdot R + a/255 \cdot r$
- $G' = (1-a/255) \cdot G + a/255 \cdot g$
- $B' = (1-a/255) \cdot B + a/255 \cdot b$
- $A' = (1-a/255) \cdot A + a/255 \cdot a$

You can see that if *a* equals *255*, (R', G', B', A') is equal to (r, g, b, a); that is, the screen's pixel color is replaced by a new color. If *a* equals *0*, (R', G', B', A') is equal to (R, G, B, A); that is, a new pixel does not affect the screen and hence is invisible.

Blending with such formulas is called **alpha-blending**. It suits well for normal collaging. But there exist other modes that are switched by using the `ofEnableBlendMode()` function.

For example, the **adding** mode, which just sums up the colors, can be enabled using the following line:

```
ofEnableBlendMode( OF_BLENDMODE_ADD );
```

While testing this mode, do not use the white color for the background. Because adding colors to white color will result in white color again! So, if you set a white background, the resulting picture will always be pure white.

For returning to the alpha-blending mode, call the following function:

```
ofEnableBlendMode( OF_BLENDMODE_ALPHA );
```

See examples of the other built-in blending modes in the openFrameworks example located at `examples/graphics/blendingExample`.

It should be noted that the built-in blending modes are useful and simple, but fixed and, therefore, limited. The most flexible tool for implementing special, parameterized, and nonstationary blending modes are fragment shaders (see *Chapter 8, Using Shaders*).

By default, blending is enabled in openFrameworks, hence alpha channel is used for drawing. If you need to disable blending and treat all the pixels as opaque, call the `ofDisableAlphaBlending()` function. To enable blending again, call the `ofEnableAlphaBlending()` function.

Disabled blending is often used for drawing FBO (see the details on FBO in the *Using FBO for offscreen drawing* section in *Chapter 2, Drawing in 2D*). The reason is to eliminating undesired secondary blending, which occurs when FBO contains transparent pixels.

When alpha-blending is enabled, you can draw the whole image as a semi-transparent image by calling ofSetColor(r, g, b, a) with a less than 255. For example, the following code draws a half-transparent image:

```
ofSetColor( 255, 255, 255, 128 );
image.draw( 0, 0 );
```

The following code demonstrates working with transparency using both alpha channel and color modulation with the alpha component. It is based on the emptyExample project of openFrameworks. Before running it, copy the sunflower-transp.png file into the bin/data folder of your project.

 This is example 04-Images/03-ImageTransp.

```
#include "testApp.h"

ofImage image;          //Declare image object

void testApp::setup(){
    image.loadImage("sunflower-transp.png");
}

void testApp::update(){
}

void testApp::draw(){
    //Set up white background
    ofBackground(255, 255, 255);

    //Draw two images without color modulation
    //(but using alpha channel by default)
    ofSetColor( 255, 255, 255, 255 );
    image.draw( 100, 0 );
    image.draw( 250, 0 );

    //Draw half-transparent image
    ofSetColor( 255, 255, 255, 128 );
    image.draw( 400, 0 );
}
```

On running the project, you will see two opaque sunflower images and one half-transparent sunflower image. All images have the background pixels removed.

Using images with alpha channel is a powerful technique for creating interactive installations in cartoon style. For example, see the images from our interactive installation, *Kuklon* (*Igor Sodazot*, *Denis Perevalov*, 2011) in the following screenshot. The installation represents an imaginary world. A funny doll that repeats the spectator's motions lives there.

The largest image shown in the following screenshot is the resultant scene, and the other images are parts from which the scene is built:

Creating and modifying images

In the preceding sections, we considered different ways of drawing images loaded from files. In this section, we see how to generate new images or alter an existing image by specifying its pixels directly.

A raster image is represented as an array of pixels in memory. If we have an image with width w pixels and height h pixels, it is represented by N = w * h pixels. Normally, the horizontal rows of an image lie sequentially in memory: the w pixels of the first row, then the second row, and so on to the h row.

The pixels of the image can hold differing amounts of information depending on the image type. In openFrameworks, the following types are used:

- The OF_IMAGE_COLOR_ALPHA type denotes a colored image with transparency. Here, each pixel is represented by 4 bytes, holding red, green, blue, and alpha color components respectively, with values from 0 to 255.

- The OF_IMAGE_COLOR type denotes colored image without transparency. Here each pixels is represented by 3 bytes, holding red, green, and blue components. Such images are used when no transparency pixels are needed. For example, JPG files and images from cameras represented in openFrameworks of this type.

- The OF_IMAGE_GRAYSCALE type denotes a grayscale image. Each pixel here is represented by 1 byte and holds only one component of color. Most often, such images are used for representing masks. In most situations, we use colored images, but if your project needs a *huge* amount of masks or halftone images use grayscale type, because it occupies less memory.

In this book, we are talking mainly about images of class ofImage, where each pixel component is represented by 1 byte, with integer values from 0 to 255 (type unsigned char). But, in some cases, more accuracy is needed. Such situations occur when using a buffer with gradual content erasing, or using an image as a height map. For such purposes, openFrameworks has an image class, ofFloatImage. The methods of the class are the same as ofImage, but each pixel component holds a float value. For an example on how to use it, see examples/graphics/floatingPointImageExample.

Also, there is the class of ofShortImage, which works with integer values in the range 0 to 65535; that is, unsigned short type. Such images are a best fit for representing data from depth cameras, where pixels hold distance to the scene objects in millimeters.

See more details on using these image types in *Chapter 9, Computer Vision with OpenCV*, and *Chapter 10, Using Depth Cameras*.

Creating images

To create image by code, we need to create a pixel array and then push it into the image using the `image.setFromPixels( data, w, h, type )` method. Here `data` is the pixels array, `w` is the image width, `h` is image height, and `type` is the image type (`OF_IMAGE_COLOR_ALPHA`, `OF_IMAGE_COLOR`, or `OF_IMAGE_GRAYSCALE`).

The `data` should be array of `unsigned char` type. If we create a four-channel image with width `w` and height `h` pixels, then array size will be $w * h * 4$ bytes. For given x from 0 to $w-1$ and y from 0 to $h-1$, we have the red, green, blue, and alpha components for the pixel (x, y) located in `data[index]`, `data[index + 1]`, `data[index + 2]`, and `data[index + 3]` respectively, where `index` equals `4 * ( x + w * y )`.

In the following example, the image is generated in each `testApp::update()` function calling and it evolves with time.

 This is example `04-Images/04-ColorWaves`.

```
#include "testApp.h"
ofImage image;          //Declare image object

void testApp::setup(){
}

void testApp::update(){
  //Creating image

  int w = 512;   //Image width
  int h = 512;   //Image height

  //Allocate array for filling pixels data
  unsigned char *data = new unsigned char[w * h * 4];

  //Fill array for each pixel (x,y)
  for (int y=0; y<h; y++) {
      for (int x=0; x<w; x++) {
          //Compute preliminary values,
          //needed for our pixel color calculation:

          //1. Time from application start
```

```
        float time = ofGetElapsedTimef();

        //2. Level of hyperbola value of x and y with
        //center in w/2, h/2
        float v = ( x - w/2 ) * ( y - h/2 );

        //3. Combining v with time for motion effect
        float u= v * 0.00025 + time;
        //Here 0.00025 was chosen empirically

        //4. Compute color components as periodical
        //functions of u, and stretched to [0..255]
        int red = ofMap( sin( u ), -1, 1, 0, 255 );
        int green = ofMap( sin( u * 2 ), -1, 1, 0, 255 );
        int blue = 255 - green;
        int alpha = 255;   //Just constant for simplicity


        //Fill array components for pixel (x, y):
        int index = 4 * ( x + w * y );
        data[ index ] = red;
        data[ index + 1 ] = green;
        data[ index + 2 ] = blue;
        data[ index + 3 ] = alpha;
      }
    }

  //Load array to image
  image.setFromPixels( data, w, h, OF_IMAGE_COLOR_ALPHA );

  //Array is not needed anymore, so clear memory
  delete[] data;
}

void testApp::draw(){
  ofBackground(255, 255, 255);      //Set up white background
  ofSetColor( 255, 255, 255 );      //Set color for image drawing
  image.draw( 0, 0 );               //Draw image
}
```

Note, for time measurement, we use the `ofGetElapsedTimef()` function, which returns the float number equal to the amount of seconds from application start. Also, we use the `ofMap()` function for mapping result of `sin(...)` (lying in [-1, 1]) into interval [0, 255]. See details in the *Basic utility functions* section in *Chapter 1*, *openFrameworks Basics*.

After running the preceding code, you will see an animated image with moving color waves, as shown in the following screenshot:

Modifying images

Instead of creating images from nothing, you can modify existing images. For such purposes, use the `image.getPixels()` function, which returns a pixel array of an image. After changing this array, call `image.update()` to apply changes in the image. Actually, `image.update()` loads the changed image into the video memory for drawing on the screen; see the *Using ofTexture for memory optimization* section for details.

This is example `04-Images/05-ImageModify`.

In the following example, we read and modify pixels of the sunflower image and draw it on the screen. We alter the image just once, at `testApp::setup()`. In the code, we did not know exactly which type has the `sunflower.png` image file, `OF_IMAGE_COLOR` or `OF_IMAGE_COLOR_ALPHA`.

For this reason, we made a universal code by computing the number of image pixel components, int components, which equals image.bpp/8. Here, the image.bpp field holds the bits per value and characterizes the number of bits allocated for each image pixel. It can be 8, 24, or 32, which corresponds to OF_IMAGE_GRAYSCALE, OF_IMAGE_COLOR, or OF_IMAGE_COLOR_ALPHA respectively. So, dividing the value 8, we get the number of pixel components 1, 3, or 4. In the example, we use a color image file, so components will be equal to either 3 or 4 (not 1).

In this example, it is convenient to use a number of components. Sometimes, it is more handy to directly check the type of image. The image type is held in the field image.type and gets the values OF_IMAGE_GRAYSCALE, OF_IMAGE_COLOR, and OF_IMAGE_COLOR_ALPHA.

Always check the type or number of color components of a given image in serious projects. Performing image modifications with incorrect assumption of its type leads to computations that rely on incorrect pixel array size. It can cause memory errors or result in corrupted images.

The code is given as follows:

```cpp
#include "testApp.h"
ofImage image;          //Declare image object

void testApp::setup(){
    image.loadImage( "sunflower.png" );   //Load image

    //Modifying image

    //Getting pointer to pixel array of image
    unsigned char *data = image.getPixels();

    //Calculate number of pixel components
    int components = image.bpp / 8;

    //Modify pixel array
    for (int y=0; y<image.height; y++) {
        for (int x=0; x<image.width; x++) {

            //Read pixel (x,y) color components
            int index = components * (x + image.width * y);
            int red = data[ index ];
            int green = data[ index + 1 ];
            int blue = data[ index + 2 ];

            //Calculate periodical modulation
```

```
            float u = abs(sin( x * 0.1 ) * sin( y * 0.1 ) );

            //Set red component modulated by u
            data[ index ] = red * u;

            //Set green value as inverted original red
            data[ index + 1 ] = (255 - red);

            //Invert blue component
            data[ index + 2 ] = (255 - blue);

            //If there is alpha component or not,
            //we don't touch it anyway
        }
    }
    //Calling image.update() to apply changes
    image.update();
}

void testApp::draw(){
    ofBackground( 255, 255, 255 );
    ofSetColor( 255, 255, 255 );
    image.draw( 0, 0 );            //Draw image
}
```

On running the project, you will see the sunflower image with non-linearly modified colors.

The preceding method for manipulating the image's pixels using `image.getPixels()` is fast, but sometimes is not very convenient, because you need to work with each pixel's color component individually. So let's consider more convenient functions, which operate with a pixel's color using `ofColor` type.

Working with the color of a single pixel

There exist functions for getting and setting color of the image's pixel without knowing the image type:

- The `image.getColor( x, y )` function reads color of pixel (x, y) of the image. It returns object of type `ofColor`, with fields r, g, b, a, corresponding red, green, blue, and alpha color components (see details in the *Colors* section in *Chapter 2, Drawing in 2D*).

- The `image.setColor( x, y, color )` function sets color of pixel (x, y) to `color` value, where `color` has type `ofColor`. After changing pixels' colors using `image.setColor()`, you need to call the `image.update()` function for the changes to take effect.

> Be careful, the overall performance of code which uses these functions can be slightly lower than code which uses the functions `image.getPixels()` and `image.setFromPixels()`.

Let's consider an example of using these functions for geometrical distortion of an image.

A simple geometrical distortion example

This example distorts the geometry of an image by shifting its horizontal lines by sine wave, which also changes with time. For achieving this, we keep the original image in `image` untouched, and use it for building distorted image `image2` in the `testApp::update()` function.

> This is example `04-Images/06-HorizontalDistortion`.

```
#include "testApp.h"

ofImage image;          //Original image
ofImage image2;         //Modified image

//--------------------------------------------------------------
```

```
void testApp::setup(){

    image.loadImage( "sunflower.png" );    //Load image
    image2.clone( image );                 //Copy image to image2
}

void testApp::update(){
    float time = ofGetElapsedTimef();

    //Build image2 using image
    for (int y=0; y<image.height; y++) {
        for (int x=0; x<image.width; x++) {
            //Use y and time for computing shifted x1
            float amp = sin( y * 0.03 );
            int x1 = x + sin( time * 2.0 ) * amp * 50.0;

            //Clamp x1 to range [0, image.width-1]
            x1 = ofClamp( x1, 0, image.width - 1 );

            //Set image2(x, y) equal to image(x1, y)
            ofColor color = image.getColor( x1, y );
            image2.setColor( x, y, color );
        }
    }

    image2.update();
}

void testApp::draw(){
    ofBackground(255, 255, 255);
    ofSetColor( 255, 255, 255 );
    image2.draw( 0, 0 );
}
```

Note, in the `testApp::setup()` function, we use the `image2.clone( image )` function, which copies `image` to `image2`. In the given example it is required for allocating `image2`.

When you run the preceding code, you will see a project in which you will see a waving sunflower image as shown in the following screenshot:

Learn how to implement the similar image distortion using shaders in the *A simple geometrical distortion example* section in *Chapter 8, Using Shaders*.

We are about to finish discussing the methods of the image's modification. Now, let's consider useful functions for resizing, cropping, and rotating the images.

The functions for manipulating the image as a whole

There are number of the functions, which perform the global image manipulations. They are as follows:

- `image.resize( newW, newH )` – resizes the image to a new size, newW × newH

- `image.crop( x, y, w, h )` – crops the image to a subimage with the top-left corner (x, y) and size w × h

- `image.rotate90( times )` – rotates the image clockwise at 90 * times degrees

- `image.mirror( vertical, horizontal )` – mirrors the image, where vertical and horizontal are bool values

- `image2.clone( image )` – copies image into image2 (we used this function in the preceding example)

Now we will discuss the relationship between the image in the ordinary memory used by the CPU and the video memory used by the video card. It is important for understanding and optimizing image processing.

Using ofTexture for memory optimization

There are two types of memory in a computer – **Random Access Memory (RAM)**, which is used by the **Central Processing Unit (CPU)**, and video memory, which is used by the video card; that is, the **Graphics Processing Unit (GPU)**. RAM is intended for making calculations and video memory is used for drawing something on the screen.

A typical GPU contains hundreds of computing cores and its number is increasing every year. This is the reason why new GPUs can have more computing power than CPUs, which has just 1 to 16 cores. Today, almost all computations can be made on the GPU using technologies such as shaders, OpenCL or NVIDIA CUDA. Hence the CPU is no longer the most important unit in a computer. For example, the visual development platform Derivative Touch Designer (for Windows only) does its processing almost entirely on the GPU.

Though programming in GPUs is a very powerful tool, it's a little tricky when compared to CPU programming. Also, debugging GPUs is not so convenient yet. So, in this book, we still mainly consider programming in CPU and only touch GPU programming when talking about shaders in *Chapter 8, Using Shaders*.

The architecture of a computer assumes all images, vector graphics, and 3D objects that will be depicted on the screen should be loaded at first into the video memory. Images in the video memory are called **textures**. By default, openFrameworks's class of Image holds two same images. These are the pixel array in RAM that can be accessed by `image.getPixels()` and its clone, the texture in the video memory that can be accessed by `image.getTextureReference()`.

So, when you change the pixel array of `image`, you need to call `image.update()` in order to apply the changes to the corresponding texture.

You may ask why is such a double representation needed? Yes, indeed, it is possible to discard the texture (using the `image.setUseTexture( false )` function) and to render the pixel array directly on the screen. But this operation needs to load the pixel array into the video memory anyway, which is a fast but nevertheless time-consuming operation. So, if we did not change the image or wish to draw it several times on the screen, it is better to have a texture for it.

You can discard a pixel array too. Pixel arrays are just tools for writing images to disks and a convenient way of changing it using CPUs. So, if you do not want to change your image, it is good idea to use only textures, without having pixel arrays in the RAM. To do so, use ofTexture instead of ofImage. In case you are using ofTexture, your image will lie in the video memory only and will not occupy any RAM. So you obtain memory optimization, which is crucial for large projects.

The usage of a texture in the code is much like the use of an instance of ofImage. The following are the functions used for working with textures:

- ofLoadImage(texture, fileName) – loads texture from an image file, fileName

- ofSaveImage(texture, fileName) – saves texture to image file, fileName

- texture.draw(x, y) or texture.draw(x, y, w, h) – draws texture

- texture.loadData(data, w, h, format) – creates texture from the pixel array data, where format is GL_RGBA, GL_RGB, or GL_LUMINANCE for 4, 3, or 1 channel images respectively.

- texture.getWidth() and texture.getHeight() are used for getting texture dimensions.

Here is example of using ofTexture for drawing images:

```
#include "testApp.h"

ofTexture  texture;      //Declare texture

void testApp::setup(){
  //Load texture from file
  ofLoadImage( texture, "sunflower.png" );
}

void testApp::update(){
}

void testApp::draw(){
  ofBackground(255, 255, 255);      //Set background color
  ofSetColor( 255, 255, 255 );
  texture.draw( 0, 0 );             //Draw texture
}
```

We had discussed the basics of textures and now will see how to use it for image warping and its application for video mapping.

Image warping and video mapping

Until now, we drew images as rigid rectangles of arbitrary shapes. But there is a possibility to draw an image as if it were made from rubber. To achieve this effect, the image is decomposed into a mesh consisting of a number of triangles or quadrangles (quads). Each triangle or quad is rendered with an arbitrary position on its vertices while preserving adjacency relation in the mesh. This gives a rubbery effect to the image.

Another way to geometrically achieve image distortion is direct pixel modification of the image, which was discussed earlier. But for big images, such methods often work too slowly.

A faster way to draw images with arbitrary modification is using shaders (see the *Creating video effects with fragment shaders* section in *Chapter 8, Using Shaders*).

Such methods can be used for implementing the video mapping technology; also known as projection mapping. This technology involves the use of projectors for projecting images on non-flat surfaces and objects such as sculptures, buildings, and custom-made constructions such as polyhedrons. In this technology, one or several projectors are mounted in a way that the desired object's surfaces are illuminated by the projector's light. Then the computer generates and sends images to the projectors to draw solid colors, textures, or even moving objects on this surfaces. Often, it is achieved by rendering normal images and then warping these on the object's surface. The parameters of warping are tuned manually or automatically on the stage when projectors and objects are physically mounted and fixed.

The following screenshot shows an example of video mapping onto a real head sculpture using one projector (project by *Igor Sodazot*, 2010):

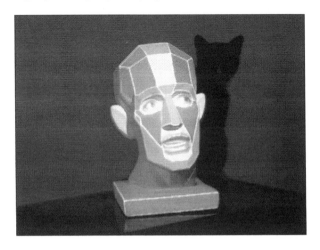

You can mention what edges of the image ideally fit the edges of the sculpture. This was achieved by warping the image's edges interactively, by manually shifting mesh vertices in the video editor.

The most popular and advanced tool for video mapping is **MadMapper**. You can send images from openFrameworks to MadMapper using the ofxSyphon addon (which performs image transfer via the **Syphon** protocol). See *Appendix A, Working with Addons* for more details.

Here we consider the simplest example of warping and video mapping; that is, warping a rectangular image. This model will be mapped onto a flat rectangular surface that is rotated in 3D with respect to the projector.

The example allows you to arbitrarily move the corners of the image that is displayed on the screen. To select one of the four corners of the image, press the key *1*, *2*, *3*, or *4*. To move the selected corner, press any cursor key. The corners' enumeration is shown as follows:

The code's basic function is `texture.draw( p[0], p[1], p[2], p[3] )`, which warps the texture to the selected corner points.

This is example 04-Images/07-VideoMapping.

```cpp
#include "testApp.h"
ofTexture      texture;
ofPoint p[4];              //Corners
int ind = 0;               //Index of selected corner, 0..3

void testApp::setup(){
  //Load texture image
  ofLoadImage( texture, "sunflower.png" );

  //Set up initial corners
  p[0].x = 100;   p[0].y = 100;
  p[1].x = 300;   p[1].y = 100;
  p[2].x = 300;   p[2].y = 300;
  p[3].x = 100;   p[3].y = 300;
}

void testApp::update(){
}

void testApp::draw(){
  ofBackground( 255, 255, 255 );

  ofSetColor( 255, 255, 255 );

  //Draw texture by specifying its target corners points
  texture.draw( p[0], p[1], p[2], p[3] );
}

//Process keys
void testApp::keyPressed(int key){
  //Select corner to edit by keys 1,2,3,4
  if ( key == '1' ) { ind = 0; }
  if ( key == '2' ) { ind = 1; }
  if ( key == '3' ) { ind = 2; }
  if ( key == '4' ) { ind = 3; }

  //Move selected corner by cursor keys
  if ( key == OF_KEY_LEFT ) { p[ ind ].x -= 10; }
  if ( key == OF_KEY_RIGHT ) { p[ ind ].x += 10; }
  if ( key == OF_KEY_UP ) { p[ ind ].y -= 10; }
  if ( key == OF_KEY_DOWN ) { p[ ind ].y += 10; }
}
```

Run the project; you will see the sunflower image. Then press keys *1, 2, 3,* or *4* to select a corner and move the corner with the cursor keys. If you have a projector, you can get video mapping of the sunflower image to any rectangular surface; for example, on the side of a carton.

If you move corners a lot, the image distortion will be high. You can see that warping is not very good along the diagonal, as there will be some unwanted additional distortion. The reason for this is that the `texture.draw()` method in the example performs warping by drawing two triangles. So the mapping mesh here consists of two triangles with a common (diagonal) edge. For smoother results, we need to construct a more complex mesh that consists of least 50 triangles and recalculate its vertices when the corners move. It can be done using bilinear interpolation and drawing a mesh using the `ofMesh` class, but it is out of the scope of this chapter. See the *Using ofMesh* section in *Chapter 7, Drawing in 3D*, for details on mesh drawing.

Using images for internal calculations

In this chapter we have considered the images mainly as building blocks of a visual scene. In this last section, we will see how images can be used in another way, as the source of data for internal calculations, not displaying on the screen directly. The main examples of such usage are masks and palettes, which we'll discuss now.

An image as a mask

Color cameras and depth cameras give color and depth images that represent the scene they capture (for example, humans in front of the camera). Such images can be processed using pixel-by-pixel methods or with the computer vision library, OpenCV. The result is often a binary image, which is called **mask**, that contains black pixels denoting the background and white pixels denoting human silhouettes. The mask can be applied for controlling physics and changing any parameter of your interactive installation. The user never sees the mask image itself, but only perceives its effect on the interactive scene's behavior. See the example of the human silhouette mask obtained using the depth camera, Microsoft Kinect:

For details on getting a color image from a camera and its processing, see *Chapter 5, Working with Videos*, and *Chapter 9, Computer Vision with OpenCV*. For details on obtaining and processing data from depth cameras, see *Chapter 10, Using Depth Cameras*.

An image as a palette

An image can be used as a palette, which sets the color of the brush or particles in your project. This means that you select some point p inside the image and slowly move it by some fixed rule of Perlin noise. After each move, you just read the pixel color from the image at the current position of p and use it for drawing with a brush or for a particle color. We often use such techniques and create many palettes for different objects and also for obtaining controllable coloring for our projects, which ensures predictable behavior.

An example of a palette used in our interactive installation and a dance performance *Abstract Wall* (made by *Kuflex*, produced by *Ksenia Lyashenko*, and shown at the Microsoft event at the Garage Center for Contemporary Culture, Moscow, 2013) are shown in the following screenshot:

The installation reacts to movements of the human body and draws flying particles with colors selected from the palette.

The method for changing colors of particles in the installation is the following: when a particle is created, its position in the palette is set randomly at the bottom of the palette image. During a particle's life, its position in the palette goes up, so the particle's color slowly changes.

> Another frequently used method for changing the particle's position in the palette is using Perlin noise. See details on Perlin noise in *Appendix B, Using Perlin Noise.*

Summary

In this chapter we learned how to load images from a file; render it on the screen with different sizes, color, and transparency; create new images; and modify existing images. We also touched upon the very basics of image warping and video mapping.

The next step is working with videos, which we will discuss in the next chapter.

5
Working with Videos

Using video footage is an easy way to add dynamic layers to an interactive project scene. And processing video is the basis of modern computer-generated video art. This chapter will cover the basic and advanced topics on playing, layering, and processing videos in the openFrameworks projects:

- Playing a video file
- Processing video frames
- Radial and horizontal slit-scan effects
- Processing a live video from the camera
- The video synthesizer
- Using image sequences

Video basics

Video is the most usable container for dynamic media today. It consists of a number of frames—moving images and soundtrack—all encapsulated in a single file. In principle, each video can be represented by a sequence of separate image files for each frame and audio files for soundtracks. But using a single file is often more comfortable.

The big advantage of using a single video file is that modern video codecs can significantly reduce the video's file size compared to the size of image sequence plus the soundtrack file sizes. Also, decoding video can be made easier using GPU instead of CPU. These two reasons give a possibility to play HD videos smoothly and at high framerates with openFrameworks. Nevertheless, in *Using image sequence* section, we will see when using an image sequence is more suitable than using a single video file.

The best known file formats for video are AVI, MP4, and MOV. All these formats are supported in openFrameworks, but in general it is preferable to use the MOV format because openFrameworks uses Apple QuickTime SDK for playing video in Mac OS X and Windows, and the MOV format is native for QuickTime.

To play videos in openFrameworks in Windows, you need to install QuickTime from `http://www.apple.com/quicktime/download/`.

If you want to use a video from sources such as `youtube.com` or `vimeo.com`, you can download it using services such as `keepvid.com`. Be careful about considering the licensee limitations when using these videos.

If you create a video file using video editors such as Adobe AfterEffects, or maybe in 3D software such as Autodesk 3DSMax, you should be aware of choosing the right codec while saving your video file. Here is the list of possible usages and corresponding codecs:

- If you want to play the video as a normal video footage, without speed changing and using alpha channel, the best option for you is using some MPEG4 codec (such as H.264), with large quality value settings in codec. It will have a good quality and a small file size. Such a codec may be crucial in case of using HD videos, because using other codecs can give a huge file, which is hard to read in real time from the disk.

  Remember, MPEG4 codecs do "deep" video compression, and use many previous frames for decoding a new frame; so changing the direction and speed of playing such videos can have a negative impact on the performance of your application.

- If you want to use video as a clip for VJ-ing, consider using codec with (Apple) Motion-JPEG.

- If you need a video with an alpha channel, use Apple-PNG format and set **Millions+ colors** or **32-bit** color mode. With this setting, the file size will be larger when using Motion-JPEG, but will give very good quality and good performance. At the time of writing this book, openFrameworks's use is limited when using such videos. Please see details in the *Using image sequence* section.

For coding videos to MOV files with different codecs, you can use Adobe Premiere. If you work in Mac OS X, you can use simple and free Squared 5's **MPEG streamclip** utility.

If you like to work with command lines, the best choice for video conversion is open source tool **ffmpeg**.

Playing a video file

The openFrameworks's `ofVideoPlayer` class is intended for playing and controlling video. The basic usage of the `ofVideoPlayer` video object is the following:

1. Loading video file, specifying its name:

   ```
   video.loadMovie( "video.mov" );
   ```

2. Starting video to play:

   ```
   video.play();
   ```

3. Decoding the needed frame to show and playing the corresponding sound chunk (best to call it in `testApp::update()`):

   ```
   video.update();
   ```

4. Drawing the current video frame:

   ```
   video.draw( x, y );
   ```

   or

   ```
   video.draw( x, y, w, h );
   ```

While drawing a video frame, you can think of the current frame of video as if it were an ordinal `ofImage` object. So, you can use the `video.width`, `video.height` values and set anchor using `video.setAnchorPercent( percentX, percentY )`, `video.setAnchorPoint( x, y )`, and `video.resetAnchor()`.

The following example shows the basic usage of `ofVideoPlayer`. It is based on an `emptyExample` project in openFrameworks. Before running it, copy the `handsTrees.mov` file into the `bin/data` folder of your project.

 This is example `05-Video/01-VideoPlayback`.

In the `testApp.h` file, inside the `testApp` class declaration, add the following line with video player object `video` declaration:

```
ofVideoPlayer video; //Declare the video player object
```

In the `testApp.cpp` file, fill the bodies of the `setup()`, `update()`, and `draw()` functions in the following way:

```
void testApp::setup(){
  video.loadMovie( "handsTrees.mov" );   //Load the video file
  video.play();      //Start the video to play
```

```
  }

  void testApp::update(){
    video.update();    //Decode the new frame if needed
  }

  void testApp::draw(){
    ofBackground( 255, 255, 255 );    //Set white background

    ofSetColor( 255, 255, 255 );
    video.draw( 0, 0 );               //Draw the current video frame
  }
```

When you run the code, you will see the movie playing on the screen:

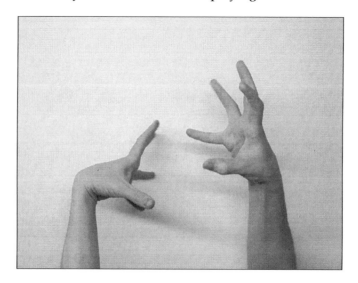

Please note, that by default, ofVideoPlayer plays video with its speed based on the time data, independently of your application rendering rate. For example, if you set the application framerate to 60 by calling ofSetFrameRate(60), but the video has the rate 30 fps, then video.update() will switch frames at rate 30, not 60 fps. So it is useful to know, whether the frame is new or not. Such information can be obtained using the Boolean function video.isFrameNew(), which returns true if a new frame was loaded during the last video.update() calling. See the example of using the video.isFrameNew() function in the *The replacing colors example* section and other examples given in the following sections.

Controlling the video playback

There are a number of additional functions in ofVideoPlayer for controlling video playing and positioning:

- The stop() function is used to stop playing the video.

- The setPaused(bPause) function sets/resets pause of video playing, where bPause has type bool. If you pause the video, you can still switch its frames using the setFrame() or setPosition() function. It is extremely useful for the exact frame number control.

- The setPosition(pos) function sets playing position in file, where pos is a float number in range [0, 1].

- The setFrame(frame) function sets current frame to frame, where frame is an integer value from 0 to video. getTotalNumFrames() - 1.

- The getCurrentFrame() function returns current frame number.

- The getTotalNumFrames() function returns number of frames in video.

- The getDuration() function returns internal duration of video in seconds as a float number.

- The isLoaded() function returns true if video is successfully loaded, this can be used for handling errors like a mistake in filename.

- The isPaused() and isPlaying() functions return value of type bool on pausing and playing state correspondingly.

- The getIsMovieDone() function returns true when the last frame of the video is achieved.

You can freely change the speed of playing using the following functions:

- The setSpeed(speed) function where speed is a float value. Value 1.0 means the normal video speed and value 2.0 means the double speed. Negative speed plays the video backwards; for example, value -1.0 means backward playing with normal speed.

- The getSpeed() function returns float value equal to the current playing speed.

Please note that you can change the speed continuously. It is an important feature for adding lifelikeness to the video backgrounds. For example, if you are playing a video of a rotating mill, you can slowly change the speed of the video to simulate wind changes using Perlin noise. See *Appendix B, Perlin Noise*, for more details.

For creating nonstop playing videos, it is possible to set up and control the loop mode using the following functions:

- The setLoopState(state) function sets the looping mode, where state can be one of the three values:
    - OF_LOOP_NONE: Looping is disabled and playing stops when the video reaches the last frame.
    - OF_LOOP_NORMAL: When playing reaches the last frame, it jumps to the first frame. This is default loop state.
    - OF_LOOP_PALINDROME: Also known as ping-pong looping, this loop goes forward and backward infinitely, and is good for creating a smooth "infinite video" from any video piece.
- The getLoopState() function returns the current loop mode.

If the video contains an audio track, you can adjust its playing volume, changing it using the setVolume(volume) method, where volume is a float number in range [0, 1].

Processing a single video frame

Now we begin to learn the methods of processing video. Values of pixels in the current video frame can be read in a way similar to the one in ofImage, using access to its pixel array data:

```
unsigned char *getPixels()
```

Also, here is the getPixelRef() method, which returns a reference to a pixel array of the current frame, represented by a special class ofPixels.

 Note that the ofImage class has getPixelRef() too and can be used in a similar way.

It is easy to get the pixel color using pixels.getColor(x, y), which returns the ofColor value of pixel (x,y). Compared to directly working with pixels data using getPixels(), it is a relatively slow operation, but is more simple and convenient. Note, ofPixels has useful properties such as getWidth() and getHeight() that are used for getting the width and height, and also the channels value, which holds the number of channels in the image (1, 3, or 4).

The vertical lines image example

See the example where we read the colors of center horizontal line pixels and draw vertical lines with the corresponding colors. The project is similar to the previous example, only `testApp::draw()` is changed:

This is example `05-Video/02-VideoVerticals`.

```
void testApp::draw(){
  //Getting reference to the pixel array
  ofPixels &pixels = video.getPixelsRef();

  //Define variables w, h equal to frame width and height
  int w = pixels.getWidth();
  int h = pixels.getHeight();

  //Scan center horizontal line
  for (int x=0; x<w; x++) {
      //Getting color of the center line
      ofColor color = pixels.getColor( x, h / 2 );

      //Draw a vertical line using this color
      ofSetColor( color );
      ofLine( x, 0, x, h );
  }
}
```

Running this example, you will see a movie with frames built from a set of colored vertical lines. The color of each line is taken from the central horizontal line of the original movie's frame:

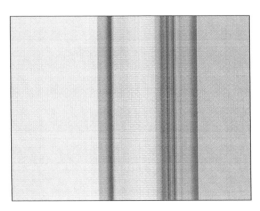

The important thing in the example is using the & symbol in the line:

```
ofPixels &pixels = video.getPixelRef();
```

This symbol means that we are getting just a reference of the pixel array data, and not copying the data itself. So this is an extremely fast operation, just like a pointer assignment. But when the next frame is obtained, we will lose old pixels data and it will be a reference on the new frame, or maybe some memory error can occur. Instead, if we call it another way, without &:

```
ofPixels pixels = video.getPixelRef();
```

The data will be copied to `pixels`, and stored there as long as we want. It is safe, but consumes a lot of memory and hence is a consuming operation (that can be noticeable for large frame size).

It is possible to change pixel colors in `ofPixels`, using `pixels.setColor( x, y, color )` with color value of type `ofColor`. But the pixel array obtained from the video frame is not intended for changing its image, so you will not see the changes drawing it with `video.draw()`. If you want to draw the changed pixels, create an `ofImage` object and load the pixels array into this image, using the `setFromPixels()` function.

The replacing colors example

Let's consider an example where we change the color components of all the framed pixels using a random-generated table and draw the resulting image. Also, the example demonstrates the usage of the `video.isFrameNew()` function.

It is based on the `emptyExample` project in openFrameworks. Before running it, copy the `handsTrees.mov` file into the `bin/data` folder of your project.

 This is example `05-Video/03-VideoReplacingColors`.

In the `testApp.h` file inside the `testApp` class declaration, add the following lines:

```
ofVideoPlayer video;    //Declare video player object
ofImage image;          //Declare image object
int table[16];          //Declare table for color replacing
```

In the `testApp.cpp` file, fill the bodies of the `setup()`, `update()`, and `draw()` functions in the following way:

```cpp
void testApp::setup(){
  video.loadMovie( "handsTrees.mov" );   //Load video file
  video.play();   //Start video to play

  //Fill the table by random values from 0 to 255
  for ( int i=0; i<16; i++ ) {
      table[i] = ofRandom( 0, 255 );
  }

}

void testApp::update(){
  video.update();      //Decode the new frame if needed

  //Do computing only if a new frame was obtained
  if ( video.isFrameNew() ) {
      //Getting pixels
      ofPixels pixels = video.getPixelsRef();

      //Scan all the pixels
      for (int y=0; y<pixels.getHeight(); y++) {
          for (int x=0; x<pixels.getWidth(); x++) {
              //Getting pixel (x,y) color
              ofColor col = pixels.getColor( x, y );

              //Change color components of col
              //using table
              col.r = table[ col.r/16 ];
              col.g = table[ col.g/16 ];
              col.b = table[ col.b/16 ];

              //Set the color back to the pixel (x,y)
              pixels.setColor( x, y, col );
          }
      }

      //Set pixel array to the image
      image.setFromPixels( pixels );
```

```
    }
}

void testApp::draw(){
  ofBackground( 255, 255, 255 );  //Set white background

  //Draw the image
  ofSetColor( 255, 255, 255 );
  image.draw(0,0);
}
```

When you start the application, you will see the movie with changed pixel colors. The rule for color changing is fixed during application execution. A color replace table is constructed at startup using random number generator; so each time you run the application, you will obtain a different result. The following screenshot shows us an example:

The rule for color replacing is held in a random-generated table:

```
for ( int i=0; i<16; i++ ) {
  table[i] = ofRandom( 0, 255 );
}
```

And the main operation of the example is changing the color using `table`:

```
col.r = table[ col.r/16 ];
col.g = table[ col.g/16 ];
col.b = table[ col.b/16 ];
```

Indeed, each color component lies in range `[0, 255]`, so `col.r/16`, `col.g/16`, and `col.g/16` lies in range `[0, 15]`. Our table has size `16`, so operation is correct. Note that if we create table of size 256, we can use simple operations as follows:

```
col.r = table[ col.r ];
col.g = table[ col.g ];
col.b = table[ col.b ];
```

The resultant image will be much more "color-sprayed". (Before running the project with such modification, you need to replace in code all constants from `16` to `256`.)

Processing multiple frames

Till now we saw examples of modification and drawing video frames just like single images. Deeper processing should involve analysis of the several frames.

If we compare two successive frames, we can find the direction and velocity of motion for each frame pixel. Such a vector field is called **optical flow**. It has many uses in video, graphics, and computer vision. Optical flow computation is a nontrivial task of computer vision, and we will learn to do it in *Chapter 9, Computer Vision with OpenCV*.

Another idea is to bufferize a number of frames and then draw parts of the frames in different parts of the screen. The famous video effect called **slit-scan** or **time displacement** is based on this principle. In effect, horizontal lines of the resulting image are built from horizontal lines of several successive frames. Often, bottom lines are taken from older frames, and top lines are made from the newest frames. So if the object was moved horizontally in the original video, in the processed video you see a slow-motion propagation from the top to the bottom of the frame. An object rotating like spinning dances will look like a twisted spiral. (See the screenshot in the *Horizontal slit-scan* section.)

The origins of the slit-scan effect lie in mechanical **slit-photography** technology developed in the 19th century. Nowadays slit-scan is made with computers, and it is used in cinematography and art.

Slit-scan is implemented in openFrameworks' addon ofxSlitScan. Also, there exist plugins for this effect in video editors such as Adobe After Effects.

Radial slit-scan example

Here we consider the implementation of a circular version of the slit-scan effect, which can be called **radial slit-scan**. The mouse position will define the center where a portion of new frame is drawn. The other pixels (x, y) are filled using the older frames, where the frame's "oldness" depends on the distance between mouse position and (x, y).

This example is based on the emptyExample project in openFrameworks. Before running it, copy the handsTrees.mov file into the bin/data folder of your project.

This is example 05-Video/04-VideoSlitScan.

In the testApp.h file, inside the testApp class declaration, add declaration of video player object video, frames buffer frames, output image image, and some other declarations:

```
ofVideoPlayer video;            //Video player object

deque<ofPixels> frames;         //Frames buffer
int N;                          //Frames buffer size

//Pixels array for constructing output image
ofPixels imagePixels;
ofImage image;                  //Output image

//Main processing function which
//computes the pixel color (x, y) using frames buffer
ofColor getSlitPixelColor( int x, int y );
```

You will note that the buffer of frames is declared here as deque<ofPixels> frames. Class deque is C++ Standard Template Library container, holding items of any class. In our case, such a class is ofPixels. You can think of frames as a dynamic array, which can change its size during runtime. It provides an indexed access to any item such as frames[i], and most importantly, it efficiently adds and removes items at its ends.

The deque class is very similar to the popular vector class of C++ Standard Template Library. The vector class can be resized and has an indexed access to its items too, and is also a little faster than deque. However, it slowly adds and removes elements to its ends, which is crucial for our example. (While using vector, see the *Using image sequence example* section.)

In the testApp.cpp file, the setup() function just reads and plays the video, and the draw() function draws processed image on the screen:

```cpp
void testApp::setup(){
  video.loadMovie( "handsTrees.mov" );  //Load video file

  //Play video with 1/4 of its normal speed
  //for better seeing slit-scan effect
  video.setSpeed( 0.25 );

  video.play();  //Start video to play

  N = 150;       //Set buffer size
}


//-------------------------------------------------------------
void testApp::draw(){
  ofBackground(255, 255, 255);        //Set white background

  //Draw image
  ofSetColor( 255, 255, 255 );
  image.draw(0,0);
}
```

Let's consider the first part of the update() function. It gradually reads frames from movies, and stores N last frames in frames buffer in such a way that newer frames have smaller indexes:

```cpp
void testApp::update(){
  video.update();              //Decode the new frame if needed

  //Do computing only if a new frame was obtained
```

```
if ( video.isFrameNew() ) {
    //Push the new frame to the beginning of the frame list
    frames.push_front( video.getPixelsRef() );

    //If number of buffered frames > N,
    //then pop the oldest frame
    if ( frames.size() > N ) {
        frames.pop_back();
    }
}
```

We use `frames.push_front( video.getPixelsRef() )` for adding pixel array of the current video frame item to the beginning, and we use `frames.pop_back()` for removing the oldest frame. These two operations always let us have the newest frame in `frames[0]`, and not more than `N - 1` older frames. (When the project starts, frames buffer is empty. With the lapse of time, its size gradually increases and later keeps equal to `N`.)

The second part of the `update()` function computes output image `image` using the `getSlitPixelColor( x, y )` function, which will be discussed later.

```
//It is possible that video player did not finish decoding
//the first frame at first testApp::update() calling,
//so we need check, if there are frames
if ( !frames.empty() ) {
    //Now constructing the output image in imagePixels

    //If imagePixels is not initialized yet, then initialize
    //it by copying from any frame.
    //This is simplest way to create a pixel array
    //of the same size and type
    if ( !imagePixels.isAllocated() ) {
        imagePixels = frames[0];
    }

    //Getting video frame size for formulas simplification
    int w = frames[0].getWidth();
    int h = frames[0].getHeight();

    //Scan all the pixels
    for (int y=0; y<h; y++) {
        for (int x=0; x<w; x++) {

            //Get "slit" pixel color
```

```
        ofColor color = getSlitPixelColor( x, y );

        //Set pixel to image pixels
        imagePixels.setColor( x, y, color );
      }
    }
    //Set new pixels values to the image
    image.setFromPixels( imagePixels );
  }
}
```

The main processing function of the example is getSlitPixelColor(x,y). It computes and returns the pixel color (x,y) corresponding to the radial slit-scan image. The function makes it work using frame buffer frames and current mouse position (mouseX, mouseY):

```
ofColor testApp::getSlitPixelColor( int x, int y ){
  //Calculate the distance from (x,y) to the current
  //mouse position mouseX, mouseY

  float dist = ofDist( x, y, mouseX, mouseY );

  //Main formula for connecting (x,y) with frame number
  float f = dist / 8.0;
  //Here "frame number" is computed as a float value.
  //We need it for getting a "smooth result"
  //by interpolating colors later

  //Compute two frame numbers surrounding f
  int i0 = int( f );
  int i1 = i0 + 1;

  //Compute weights of the frames i0 and i1
  float weight0 = i1 - f;
  float weight1 = 1 - weight0;

  //Limiting frame numbers by range from 0 to n=frames.size()-1
  int n = frames.size() - 1;
  i0 = ofClamp( i0, 0, n );
  i1 = ofClamp( i1, 0, n );

  //Getting the frame colors
  ofColor color0 = frames[ i0 ].getColor( x, y );
```

```
    ofColor color1 = frames[ i1 ].getColor( x, y );

    //Interpolate colors - this is the function result
    ofColor color = color0 * weight0 + color1 * weight1;

    return color;
}
```

This example is quite CPU-intensive, so we suggest to run it in the **Release** mode of your development environment. Of course, it runs in the **Debug** mode too, but can give slow performance.

 To improve performance further, you can implement the algorithm using fragment shader; see the *Processing several images* section in *Chapter 8, Using Shaders*.

Run this example and place the mouse cursor somewhere in the central area of the video frame. You will see radial waves of motion centered in the mouse position.

Now begin to move the mouse cursor from left to right hands and back. You will see how your movement changes time-space distribution of this interactive picture. When you move your mouse to some point, this part of the image shows "future", and other parts of the image gradually go to the "past", in respect to the video. It is simple to understand from algorithmic point of view: the closer the pixel is to mouse position, the newer the corresponding frame is for its color. The example of the resulting frame is shown in the following screenshot. The mouse cursor is pointing to the center of the right hand, so this region is undistorted:

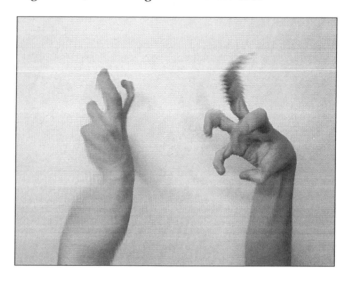

The most important function of the example is `getSlitPixelColor( x, y )`, which returns the color of the pixel (x, y) computed from colors of the buffered frames. The main formula is:

```
float f = dist / 8.0;
```

It computes the desired frame number for getting color for pixel (x,y) depending on coordinates (x, y). It is equal to the distance between the pixel and the mouse position to the frame number, divided by `8.0`. If you change the constant `8.0` to another value, you will notice the change in the speed of the radial wave.

Horizontal slit-scan

Change the main formula in `getSlitPixelColor( x, y )` using the following line:

```
float f = y / 8.0;
```

It gives "classical" horizontal slit-scan effect (which is independent of the mouse position and hence is not interactive). The example of using this formula is shown in the following screenshot. You can observe the specific twisting of the hands and fingers.

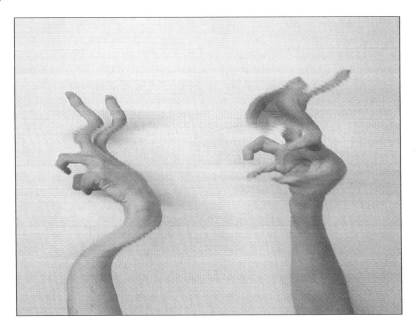

Play with the formula and try other slit-scan effects by yourself.

Discussing color interpolation

The last important thing to discuss in the example is color interpolation. Notice that we compute frame number as a float, but not as an integer value:

```
float f = dist / 8.0;
```

The reason for this is our desire to visually smoothen borders between the frames to get better results. (Check how the borders look by making truncating `float f = int(dist / 8.0);`). We achieve this using color interpolation between two successive frames with numbers `i0` and `i1` around `f`:

```
int i0 = int( f );
int i1 = i0 + 1;
```

Then we compute weights for these frame numbers in a way that the sum of `weight0` and `weight1` is equal to 1. If `f` is closer to `i0` than to `i1`, `weight0` is greater than `weight1` and vice versa:

```
float weight0 = i1 - f;
float weight1 = 1 - weight0;
```

The correspondence between `f`, `i0`, `i1`, and `weight`s is shown in the following diagram:

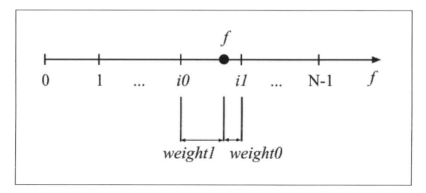

Finally, we construct the resulting color by interpolating colors of frames `i0` and `i1` using weights:

```
ofColor color = color0 * weight0 + color1 * weight1;
```

Despite using color interpolation, you can notice "interlacing-like" artifacts in the resulting video. The reason for this is that we need to show in image continuous space-time motion, using just frames made in discrete moments of time. For reduction such as an "interlacing-like" effect, we need to shift the pixels slightly during color interpolation, using optical flow between frames i0 and i1. You will be able to construct such an algorithm after learning optical flow in *Chapter 9, Computer Vision with OpenCV*.

Processing a live video from the camera

External and built-in webcams are the sources of live video. There are several cases of using this capability:

- Transform input frames and show it on the screen. You then get a kind of "magic mirror" interactive project.

- Add some objects over live video. In this way, you obtain a kind of **Augmented Reality (AR)** application with 3D or cartoon objects added over video.

- Analyze human silhouette and gestures, find human faces, and perform some action based on this knowledge. For example, it can be the cartoon character repeating your mimics, or gesture-based drawing interactive installation.

It is enough to use video processing methods described in the preceding sections for creating simple art and interactive projects. For more advanced processing, there is a need to use deeper image analyzing techniques, which will be considered in *Chapter 9, Computer Vision with OpenCV*.

Now we will consider how to capture live video using openFrameworks. It can be done with class ofVideoGrabber. The typical usage is as follows:

1. Define grabber object in the testApp class definition:

   ```
   ofVideoGrabber grabber;
   ```

2. Start capture in testApp::setup():

   ```
   //Select camera by its id in system
   grabber.setDeviceID( 0 );

   //Select desired grabbing frame rate
   grabber.setDesiredFrameRate( 30 );

   //Start grabbing with desired frame width and height
   grabber.initGrabber( 640, 480 );
   ```

3. Update and process frames in `testApp::update()`:

```
grabber.update();   //Update grabber
if ( grabber.isFrameNew() ) { //Check for the new frame

    //Get pixels array
    ofPixels pixels = grabber.getPixelsRef();
    //Do some processing
    //...
}
```

4. Draw current frame in `testApp::draw()`:

```
grabber.draw( 0, 0 );
```

Additionally, the `grabber.listDevices()` function shows a list of cameras in console. It is very useful for properly choosing the camera ID in `grabber.setDeviceID()`.

Also, you can call `grabber.setVerbose( true );` for printing in console details and warnings about grabbing.

The video synthesizer example

Let's consider the example of using live video captured from camera. We will build a video synthesizer performing fusion of live video with a prerecorded video. Namely, we will use colors of live video pixels for shifting pixels of the prerecorded video.

The example is based on a `emptyExample` project in openFrameworks. Before running it, copy the `handsTrees.mov` file into the `bin/data` folder of your project and connect a webcam. If you use laptop with built-in webcam, it will most probably work by itself.

 This is example `05-Video/05-VideoCameraSynth`.

In the `testApp.h` file, inside the `testApp` class declaration, add declaration of video grabber `grabber`, video player object `video`, output image `image`, and function `synthesizeImage()`:

```
ofVideoGrabber    grabber;      //Video grabber

ofVideoPlayer    video;        //Prerecorded video

ofImage image;    //Resulted synthesized image

//Synthesize image from grabber and video frames
void synthesizeImage();
```

The `setup()`, `update()`, and `draw()` functions in the `testApp.cpp` file demonstrate how to run camera, read camera frames, and draw camera and resulting images on the screen. Note how calling the `synthesizeImage()` function in `update()` computes the output image:

```
void testApp::setup(){

    //Show in console all details and warnings on the grabbing
    grabber.setVerbose(true);

    //Select camera by its id in system
    grabber.setDeviceID(0);

    //Select desired camera frame rate
    grabber.setDesiredFrameRate(30);

    //Start grabbing with desired frame width and height
    grabber.initGrabber(640,480);

    //Show in the console list of connected cameras
    //if you camera did not connect, please see the list
    grabber.listDevices();


    //Load and start prerecorded movie to play
    video.loadMovie( "handsTrees.mov" );
```

```
      video.play();
   }

   //-------------------------------------------------------------
   void testApp::update(){
      grabber.update();                    //Update grabber state
      if ( grabber.isFrameNew() ) {  //Check for new frame
         //Create image using grabber and video frames
         synthesizeImage();
      }
      video.update();       //Update video state
   }

   //-------------------------------------------------------------
   void testApp::draw(){
      //Set white background
      ofBackground( 255, 255, 255 );

      //Draw processed image
      ofSetColor( 255, 255, 255 );
      image.draw( 0, 0 );

      //Draw live unchanged video frame at right,
      //in a half of its size
      grabber.draw( image.width + 10, 0, 320, 240 );
   }
```

The custom, and the most interesting function of the example is synthesizeImage().
It creates synthesized image using grabber and video frames. The pixels of the
video frames are geometrically modulated by shifting along x axis, using red color
component of the pixels of the grabber frame:

```
   void testApp::synthesizeImage(){

      //Initialize output pixels
      ofPixels pixels = grabber.getPixelsRef();

      //Get pixel arrays for grabber and video
      ofPixels &pixelsGrab = grabber.getPixelsRef();
```

```cpp
ofPixels &pixelsVideo = video.getPixelsRef();

//Get width and height for formulas shortening
int w = pixelsGrab.getWidth();
int h = pixelsGrab.getHeight();

//We proceed only if video and grabbing frames
//have equal sizes
if ( !( w == pixelsVideo.getWidth()
     && h == pixelsVideo.getHeight()) ) {
    return;
}

//Scan pixels
for (int y=0; y<h; y++) {
    for (int x=0; x<w; x++) {
        //Get grabber color
        ofColor colorGrab = pixelsGrab.getColor( x, y );

        //Shift x-coordinate by red component
        int x1 = x + ( colorGrab.r - 127 );

        //Truncate x1 to bounds
        x1 = ofClamp( x1, 0, w-1 );

        //Get color of pixel (x1, y) from video
        ofColor color = pixelsVideo.getColor( x1, y );

        //Set color to output pixel (x, y)
        pixels.setColor( x, y, color );
    }
}
//Update image pixels
image.setFromPixels( pixels );
}
```

Run the example. In the left part of the screen, you will see the result of fusion live video with a prerecorded video. In the right part of the screen, you will see a small picture along with a live video from the camera:

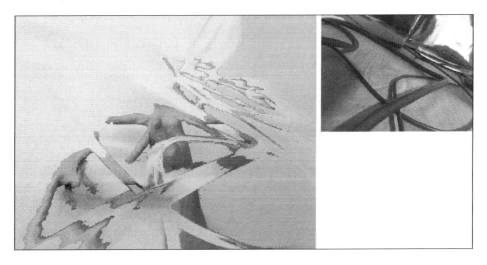

Let's continue the experiments, and direct camera straight on the left (transformed) image on the screen. (If you have a laptop with embedded camera, you can use mirror.) Screen-to-camera feedback loop will then occur. This nonlinear feedback loop results in some organic morphing-like transformation of the prerecorded video. You can rotate camera, move it closer or further, and explore the results. Actually, now you are controlling the simple video synthesizer. The synthesizer's controller is the webcam, which you are controlling by your hand. The example of its working is shown in the following screenshot:

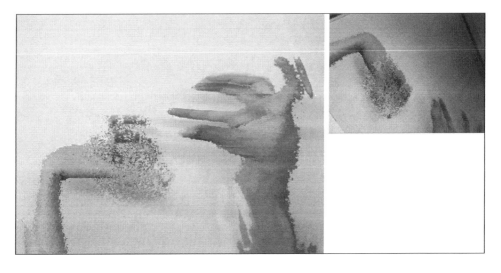

Usually various color artifacts in the screen-to-camera chain are unwanted. But in our situation we have the opposite. Artifacts are the source of interesting effects, like the vivid ripples in output. See the example in the following screenshot:

Using image sequence

In the previous sections, we have considered how to work with videos stored in video files or captured by cameras. Here we will consider working with the third source of video – image sequences.

Sometimes using ofVideoPlayer for drawing movies is not appropriate. Two main cases are:

- You need to render a big amount of movies on one screen simultaneously. For example, in a 2D computer arcade game, there can be about 100 moving characters and objects. You can play about 10 different video files in openFrameworks simultaneously, but 100 is too much for it; so some other solution is needed.

- You need to draw many layers of videos using alpha channel. But at the time of writing this, openFrameworks does not support videos with alpha channel within its standard class ofVideoPlayer. There is support in openFrameworks for only Mac OS X, with class ofQTKitPlayer and example examples/video/osxHighPerformanceVideoPlayerExample. Also, there is an addon ofxAlphaVideoPlayer, but it is not included in the openFrameworks distribution. So some universal solution for video with alpha channel is desirable.

The simplest solution for these cases is using image sequences. Image sequence is a number of images located in the folder and numbered, such as:

```
image001.png
image002.png
...
image050.png
```

You can load the images into one array, and draw these one by one, creating a full illusion of movie playing. For resolving the case of large number of videos, you can load many image sequences and draw corresponding images on the screen. For resolving the case of the alpha channel, you just should use images with the alpha channel.

Using image sequences has several constrains:

- Reading images is a time-consuming operation, so for faster sequence drawing, you should normally read a whole image sequence at `testApp::setup()`.

- The number of loaded images is limited by the size of the video memory of your graphics card. If you have n images with width w and height h, colored and with alpha channel, the sequence will occupy $n * w * h * 4$ bytes in the memory. Note that you should use `ofTexture` for image sequence instead of `ofImage`, in order to not occupy RAM.

 You should never occupy all of your video memory, because some amount of it is needed for usage by your operating system. If you do so during your application execution, your computer can suddenly go slow and even hang on, until you restart it.

Using image sequence example

Till now, there is no standard openFrameworks class for working with image sequences. So we show here a simple example of working with one looped image sequence. The following code loads images from a folder into an array, and then draws these one by one. The index of the currently drawn image is computed using the current time.

Running this example, you will see a toy elephant movie with flying wool cloud. Actually the cloud is an image sequence, drawn over a normal video:

The example is based on an `emptyExample` project in openFrameworks. Before running it, copy the `elephant.mov` file and the `woolCloudSeq` folder into the `bin/data` folder of your project.

[This is example `05-Video/06-VideoImageSequence`.]

In the `testApp.h` file, inside the `testApp` class declaration, add declaration of video player object `backVideo` and image sequence array `seq`, which is `vector` of textures:

```
//Video which will play as the background layer
ofVideoPlayer   backVideo;

//Image sequence which will be overlaid on backVideo
vector<ofTexture> seq;
```

The `setup()` function in the `testApp.cpp` file loads and starts the `backVideo` movie and reads contents of the `data/woolCloudSeq` folder into dynamic vector of images `seq`. The `update()` function just loads frames of the `backVideo` movie:

```
void testApp::setup(){
  //Load background
  backVideo.loadMovie( "elephant.mov" );
```

```
    backVideo.play();

    //Set the screen size equal to the backVideo dimensions
    ofSetWindowShape( backVideo.width, backVideo.height );

    //Read image sequence from the folder

    //1. Create object for reading folder contents
    ofDirectory dir;

    //2. Get the number of files in the folder data/woolCloudSeq
    int n = dir.listDir("woolCloudSeq");

    //3. Set the array size to n
    seq.resize( n );

    //4. Load images
    for (int i=0; i<n; i++) {
        //Getting i-th file name
        string fileName = dir.getPath( i );

        //Load i-th image
        ofLoadImage( seq[i], fileName );
    }
}

//---------------------------------------------------------------
void testApp::update(){
  backVideo.update();  //Decode the new frame if needed
}
```

In the preceding code, the list of images in the folder is obtained using `ofDirectory` `dir` object. We get the number of files using the following function:

```
int n = dir.listDir( "woolCloud" );
```

Calling this function does not only return the amount of files, but also stores the list of file names inside `dir`. After this, we can read all the file names using the function:

```
string fileName = dir.getPath( i );
```

The image sequence is implemented here using `vector<ofTexture>` seq. **Class**
`vector` is C++ Standard Template Library container, holding items of any class.
It is very good for representing arrays with rare changed sizes. We resize the array
with the following function:

```
seq.resize( n );
```

Then fill each item, loading the corresponding image from the file:

```
ofLoadImage( seq[i], fileName );
```

The visual layering of the image sequence over the `backVideo` movie is made in the
`draw()` method as follows:

```cpp
void testApp::draw(){
  //Draw background video
  ofSetColor( 255, 255, 255 );
  backVideo.draw(0,0);

  // Calculate sequence frame number i,
  //based on the current time

  //1. Get the number of seconds from application start
  float time = ofGetElapsedTimef();

  //2. Get the size of image sequence
  int n = seq.size();

  //3. Calculate the sequence duration
  //Our sequence will render 12 frames per second, so:
  float duration = n / 12.0;

  //4. Calculate looped playing position in sequence,
  //in range [0..duration]
  float pos = fmodf( time, duration );

  //5. Convert pos in the frame number
  int i = int( pos / duration * n );

  //Wool cloud will move, so calculate its position
  //depending on time
  float x = ofNoise( time * 0.5 + 10.0 ) * ofGetWidth();
  float y = ofNoise( time * 0.3 + 20.0 ) * ofGetHeight() / 4.0;

  //Enable alpha blending
```

```
ofEnableAlphaBlending();

//Draw a sequence frame centered at (x,y)
seq[i].setAnchorPercent( 0.5, 0.5 );
seq[i].draw( x, y );
}
```

The most important thing here is computing the image sequence frame number depending on the time. For calculating it, we use the fmod(a, b) function.

> The fmod() function is a float analog of a % operation in C++. For integer a and b, operation a % b returns residue of a divided by b. fmodf(a, b) does the same, but for float a and b, and the result is float too.
>
> For example, calling fmodf(3.2, 1.0) will return 0.2.

In our case, fmodf(time, duration) returns the value in range [0, duration), and after reaching the duration value, its result jumps back to 0, giving the necessary looping effect.

Another thing to mention is how we make a cloud move across the screen. To achieve this, we are changing cloud's drawing center coordinates (x, y) for drawing depending on the time. That is, x and y are computed using values of the smoothly changed ofNoise() function, which is a Perlin noise function. See *Appendix B, Perlin Noise*, for details.

We use different shift values (10.0 and 20.0) in the function in order x and y to change independently. Values 0.5 and 0.3 set the speed of changing x and y. The ofNoise() function returns value in range [0, 1], so finally we multiply the ofNoise results on ofGetWidth() and ofGetHeight() / 4.0 so that the cloud flies in the high quarter of the screen:

```
float x = ofNoise( time * 0.5 + 10.0 ) * ofGetWidth();
float y = ofNoise( time * 0.3 + 20.0 ) * ofGetHeight() / 4.0;
```

Summary

In this chapter, we learned how to work with three sources of video: video file, live video grabbed from camera, and image sequence. We considered several examples of processing video, including replacing colors and slit-scan effect. Also, we discovered a simple video synthesizer, which uses screen-to-camera feedback loop to create vivid effects on prerecorded video.

In the next chapter, we will explore how to work with sound, including playing sound samples, capturing sounds from microphones, and transcoding sounds into images and back.

6

Working with Sounds

Sounds are a necessary part of many interactive and entertainment projects. They increase the level of immersion and add feedback to the interactions. Also, sounds play a central role in sound art projects. In this chapter you will learn how to play sound samples, synthesize new sounds, and get sounds from the microphone. Also, you will learn how to get information from sound using its spectrum and use it for controlling visualization parameters:

- Playing sound samples
- Generating sounds
- Using a microphone
- Getting spectral data from sound

Sound basics

From a physical point of view, sound is a wave of air density changing, which propagates in the space from the sound source to our ears. In computers and other digital devices, a sound is represented as an array of numbers which describe the sound wave amplitude at discrete moments in time. These numbers are called **digital audio samples**.

 Digital sound representation using audio samples is called **Pulse Code Modulation (PCM)**. It is a historical term, meaning that we code the amplitudes using digital numbers.

An array of audio samples with additional information such as its discretization time step and number of channels (mono, stereo, and so on) is called a **sound sample**. Sound samples can be used as the elementary bricks for construction of sound and music. The most notable example is hip-hop music, which is based on samples. Many computer games also use samples for sounding player actions.

openFrameworks has good capabilities for playing samples. So using samples is a simple and straightforward way to add voices, effects, and the sound of real instruments to your interactive project.

The most widely used sound sample file formats are MP3, WAV, and AIFF. The WAV and AIFF formats store an uncompressed audio sample array with additional information, and they are usable in all cases, especially when high-quality sounds are needed.

MP3 is a format for playing music. It represents sound in a compressed form with losing quality, so such files are not appropriate for further sound processing. Also MP3 sounds consume more CPU memory on decoding data while playing. As MP3 files are much more compact than WAV and AIFF, they are great for long background sounds in your projects.

You can get many free and paid sound samples from the Web. Be careful about considering the licensee limitations when using these. Anyway, the good option is to record, synthesize, and process your own sounds, using sound recording and editing software and software synths that are widely available for computers and mobile devices.

Now we will consider how to use and play samples in openFrameworks. Low-level sound generation and recording is considered later in the *Generating sounds* section.

Playing sound samples

The openFrameworks' `ofSoundPlayer` class is designed for playing and controlling sound samples. The basic usage of the `ofSoundPlayer` sound object is the following:

- Loading a sound sample, specifying its filename using:

    ```
    sound.loadSound( fileName );
    ```

- Playing the sample using:

    ```
    sound.play();
    ```

- Updating the sound engine using the global function:

    ```
    ofSoundUpdate();
    ```

    You need to call the `ofSoundUpdate();` function in `testApp::update()` for all the samples to play correctly.

There are a number of functions for controlling sample playback. They are as follows:

- The `stop()` function stops sample playing.

- The `getIsPlaying()` function returns `true` if our sample is currently playing.

- The `setPaused( pause )` function enables or disables pause in sample playing, with `pause` of type `bool`.

- The `setPosition( pos )` function sets sample playing position, where `pos` is a `float` value from `0.0` to `1.0`. Here `0.0` means the start of the sample and `1.0` means the end of the sample.

- The `getPosition()` function returns the current playing position as a `float` value from `0.0` to `1.0`.

- The `setPositionMS( ms )` function sets the sample playing position in milliseconds, where `ms` has type `int`.

- The `getPositionMS()` function returns the `int` value with the current sample playing position in milliseconds.

- The `setLoop( looping )` function enables or disables the sample loop mode in which the sample repeats infinitely, `looping` has a type `bool`.

- The `setMultiPlay( multi )` function is a very important function. It enables or disables the special mode for playing multiple copies of the sample simultaneously. The `multi` attribute has a type `bool`. By default, this mode is disabled, so if you start playing with `sample.play()`, wait some time and call it again, then you will hear that the first sound has stopped and the second sound has started. If you call `setMultiPlay( true )` before playing, then you will hear two samples playing simultaneously.

> If you enable the multiplay mode for the `sample` and play many sounds by calling `sample.play()`, please note that you can change the playing parameters of the last sound that started. So you should call `sample.play()` and then change its parameters before the next call of `sample.play()`.

To stop all the playing samples, call the `ofSoundStopAll()` global function.

There are two functions for controlling the process of loading samples from files. They are especially useful when your project uses many sample files:

- The `isLoaded()` function returns `true` if the sound is successfully loaded and is ready to play.

- The `unloadSound()` function unloads a sample from the memory. This function is useful for memory saving in mobile devices. On PCs, it is not so crucial. Note that the `loadSound()` function unloads the previous loaded sample automatically, so you will probably never use this function on a PC.

Until now, we learned how to play sound samples in an unchangeable way. But when you play the sample several times, it will sound exactly the same and can be boring, especially for short samples. One method for adding diversity in the output sound is by loading many different samples and selecting them to play randomly. Another great method is to use not as many samples, but to change its parameters such as speed, volume, and stereo panorama:

- The `setSpeed( speed )` function sets the speed of sample playing. Here `speed` has type `float`. If `speed` is equal to `1.0`, the sample plays unchangeable. Value `2.0` means the sample plays two times faster and with doubled tone. Value `-1.0` means the sample plays reversed.

- The `setVolume( vol )` function sets the volume of the sample, where `vol` is a `float` value from `0.0` to `1.0`.

- The `setPan( pan )` function sets stereo panorama position of the sample, where `pan` is a `float` value from `-1.0` (left) to `1.0` (right). The default value is `0.0` (center).

- The `getSpeed()`, `getVolume()`, and `getPan()` functions return the current value of the corresponding parameter of the sample.

The global function `setSoundVolume( vol )` changes the overall volume of all the sounds playing. Note that it affects only the samples playing and has no effect on sound generation (which is discussed in the *Generating sounds* section).

Let's consider an example of playing sound samples and changing their parameters based on a simple physical model.

The bouncing ball example

Consider a ball bouncing on the floor. Let the ball jump in the left or right direction after each bounce and let's play a sound sample at each bounce, with the speed (and hence a tone) of the sample depending on the ball position. Over time, some random sequences of samples with different tones will be played. It is a piece of computer-generated music, based on physical modeling.

 This is example `06-Sound/01-BouncingBall`.

The example is based on the `emptyExample` project in openFrameworks. Before running it, copy the `bounce.wav` file into the `bin/data` folder of your project.

In the `testApp.h` file, in the class `testApp` declaration, add declarations of sound samples and the ball moving function, after the `#include "testApp.h"` line:

```
ofSoundPlayer sound;        //Sound sample
bool updateBall();          //Move ball function
```

Now let's consider the `testApp.cpp` file. For simplicity, we place the model constants and variables not in the `testApp` class definition, but right into the beginning of the `.cpp` file:

```
float mass = 0.007;    //Mass of point
float g = 9.8;         //Gravity force
float time0;           //Time value, used for time step computing
ofPoint pos, vel;      //Ball position and velocity
```

The `setup()` function does the sound sample loading and model initialization:

```
void testApp::setup(){
  //Set up sound sample
  sound.loadSound( "bounce.wav" );  //Load sound sample
  sound.setMultiPlay( true );       //Set multiplay mode

  //Model setup
  time0 = ofGetElapsedTimef();      //Get current time
  pos = ofPoint( ofGetWidth() / 2, 100 ); //Ball's initial position
  vel = ofPoint( 0, 0 );            //Initial velocity

  //Set up background to not clear each frame
  ofSetBackgroundAuto( false );
  ofBackground( 255, 255, 255 );    //Clear background to white
}
```

Note that we use the `ofSetBackgroundAuto( false )` function calling, which disables clearing of the screen at each `testApp::draw()` calling, so the drawing will be accumulated on the screen (see details in the *Drawing with an uncleared background* section in *Chapter 2, Drawing in 2D*).

The `update()` function moves the ball, and if bouncing occurs then the sample starts to play. The important thing here is calling `ofSoundUpdate()` to update the sound engine for each `update()` call, for the samples to play correctly:

```
void testApp::update(){
  //Update ball position and check if it is bounced
  bool bounced = updateBall();
  if ( bounced ) {
      //Start sample playing
      sound.play();
      //Set play speed, in dependence of x
      float speed = ofMap( pos.x, 0, ofGetWidth(), 0.2, 2 );
      sound.setSpeed( speed );
  }
  //Update sound engine
  ofSoundUpdate();
}
```

The `draw()` function draws the floor line and the ball:

```
void testApp::draw(){
  float bottom = 300.0; //The floor position on the screen
  //Draw the floor line in black color
  ofSetColor( 0, 0, 0 );
  ofLine( 0, bottom, ofGetWidth(), bottom );
  //Draw the ball in red color
  ofSetColor( 255, 0, 0 );
  ofFill();
  ofCircle( pos.x, bottom - pos.y, 3 );
}
```

The last function to consider is `updateBall()`. It changes the position and the velocity of the ball using the Euler method, according to Newton's second law of motion, with gravitational force.

Details on the Euler method can be seen in the *Defining the particle functions* section in *Chapter 3, Building a Simple Particle System*. The information on the second Newton's law of motion and gravity force can be seen at http://en.wikipedia.org/wiki/Newton's_laws_of_motion and http://en.wikipedia.org/wiki/Gravitational_field.

When the ball bounces on the floor, it bounces in the y axis and changes its x velocity randomly. When the ball jumps out of the screen, it appears on the opposite side of the screen. The function returns `true` if the ball is bounced off the floor:

```
bool testApp::updateBall() {
    bool bounced = false;

    //Compute dt
    float time = ofGetElapsedTimef();
    float dt = ofClamp( time - time0, 0, 0.1 );
    time0 = time;

    //Compute gravity force acceleration
    //using the second Newton's law
    ofPoint acc( 0, -g/mass );

    //Change velocity and position using Euler's method
    vel += acc * dt;
    pos += vel * dt;

    //Check if the ball bounced off floor
    if ( pos.y < 0 ) {
        //Elastic bounce with momentum conservation
        pos.y = -pos.y;
        vel.y = -vel.y;
        //Set random velocity by x axe in range [-300, 500]
        vel.x = ofRandom( -300, 500 );
        bounced = true;
    }

    //Check if the ball is out of screen
    if ( pos.x < 0 ) { pos.x += ofGetWidth(); }
    if ( pos.x > ofGetWidth() ) { pos.x -= ofGetWidth(); }
    return bounced;
}
```

The dt is a time step value, which is computed as a time difference between the current time and the time of the previous calling of the `updateBall()` function.

We use the `ofClamp()` function for limiting its value by `0.1`. The reason for this is that sometimes `time - time0` can be a large value. (For example, if the user drags the window or hides the application's window, `testApp::update()` callings can be paused - it depends on the operating system.) So if we don't limit this, formulas in the Euler method will work in an unstable manner, and the model literally explodes.

Run the example. You will see a flying red dot which bounces of the line (the floor) and also draws its trajectory on the screen. Each time the bouncing occurs, you will hear a sound. Over time you will see the ball's path as shown in the following screenshot:

Run the example a few more times. You will notice that the resulting trajectories and the music differ. But the structure of the music will be the same. Actually it is the **structured randomness** effect, which is typical for many creative coding and generative art projects.

You can play with parameters such as mass, the y value of the ball's initial position (`100`), the range of dependence of the sample speed of `pos.x`, range for random velocity, and explore how model behavior and the music structure changes.

The singing voices example

There is a simple but fruitful method to make interesting and evolving sounds with samples. It is based on playing several different samples simultaneously and changing the parameters continuously inside `testApp::update()`. Let's consider the simplest case of changing just the volumes of the samples. Namely, let's get a number of vocal samples singing different notes, start playing them, and randomly change the volume of each sample. The resulting sound will be like a live choir singing a tonic chord.

This is example `06-Sound/02-SingingVoices`.

This example is based on the `emptyExample` project in openFrameworks. Before running it, copy the files `vox1.wav` to `vox6.wav` into the `bin/data` folder of your project.

For simplicity, we place all constants and variables not in the class `testApp` definition, but right at the beginning of the `testApp.cpp` file, after the `#include "testApp.h"` line:

```
const int N = 6;           //Number of the samples
ofSoundPlayer sound[ N ];  //Array of the samples
float vol[ N ];            //Volumes of the samples
```

 It is a best practice to use `vector` instead of fixed arrays whenever it is possible. So it would be better to declare `sound` and `vol` as follows:

```
vector<ofSoundPlayer> sound;
vector<float> vol;
```

Currently, such an approach does not work properly in openFrameworks for Mac OS X—the project plays just one sound due to an undesired interrelation between `vector` and `ofSoundPlayer`.

The `setup()` function loads samples and sets up their parameters. Note how we place the samples uniformly in stereo panorama ranging from `-0.5` to `0.5` using `setPan()`:

```
void testApp::setup(){

    //Load and set up the sound samples
    for ( int i=0; i<N; i++) {
        sound[i].loadSound(
                "vox" + ofToString( i + 1 ) + ".wav" );
        sound[i].setLoop( true );

        //Do some stereo panoraming of the sounds
        sound[i].setPan( ofMap( i, 0, N-1, -0.5, 0.5 ) );

        sound[i].setVolume( 0 );
        sound[i].play();     //Start a sample to play
    }
    //Decrease overall volume to eliminate volume overload
    //(audio clipping)
    ofSoundSetVolume( 0.2 );
}
```

The update() function slowly changes the values of the vol array using Perlin noise (see more details in *Appendix B, Perlin Noise*), and sets its values to the sample's volumes:

```
void testApp::update() {
   float time = ofGetElapsedTimef();     //Get current time

   //Update volumes
   float tx = time*0.1 + 50;   //Value, smoothly changed over time
   for (int i=0; i<N; i++) {
        //Calculate the sample volume as 2D Perlin noise,
        //depending on tx and ty = i * 0.2
        float ty = i * 0.2;
        vol[i] = ofNoise( tx, ty );     //Perlin noise

        sound[i].setVolume( vol[i] );  //Set sample's volume
   }

   //Update sound engine
   ofSoundUpdate();
}
```

The first parameter for noise computation is as follows:

```
float nx = time*0.1 + 50;
```

It starts from 50 and increases by 0.1 for each second. These two constants set the initial distribution and the speed of fluctuations.

The second parameter is as follows:

```
float ty = i * 0.2;
```

It is equally distributed from 0.0 to (N-1) * 0.2. Parameter 0.2 specifies the smoothness of just the volumes distributed in the given time. Increasing this value leads to smoothness decreasing.

The draw() function draws current volumes as narrow vertical rectangles:

```
void testApp::draw() {
   ofBackground( 255, 255, 255 );   //Set the background color

   //Draw volumes as vertical lines
   ofSetColor( 0, 0, 0 );
   for (int i=0; i<N; i++) {
        ofRect( i * 20 + 100, 400, 5, -vol[i] * 300 );
   }
}
```

When you run this example, you will hear an evolving sound and see slow moving lines which correspond to the current levels of each of the six playing samples:

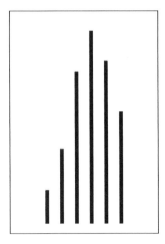

Note that normally `testApp::update()` runs not more than 60 frames per second. And changes of sound parameters at such a rate can be audible. So the described technique of controlling volumes is very simple, but resulted changes in sound can be not so smooth as it should be. To reach the perfect sound, you need to change the parameters smoothly for each audio sample. See the example of such parameters changing techniques in the *The PWM synthesis example* section.

Generating sounds

We saw earlier how to play sound samples and change their parameters. Though this technique is simple and easy to begin with, it is not enough for making breakthrough sound art projects. One way to achieve this is by generating and synthesizing sounds and not using samples at all. Another way is to use samples as raw material for processing methods such as morphing and granular synthesis. Both ways are based on using low-level algorithms, which construct sounds as an array of audio samples in real time.

openFrameworks uses low-level sound input and output, and we use C++ for processing it, so our sound processing pipeline can perform almost any trick with sounds, will work fast, and with only small lags.

There is one thing that is currently not so convenient to implement with openFrameworks. This is processing a sound stream using a variety of standard filters and effects. To do this, you need to program filters yourself or use libraries or addons. Also, you can use software such as Max/MSP or Ableton Live for sound generation and then control it from openFrameworks via OSC protocol. See *Chapter 11, Networking* for more details.

For generating sound in real time, you need to start the sound output stream and then provide audio samples for the sound when it is requested by openFrameworks. The corresponding additions to the project's code are as follows:

1. Add a sound stream object and function for audio output to the `testApp` class declaration as follows:

    ```
    ofSoundStream soundStream;

    void audioOut( float *output, int bufferSize, int nChannels );
    ```

2. At the end of the `testApp::setup()` function definition add:

    ```
    soundStream.setup( this, 2, 0, 44100, 512, 4 );
    ```

    Here `this` is a pointer to our `testApp` object which will receive requests of audio data from openFrameworks by calling our `testApp::audioOut` function.

    Subsequently, `2` is the number of output channels (hence, stereo output), `0` is the number of input channels (hence, no input), and `44100` is a sample rate, that is, the number of audio samples played per second. The value `44100` means CD quality and is good in most situations. The last two parameters `512` and `4` are the size of the buffer for audio samples and the number of buffers respectively. This is discussed later.

3. Add the function definition as follows:

    ```
    void testApp::audioOut(
            float *output, int bufferSize, int nChannels ){

      //... fill output array here

    }
    ```

This is the function that should fill the output array with the audio samples' data. This function actually generates the sound. Values of output should lie in the range from -1.0 to 1.0. In the opposite case, audio clipping will occur (you will hear clicks in sound). The size of output is equal to bufferSize * nChannels, and the samples in the channels are interleaved. Namely, if nChannels is equal to 2, then this is a stereo signal, so output[0] and output[1] mean the first audio samples for the left and the right channels. Correspondingly, output[2] and output[3] mean the second audio samples, and so on.

Also, there are a number of functions for managing audio devices. They are as follows:

- The soundStream.listDevices() function prints to console the list of devices.
- The soundStream.setDeviceID(id) function selects a device, where id has type int. You should call this before soundStream.setup(). If no soundStream.setDeviceID(id) was called, then the default system device is used.
- The soundStream.stop() function stops calling audioOut().
- The soundStream.start() function starts calling audioOut() again.
- The soundStream.close() function ends using audio device by soundStream object.

There are two important things about the sound generating function audioOut(). Firstly, the function is called by openFrameworks independent of the update() and draw() functions' calls. Namely, it is called at the request of the sound card, when the next buffer with audio samples for playing is needed:

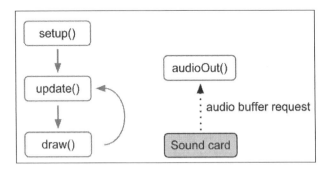

Secondly, audioOut() should work fast. In the opposite case, the sound card did not receive the buffer in time, and you will hear clicks in the output sound. You can tune this by changing the two last parameters in the following line:

```
soundStream.setup( this, 2, 0, 44100, 512, 4 );
```

512 is a buffer size. If the buffer is bigger (for example, 1024), then it is rarely requested, so you have more time for filling this, so more robustness. On the contrary, a lower value of the buffer size, for example, 256, leads to the better responsivity (smaller latency) of audio. The reason is that the delay between buffer filling and its playing through the audio system will be smaller. The last parameter, 4, is the number of buffers used by the sound card for storing sound. Similarly, increasing the parameter leads to better robustness and decreasing them leads to better audio responsivity.

Now, we will consider an example of sound generation.

Warning

When using ofSoundStream for sound output in your projects, be careful! Due to possible errors in the projects' code and for other reasons, it can suddenly generate clicks and very loud sounds. To avoid the hazard of damaging your ears, *do not* listen to the output of such projects using headphones.

The PWM synthesis example

Let's build a simple sound generator using **Pulse Width Modulation (PWM)**. In electronics, PWM is a method of sending analog values through wires using just two levels of voltage (logical 1 and 0). The value is coded by changing the length of the pulse with logical value 1, with the overall cycle length fixed. In the following diagram, coding *val* in range from *0* to *1*, with fixed cycle length *c* is shown. You can see that an output signal is a periodic wave, with the wavelength equal to *c*, and the wave consists of two segments with values *1* and *0*, with lengths *val * c* and *c - val * c* respectively:

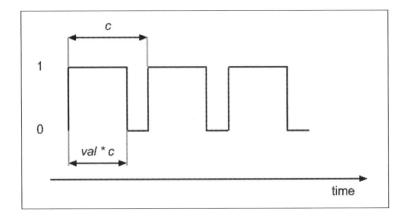

Such a signal can be considered as a sound wave, with the wave frequency equal to $1.0/c$.

If *val* is equal to *0.5*, then *1* and *0* values have equal length in the wave, and such a waveform is called a **square wave**.

 PWM sound waves and especially square waves are widely used in subtractive synthesizers as the basic waveforms for sound generation. They have a fat and distinct electronic sound. Among them, sinusoidal, triangle, and saw-shaped waves are also used.

Let's consider an example of PWM sound generation. The frequency and PWM value of the wave will depend on x and y mouse coordinates, so when you move the mouse, you will hear the sound changing.

 This is example `06-Sound/03-PWMSynth`.

Warning: To avoid the hazard of damaging your ears due to the possibility of suddenly generated very loud sounds, *do not* listen to the output of the project with headphones.

This example is based on the `emptyExample` project in openFrameworks.

Add the next code to `testApp.h`, in the class `testApp` declaration. Note that the sound control parameters are `userFreq` and `userPwm`— a frequency and PWM value. And there are separate variables for these parameters `freq` and `pwm` which will change relatively slowly. This lets us always obtain a smooth sound, even when the user changes sound parameters fast (that is, moves the mouse rapidly).

```
//Function for generating audio
void audioOut( float *output, int bufferSize, int nChannels );

ofSoundStream soundStream;   //Object for sound output setup

//User-changing parameters
float userFreq;              //Frequency
float userPwm;               //PWM value
//Parameters, used during synthesis
float freq;                  //Current frequency
float pwm;                   //Current PWM value
float phase;                 //Phase of the wave

//Buffer for rendering last generated audio buffer
vector<float> buf;
```

At the beginning of the `testApp.cpp` file, after the `#include "testApp.h"` line, add declarations of some constants as follows:

```
int bufSize = 512;           //Sound card buffer size
int sampleRate = 44100;      //Sound sample rate
float volume = 0.1;          //Output volume
```

The `setup()` function sets the initial values and starts the sound output:

```
void testApp::setup(){
  userFreq = 100.0;          //Some initial frequency
  userPwm = 0.5;             //Some initial PWM value

  freq = userFreq;
  pwm = userPwm;
  phase = 0;
  buf.resize( bufSize );

  //Start the sound output
  soundStream.setup( this, 2, 0, sampleRate, bufSize, 4 );
}
```

The `update()` function is empty, and the `draw()` function draws the buffer with audio sample values on the screen:

```
void testApp::draw(){
  ofBackground( 255, 255, 255 );  //Set the background color
  //Draw the buffer values
  ofSetColor( 0, 0, 0 );
  for (int i=0; i<bufSize-1; i++) {
      ofLine( i, 100 - buf[i]*50, (i+1), 100 - buf[i+1]*50 );
  }
}
```

Also we need to fill the `mouseMoved()` function to change the parameters according to the mouse move. The `userFreq` frequency will change in a range from 1 to 2000 Hz, and the PWM value `userPwm` will change in a range from 0 to 1:

```
void testApp::mouseMoved( int x, int y ){
  userFreq = ofMap( x, 0, ofGetWidth(), 1, 2000 );
  userPwm = ofMap( y, 0, ofGetHeight(), 0, 1 );
}
```

Finally, add the `audioOut()` function that generates the sound. You can see how we change the `freq` and `pwm` values with each cycle loop to approach `userFreq` and `userPwm` smoothly. Also note that `phase` is a value in a range from 0 to 1 and it changes in correspondence with `freq` and `sampleRate` at each audio sample generation.

```
void testApp::audioOut( float *output,
        int bufferSize, int nChannels ){
  //Fill output buffer,
  //and also move freq to userFreq and pwm to userPWM slowly
  for (int i=0; i<bufferSize; i++) {
      //freq smoothly reaches userFreq
      freq += ( userFreq - freq ) * 0.001;
      //pwm smoothly reaches userPwm
      pwm += ( userPwm - pwm ) * 0.001;

      //Change phase, and push it into [0, 1] range
      phase += freq / sampleRate;
      phase = fmodf( phase, 1.0 );

      //Calculate the output audio sample value
      //Instead of 1 and 0 we use 1 and -1 output values
      //for the sound wave to be symmetrical along y-axe
      float v = ( phase < pwm ) ? 1.0 : -1.0;

      //Set the computed value to the left and the right
```

```
        //channels of output buffer,
        //also using global volume value defined above
        output[ i*2 ] = output[ i*2 + 1 ] = v * volume;

        //Set the value to buffer buf, used for rendering
        //on the screen
        //Note: bufferSize can occasionally differ from bufSize
        if ( i < bufSize ) {
            buf[ i ] = v;
        }
    }
}
```

Run the code and move the mouse left-right and up-down. You will hear a distinctive PWM sound and will see its waves:

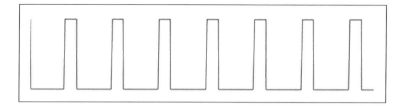

Move the mouse and explore the sound when the mouse is in the center of the screen and in the screen borders. Because the x coordinate of the muse sets the frequency and the y coordinate of the mouse sets the PWM value, you will notice that moving the mouse in the middle of the screen gives a fat square sound, and moving the mouse at the very top and bottom of the screen gives glitch-like pulse signals.

If you change the values `0.001` to `0.0001` in lines `freq += ( userFreq - freq ) * 0.001;` and `pwm += ( userPwm - pwm ) * 0.001;` then `freq` and `pwm` will slowly move to `userFreq` and `userPwm`. So while moving the mouse, you will hear a glide effect used in synthesizers. On the contrary, if you set these values to `1.0`, `freq` and `pwm` will just be equal to `userFreq` and `userPwm`, and you will hear a raw sound, rapidly changing with the mouse moving.

In some compilers, you need to perform the **Rebuild** command for your project in order for the `audioOut ()` function to be linked to the project correctly. If the linking is not correct, you will just see a straight line on the screen and hear nothing. If you see the PWM waves on the screen but do not hear the sound, check your sound equipment and its volume settings.

You can extend the example by adding control to its parameters by using some analysis of live video taken from the camera or 3D-camera data.

We will go further and see an example of transcoding image data into a sound signal directly.

Image-to-sound transcoder example

Let's get an image and consider its center horizontal line. This is a one-dimensional array of colors. Now get the brightness of each color in the array. We will obtain an array of numbers, which can be considered as PCM values for some sound, and used for playing in the `audioOut()` function.

Certainly, there exist other methods for converting visual data to audio data and back. Moreover, there exist ways to convert audio and video to commands, controlling robot motors, 3D printers, smell printers, and any other digital devices. All such transformations between different information types are called **transcoding**. Transcoding is possible due to the digital nature of representation of all the information in the computer. For example, number 102 can be simultaneously interpreted as a pixel color component, an audio sample value and an angle for a robot's servo motor. For detailed philosophical considerations on transcoding, see the book *The Language of New Media, Leo Manovich, The MIT Press*.

Such an algorithm is a transcoding of image to audio data. Let's code it using frames from a camera as input images. For details on using camera data, see *Chapter 5, Working with Videos*.

This is example `06-Sound/04-ImageToSound`.

Warning: To avoid the hazard of damaging your ears due to the possibility of suddenly generated very loud sounds, *do not* listen to the output of the project with headphones.

This example is based on the `emptyExample` project in openFrameworks. Add the following code to `testApp.h` in the class `testApp` declaration:

```
//Function for generating audio
void audioOut( float *output, int bufferSize, int nChannels );

ofSoundStream soundStream;  //Object for sound output setup

ofVideoGrabber grabber;     //Video grabber
```

At the beginning of testApp.cpp, after the #include "testApp.h" line, add constants and variables:

```
//Constants
const int grabW = 1024;         //Width of the camera frame
const int grabH = 768;          //Height of the camera frame
const int sampleRate = 44100;   //Sample rate of sound
const float duration = 0.25;    //Duration of the recorded
                                //sound in seconds
const int N = duration * sampleRate;  //Size of the PCM buffer
const float volume = 0.5;              //Output sound volume
const int Y0 = grabH * 0.5;     //y-position of the scan line

//Variables
vector<float> arr;      //Temporary array of pixels brightness
vector<float> buffer;   //PCM buffer of sound sample
int playPos = 0;        //The current position of the buffer playing
```

The setup() function sets the buffer arrays' sizes, runs the video grabber, and starts the sound output:

```
void testApp::setup(){
  //Set arrays sizes and fill these by zeros
  arr.resize( grabW, 0.0 );
  buffer.resize( N, 0.0 );

  //Start camera
  grabber.initGrabber( grabW, grabH );

  //Start the sound output
  soundStream.setup( this, 2, 0, sampleRate, 512, 4 );
}
```

The update() function reads a frame from the camera and writes the brightness of the central line into the buffer. It saves the pixel's brightness values into array arr, which has a size equal to the image width grabW. Next, arr is stretching the buffer array, which has size N, using **linear interpolation**.

Also, the values of the buffer are shifted so the mean value of its values will be equal to zero. Such a transformation is the simplest method for **DC-offset removal**. Methods of DC-offset removal are always used in sound recording for centering recorded signals. This is a crucial procedure in the case of mixing several sounds because it helps to reduce a dynamic range of mixed signals without any changes being heard:

```
void testApp::update(){
    grabber.update();                    //Update camera
    if ( grabber.isFrameNew() ) {        //Check for new frame

        //Get pixels of the camera image
        ofPixels &pixels = grabber.getPixelsRef();

        //Read central line's pixels brightness to arr
        for (int x=0; x<grabW; x++) {
            //Get the pixel brightness
            float v = pixels.getColor( x, Y0 ).getLightness();
            //v lies in [0,255], convert it to [-1,1]
            arr[x] = ofMap( v, 0, 255, -1, 1, true );
        }

        //Stretch arr to buffer, using linear interpolation
        for (int i=0; i<N; i++) {
            //Get position in range [0, grabW]
            float pos = float(i) * grabW / N;

            //Get left and right indices
            int pos0 = int( pos );
            int pos1 = min( pos0 + 1, N-1 );

            //Interpolate
            buffer[i] = ofMap( pos, pos0, pos1,
                               arr[pos0],arr[pos1] );
        }

        //DC-offset removal
        //Compute a mean value of buffer
        float mean = 0;
        for (int i=0; i<N; i++) {
            mean += buffer[i];
        }
```

```
        mean /= N;

        //Shift the buffer by mean value
        for (int i=0; i<N; i++) {
            buffer[i] -= mean;
        }
    }
}
```

The `draw()` function draws the camera image, marks the scan line area by a yellow rectangle, and draws the buffer as a graph in the top part of the screen. See the `draw()` function code in the example's text.

Finally, the `audioOut()` function reads the values from the buffer and pushes them into the `output` array. The playing position is held in the `playPos` value. When the end of the buffer is reached, the `playPos` is set to 0, so the buffer plays in a loop:

```
void testApp::audioOut(
        float *output, int bufferSize, int nChannels ) {
    for (int i=0; i<bufferSize; i++) {
        //Push current audio sample value from buffer
        //into both channels of output.
        //Also global volume value is used
        output[ 2*i ] = output[ 2*i + 1 ]
                    = buffer[ playPos ] * volume;
        //Shift to the next audio sample
        playPos++;
        //When the end of buffer is reached, playPos sets to 0
        //So we hear looped sound
        playPos %= N;
    }
}
```

Run the example and direct the camera somewhere. You will see the camera image with the scan area selected by a yellow rectangle. At the top of the screen, you will see the corresponding graph of sound, and will hear this sound in a loop. Note how bright and dark pixels in the scan line correspond to the high and low graph values. Most likely, the sound you hear will be quite strange. This is because our ears are trained to hear periodic signals but normally, data from a camera image is not periodic.

Now, direct the camera to this stripes image (yes, direct the camera right to this picture in the book, or print it on a paper from the file `stripesSin0To880Hz.png`):

If you fit the scan line to the horizontal line of the image, you will hear a sound tone, swiping from a low to a high tone, and see the image as shown in the following screenshot:

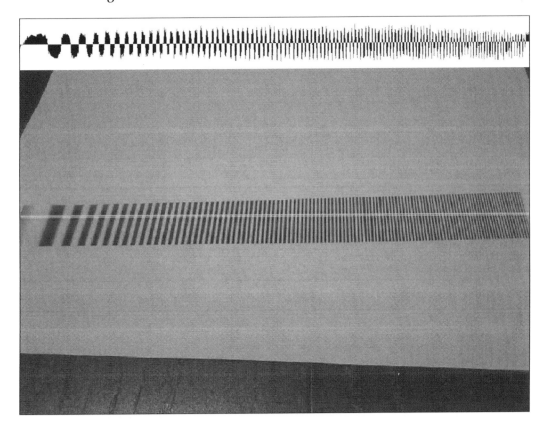

Actually, the stripes correspond to a sine wave with the frequency changed from 0 to 800 Hz, with a duration of one-fourth of a second. The corresponding graph of its PCM is shown in the following screenshot:

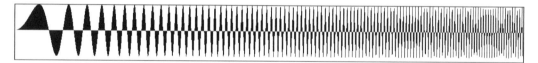

You can see that the graph of the sound, transcoded from the camera (at the top of the previous screenshot), is noised but nevertheless, is similar to the original graph.

Now move the camera closer to the stripes image. You will notice how the tone of the sound decreases. If you move the camera very close, you will hear a bass sound.

Here is one more stripes image to play with. It codes *ar* sound (`stripesAr.png file`):

> You can prepare stripe images by coding your own sounds using the loop sampler example. This is discussed in *The loop sampler example* section.

We hope that after you finish playing with this example you will understand and feel the nature of a PCM-sound representation in a better way.

Now we will consider how to get sound data from a microphone and other input sound devices.

Using a microphone

The way to input sound data from a microphone or other audio input device is similar to the sound output considered earlier, with small changes:

1. Add a sound stream object and function for the audio input to the `testApp` class declaration as follows:

    ```
    ofSoundStream soundStream;

    void audioReceived( float *input, int bufferSize, int nChannels );
    ```

2. At the end of the `testApp::setup()` function definition, add the following:

```
soundStream.setup( this, 0, 1, 44100, 512, 4 );
```

Here, `this` is a pointer to our `testApp` object which will receive the microphone's sound data by calling our `testApp::audioReceived` function.

Subsequently, `0` is the number of output channels (hence, no output), `1` is the number of input channels (hence, mono input), `44100` is a sample rate, that is, the received number of audio samples per second.

The last two parameters `512` and `4` are the size of the buffer for audio samples and the number of buffers.

3. Add function definition as follows:

```
void testApp::audioReceived(
        float *input, int bufferSize, int nChannels ){

   //... use input array here

}
```

This is a function that can use the `input` array of the audio sample's data. It is a function which actually processes sound.

Values of `input` lie in the range from `-1.0` to `1.0`. The size of the `input` is equal to the `bufferSize * nChannels`, and samples in the channels are interleaved. Namely, if `nChannels = 2`, then this is a stereo signal, so `input[0]` and `input[1]` mean the first audio samples for the left and right channels. Correspondingly, `input[2]` and `input[3]` mean the second audio samples, and so on.

Functions `listDevices()`, `setDeviceID( id )`, `stop()`, `start()`, and `close()`, discussed in the *Generating sounds* section are applicable here as well.

Note that the `audioReceived()` function is called by openFrameworks independent of calling the `update()` and `draw()` functions. Namely, it is called when the next buffer with audio samples is received from the sound card:

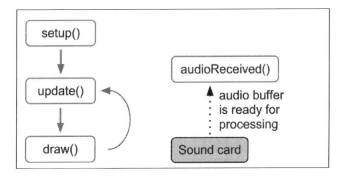

If you need both sound output and input, just specify the nonzero number of the output and input channels:

```
soundStream.setup( this, 2, 1, 44100, 512, 4 );
```

Add both `audioOut()` and `audioReceived()` functions to your `testApp` class.

Let's see an example of using sound input.

The loop sampler example

Sound samplers are music devices which record and replay sound samples. Let's make a simple sampler which records and plays one short sound. Recording and playing are made in a loop. Additionally, the current sound is drawn as a graph and also as a stripe image, so you can use it for making input pictures for an image-to-sound transcoder example as described earlier.

This is example `06-Sound/05-LoopSampler`.

Warning: To avoid the hazard of damaging your ears due to the possibility of suddenly generated very loud sounds, *do not* listen to the output of the project with headphones.

This example is based on the `emptyExample` project in openFrameworks. As it receives and generates sound, add the next code to `testApp.h` in the class `testApp` declaration:

```
//Function for receiving audio
void audioReceived( float *input, int bufferSize, int nChannels );

//Function for generating audio
void audioOut( float *input, int bufferSize, int nChannels );

//Object for sound output and input setup
ofSoundStream soundStream;
```

At the beginning of `testApp.cpp`, after the `#include "testApp.h"` line, add constants and variables. The main thing here is the `buffer` array, which is used as storage for sound recording and also as a data source for sound playing. This buffer has a size which is generally not equal to the size of the `input` and `output` buffers passed in the `audioReceived()` and `audioOut()` functions. This means we need to use variables for holding the current recording and playing position, `recPos` and `playPos` respectively. Also, there are two modes of work selectable from the keyboard, sample recording and playing. To manage this, we define the flags `recordingEnabled` and `playingEnabled`:

```
//Constants
const int sampleRate = 44100;      //Sample rate of sound
const float duration = 0.25;       //Duration of the recorded
                                   //sound in seconds
const int N = duration * sampleRate;    //Size of the PCM buffer

//Variables
vector<float> buffer;   //PCM buffer of sound sample
int recPos = 0;         //Current recording position in the buffer
int playPos = 0;        //Current playing position in the buffer

int recordingEnabled = 1;    //Is recording enabled
int playingEnabled = 0;      //Is playing enabled
```

The `setup()` function sets the `buffer` size and starts the sound output and input:

```
void testApp::setup(){
    //Set buffer size and fill it by zeros
    buffer.resize( N, 0.0 );

    //Start the sound output in stereo (2 channels)
    //and sound input in mono (1 channel)
    soundStream.setup( this, 2, 1, sampleRate, 256, 4 );
}
```

In order to record sound updates on the screen more rapidly, we set the sound card buffer size equal to 256 (not 512 as in the previous examples). If you hear some clicks in the sound, it means that the application is too expensive for your computer (due to CPU or sound card), so increase the value back to 512.

The update() function is empty. The draw() function draws a graph of the buffer and its stripe image. A stripe image is drawn by vertical lines of different colors. Note that the width of the screen w = 1024 is less than the sound buffer size N, so we are shrinking the buffer on the screen using the conversion formula:

```
i = float(x) * N / w
```

Also, while converting the buffer values into color values of the lines, we apply square root transformation. It makes small changes of audio samples more visually distinct. Image-to-sound transcoding works better with such a transformed image too. See the draw() function code in the example's text.

The most important functions of the example are audioReceived() and audioOut(). They record and play audio samples to and from the buffer array:

```
//Audio input
void testApp::audioReceived(
  float *input, int bufferSize, int nChannels ) {

  //If recording is enabled by the user,
  //then store received data
  if ( recordingEnabled ) {
      for (int i=0; i<bufferSize; i++) {
          buffer[ recPos ] = input[i];
          recPos++;
          //When the end of buffer is reached, recPos sets
          //to 0, so we record sound in a loop
          recPos %= N;
      }
  }
}


//Audio output
void testApp::audioOut(
      float *output, int bufferSize, int nChannels) {

  //If playing is enabled by the user, then do output sound
  if ( playingEnabled ) {
      for (int i=0; i<bufferSize; i++) {
          output[ 2*i ] = output[ 2*i+1 ]
                        = buffer[ playPos ];
          playPos++;
          //When the end of buffer is reached, playPos sets
          //to 0, so we hear looped sound
          playPos %= N;
      }
  }
}
```

Finally, add a reaction on the keyboard. Keys *1* and *2* will switch between the recording and playing modes. Key *S* will save the screen image to the `grab.png` file, so you can print it and use it as an input in the *Image-to-sound transcoder* example:

```cpp
void testApp::keyPressed( int key ){

    //Enable recording mode
    if ( key == '1' ) {
        recordingEnabled = 1; playingEnabled = 0;
    }

    //Enable playing mode
    if ( key == '2' ) {
        recordingEnabled = 0; playingEnabled = 1;
    }

    //Save screen image to the file
    if ( key == 's' ) {
        ofImage grab;
        grab.grabScreen( 0, 0, ofGetWidth(), ofGetHeight() );
        grab.saveImage( "grab.png" );
    }
}
```

If you use a laptop, then it is highly possible that you may have an built-in microphone. If not, then before running the application, connect a microphone or web camera to your computer (most web cameras have microphones). Run the application and say something into the microphone. You will see a graph of the sound and also a stripe image as shown in the following screenshot:

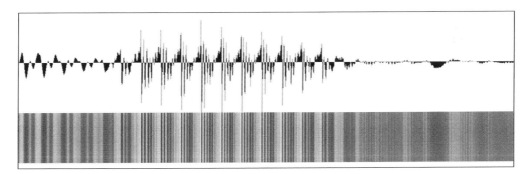

Continue talking into the microphone and press 2. The recording will be stopped and the last recorded sound sample will play in a loop. As the recording is performed in a looped buffer with a length duration = 0.25 seconds, the resulting duration of the sample will be 0.25 seconds too.

Now press *S* and the image will be saved into the grab.png file in the bin/data folder of the application. Press *1* and the recording will start again.

> If your application hangs at the start, you might have selected an improper sound device. For example, it can happen if you run the application in Microsoft Windows 7 and no input device is connected. Also, some sound devices are output or input only. Use soundStream.listDevices() to show the list of available devices, and then call soundStream.setDeviceID(id) with proper id. If you use an input-only device, try to run the example with sound output disabled. To do so, change the number of output channels from 2 to 0 in soundStream.setup() calling in the testApp::setup() function:
>
> ```
> soundStream.setup( this, 0, 1, sampleRate, 256, 4 );
> ```

Saving a recorded sample to the file

Let's talk about saving the recorded sound sample into a file. Currently, openFrameworks does not have a function for writing sound samples to WAV or MP3 files. To do so, you need to download and use an addon such as ofxSndFile.

Another simple but not so comfortable way is to save your file as a RAW file containing only audio samples, and then open it in an audio editor, specifying its sample rate and audio samples' type. To do so in the preceding example, add the following code to the keyPressed(int key) function:

```
//Write the sound sample to raw-file
if ( key == 'f' ) {
  //Create a file for writing
  //Here "wb" means that we open binary file for writing
  FILE *file = fopen( ofToDataPath("sound.raw").c_str(), "wb" );
  //Write the buffer into file
  fwrite( &buffer[0], N, sizeof( buffer[0] ), file );

  //Close the file
  fclose( file );
}
```

Now if you run the application and press *F*, the current sound sample will be written to the sound.raw file in the bin/data folder of the application. You can open it in a sound editor such as Audacity (free) or Sony Sound Forge (commercial) and while opening, specify the sample parameters:

- Sample rate: 44100 Hz
- Sample type or encoding: 32-bit float
- Channels: 1 channel (mono)
- Byte order: Little-endian

Finally, using the editor, you can save it as a WAV or an MP3 file.

Now we will consider how to get meaningful information from sound and use it for adding a real-time reaction to sound into your projects.

Getting spectral data from sound

PCM sound representation is good for sound storage and playing. It lets us operate sound samples like a piece of magnetic tape—to cut, shuffle its parts, reverse, and glue back together. Also it lets us change and measure the overall volume of the sound. But PCM is inadequate for more advanced sound analysis and processing. The reason being that humans cannot hear separate audio samples, only frequencies in sound in short time intervals. The collection of amplitudes of each frequency in a short time interval is called **spectrum** of the sound. Therefore, sound processing methods should work using frequencies-spectrum language. This differs sound processing from image and video processing as they work well with pixels independently.

In this section, we will not dip into the mathematical aspects of spectrum computing, but will learn how to compute it using the openFrameworks functions and use it in projects.

The spectrum in openFrameworks is calculated for sound, which is formed by playing samples using the ofSoundPlayer objects.

 If you need to calculate the spectrum for your own generated audio with the audioOut() function, you need to do it by yourself, with Fast Fourier Transform implementation, which you can find on the Internet.

The spectrum is an array of float numbers. It is obtained using the ofSoundGetSpectrum(N) function, where N is the number of spectrum bands. Normally, N is the power of two:

```
float *val = ofSoundGetSpectrum( 256 );
```

Here val is an array of size 256. First array items correspond to lower frequencies, and last array items correspond to higher frequencies. With increasing N, you will have a more detailed description of the spectrum, but the data accuracy in time will decrease. The values of the spectrum are normalized so you can think they lie in the range [0, 1], though for loud sounds, values can exceed 1.

Note that you should not release the memory of val, because it is managed by a sound engine.

Having a spectrum array, you can get its values and use these for changing the controlling parameters for physics and visualization in your project. It is a good idea to smooth the spectrum because it jitters. Also, when using it for crucial projects, you do not need to use one spectrum band but perform smoothing (filtration) spectrum values over a number of bands.

The technology of filtering the regions of a spectrum is widely used in the VJ software for detecting a track's BPM (beats per minute, or tempo), and tracking separate beats of drums and other instruments. If you need to do a really advanced sound analysis of the music track for visualization, it may be a good idea to use Max/MSP, VDMX, or any other VJ software for analysis, and then send its result to your openFrameworks project via the OSC protocol. For more details on using the OSC protocol, see *Chapter 11, Networking*.

Dancing cloud example

This is an example of an audio-reactive visual project. We are going to play a music track, get its spectrum, and use it for controlling point cloud parameters. So the cloud is rendered on the screen and shakes synchronously with drum beats in the music.

This is example 06-Sound/06-DancingCloud.

The example is based on the emptyExample project in openFrameworks. Before running it, copy the surface.wav file into the bin/data folder of your project.

In the `testApp.h` file, in the class `testApp` declaration, add declarations of a sound sample:

```
ofSoundPlayer sound;   //Sound sample
```

Now let's consider the `testApp.cpp` file. For simplicity, we place the constants and variables not in class `testApp` definition, but right into the cpp file, after the `#include "testApp.h"` line:

```
const int N = 256;        //Number of bands in spectrum
float spectrum[ N ];      //Smoothed spectrum values
float Rad = 500;          //Cloud radius parameter
float Vel = 0.1;          //Cloud points velocity parameter
int bandRad = 2;          //Band index in spectrum, affecting Rad value
int bandVel = 100;        //Band index in spectrum, affecting Vel value

const int n = 300;        //Number of cloud points

//Offsets for Perlin noise calculation for points
float tx[n], ty[n];
ofPoint p[n];             //Cloud's points positions

float time0 = 0;          //Time value, used for dt computing
```

You can see that the spectrum is stored in the `spectrum` array, with size `N = 256`. Cloud has two control parameters—radius `Rad` and velocity `Vel`. Radius depends on the spectrum band `bandRad = 2`, and velocity depends on spectrum band `bandVel = 100`. These bands were selected specifically for the given music track, so `Rad` and `Vel` jump up on the base drum and snare drum beats respectively. Visually, the cloud expands on the base drum beat, and the points in the cloud begin to shuffle on the snare drum beat. The cloud is made from array points `p`, with size `n = 300`. Points are moved by Perlin noise (see more details in *Appendix B, Perlin Noise*).

The `setup()` function does sound sample loading and sets Perlin noise offsets for points initialization:

```
void testApp::setup(){
   //Set up sound sample
   sound.loadSound( "surface.wav" );
   sound.setLoop( true );
   sound.play();

   //Set spectrum values to 0
   for (int i=0; i<N; i++) {
       spectrum[i] = 0.0f;
```

```
    }

    //Initialize points offsets by random numbers
    for ( int j=0; j<n; j++ ) {
        tx[j] = ofRandom( 0, 1000 );
        ty[j] = ofRandom( 0, 1000 );
    }
}
```

The `update()` function gets the spectrum of the currently played sound, computes its smoothed values to the `spectrum` array, and recalculates the `Rad` and `Vel` parameters. Finally, it calculates new point positions:

```
void testApp::update(){
    //Update sound engine
    ofSoundUpdate();

    //Get current spectrum with N bands
    float *val = ofSoundGetSpectrum( N );
    //We should not release memory of val,
    //because it is managed by sound engine

    //Update our smoothed spectrum,
    //by slowly decreasing its values and getting maximum with val
    //So we will have slowly falling peaks in spectrum
    for ( int i=0; i<N; i++ ) {
        spectrum[i] *= 0.97;      //Slow decreasing
        spectrum[i] = max( spectrum[i], val[i] );
    }

    //Update particles using spectrum values

    //Computing dt as a time between the last
    //and the current calling of update()
    float time = ofGetElapsedTimef();
    float dt = time - time0;
    dt = ofClamp( dt, 0.0, 0.1 );
    time0 = time; //Store the current time

    //Update Rad and Vel from spectrum
    //Note, the parameters in ofMap's were tuned for best result
    //just for current music track
    Rad = ofMap( spectrum[ bandRad ], 1, 3, 400, 800, true );
```

```
    Vel = ofMap( spectrum[ bandVel ], 0, 0.1, 0.05, 0.5 );

    //Update particles positions
    for (int j=0; j<n; j++) {
        tx[j] += Vel * dt;   //move offset
        ty[j] += Vel * dt;   //move offset
        //Calculate Perlin's noise in [-1, 1] and
        //multiply on Rad
        p[j].x = ofSignedNoise( tx[j] ) * Rad;
        p[j].y = ofSignedNoise( ty[j] ) * Rad;
    }
}
```

The `draw()` function draws a spectrum and the cloud. Cloud's points are rendered as small circles. Additionally, pairs of points with distance less than the threshold `dist = 40` are joined by a line segment:

```
void testApp::draw(){
    ofBackground( 255, 255, 255 );   //Set up the background

    //Draw background rect for spectrum
    ofSetColor( 230, 230, 230 );
    ofFill();
    ofRect( 10, 700, N * 6, -100 );

    //Draw spectrum
    ofSetColor( 0, 0, 0 );
    for (int i=0; i<N; i++) {
        //Draw bandRad and bandVel by black color,
        //and other by gray color
        if ( i == bandRad || i == bandVel ) {
            ofSetColor( 0, 0, 0 ); //Black color
        } else {
            ofSetColor( 128, 128, 128 ); //Gray color
        }
        ofRect( 10 + i * 5, 700, 3, -spectrum[i] * 100 );
    }

    //Draw cloud

    //Move center of coordinate system to the screen center
    ofPushMatrix();
```

```
ofTranslate( ofGetWidth() / 2, ofGetHeight() / 2 );

//Draw cloud's points
ofSetColor( 0, 0, 0 );
ofFill();
for (int i=0; i<n; i++) {
    ofCircle( p[i], 2 );
}

//Draw lines between near points
float dist = 40;    //Threshold parameter of distance
for (int j=0; j<n; j++) {
    for (int k=j+1; k<n; k++) {
        if ( ofDist( p[j].x, p[j].y, p[k].x, p[k].y )
                    < dist ) {
            ofLine( p[j], p[k] );
        }
    }
}

//Restore coordinate system
ofPopMatrix();
}
```

When running this example, you will hear a music track and will see the moving point cloud in the center of the screen. At the bottom of the screen, you will see the sound spectrum:

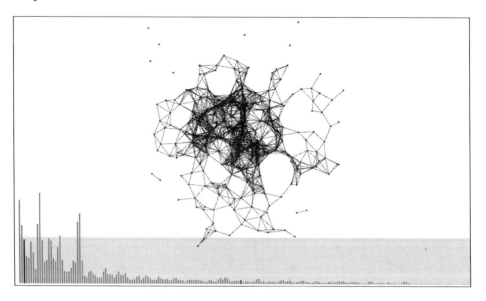

You can see that spectrum bands `bandRad = 2` and `bandVel = 100` are drawn in black (numeration from 0). Note that band 2 jumps on the base drum beat, and band 100 jumps on the snare drum beat, but in a lesser range, and the cloud extends and shuffles in correspondence to these beats.

You can extend the example by associating the radius and color of the point's circles with some spectrum bands.

Summary

In this chapter, we learned how to load, play, and control sound samples and considered two generative music examples. Also, we studied low-level sound input and output, and explored this using examples of PWM synthesis and image-to-sound and sound-to-image transcoding examples. Finally, we talked about sound spectrum notion and built a audio-reactive visual project with a point cloud moving according to the music track.

In the next chapter, we will learn how to draw 3D objects using openFrameworks.

7
Drawing in 3D

3D graphics often looks more impressive than 2D graphics because 3D has unique expressive capabilities, such as depth, perspective, and shading. Also, the third dimension allows objects to interweave and twist in the space in ways that are hard to achieve using 2D graphics. In this chapter we will cover the basics of rendering and animating 3D surfaces and primitive clouds with openFrameworks. We'll cover the following topics:

- Simple 3D drawing
- Using ofMesh
- Enabling lighting and setting normals
- Texturing
- Working with vertices

3D basics

Working with 3D means working with objects modeled in the three-dimensional scene, where the dimensions are horizontal (x), vertical (y), and depth (z). The resulting 3D scene is projected either onto a 2D image to show it on the screen, two 2D images for stereoscreen, or even printed as a 3D object using a 3D printer.

Representation of 3D objects

Each 3D object is represented using a number of elementary primitives such as points, line segments, triangles, or other polygons. Methods of the object's representation are as follows:

- An object is a number of surfaces assembled from polygonal primitives such as triangles and quadrangles (often called **quads**). This method is used in 3D-modeling software for representing "surface" objects, such as a human body, a car, a building, and also clothes and a rippled water surface.

- An object is a number of **curves** assembled from line segments. Such a representation is used for modeling hair and fur.

- An object is a huge number of small points called **particles**. This is representation of objects without distinct shape: smoke, clouds, fire, and a waterfall (see *Chapter 3, Building a Simple Particle System*).

These methods refer to realistic representation of real-world objects. We are interested in experimental 3D, so we can play with representations freely. For example:

- Triangles can be used to draw some clouds made from triangles but not smooth surfaces

- Thousands of long curves can interweave inside a volume with specified bounds, creating an evolving "hairy" 3D object

- Particles can represent a rigid 3D object that suddenly changes its shape in a complex way

In openFrameworks, you can represent and draw 3D objects by yourself; see the *Simple 3D drawing* section. But normally it is preferable to use a powerful ofMesh class, which lets you represent and draw surfaces, curves, particles, and distinct primitives at the fastest speed; see the *Using ofMesh* section. Also you can manipulate the static and animated 3D models stored in files such as 3DS; see the *Additional topics* section.

3D scene rendering

In this chapter we will consider rendering a 3D scene on a 2D screen (and will not consider stereoscreens and 3D printers).

Recall that, when we draw a flat 2D scene, we just imprint objects such as images and curves onto the screen at the specified coordinates. And the order of the object's drawing defines its visibility; the last object is visible as a whole and can occlude the objects drawn before it.

The rendering of a 3D scene differs from the case of a 2D scene because the object's visibility here is defined by its z coordinate (depth). By default, in openFrameworks, points with a zero value for the z coordinate forms an xy plane, which is used for 2D drawing. Increasing and decreasing the value of the z coordinate leads to moving the objects closer or farther correspondingly.

openFrameworks graphics is based on **Open Graphics Library** (**OpenGL**), which renders objects using z-buffering technology. This technology just stores z values for each screen pixel in a special buffer, called **z-buffer** (or **depth buffer**). During rendering, if the z value of the object's pixel is greater than the z value in the buffer, the pixel is rendered and the z-buffer is updated to this value. Otherwise, the object's pixel is not rendered.

By default, the z-buffering is disabled. To enable it, call the following function:

```
ofEnableDepthTest();
```

When enabled, the z-buffer clears automatically at each frame, together with the background drawing (if you do not call ofSetBackgroundAuto(false)). To disable z-buffering, use the ofDisableDepthTest() function.

There is another 3D rendering technology, called **ray tracing**. Instead of directly projecting the pixels of primitive onto the screen, it simulates light ray propagation from the light sources to the camera. Such a method is a natural way to construct shadows and other natural-world lighting effects. It is used for the highest quality 3D graphics and is available in 3D animation software. But its real-time implementations are currently very resource intensive, and we do not consider them here.

The volumetric nature of the 3D objects introduces new attributes into the 3D scene. These are lights, the object's materials interacting with lights, the 3D scene perspective, and virtual cameras. See the *Enabling lighting and setting normals* and *Additional topics* sections for more information.

Note, the modern approach in 3D that includes advanced lighting and shading, object's shape manipulation, and the rendered scene postprocessing requires using shaders; see *Chapter 8, Using Shaders*, for further details.

openFrameworks is a thin wrapper over OpenGL, so it provides low-level functionality, which is great for working with custom-generated 3D graphics. However, if you need to work with 3D worlds consisting of many life-like models and characters, it is probably better to use some other 3D engine, such as Unity 3D. We use Unity 3D for complex 3D world rendering and add interactivity by controlling it from openFrameworks' project, which processes sensors such as depth cameras. openFrameworks and Unity 3D are connected via OSC network protocol; see *Chapter 11, Networking*.

Now we will consider a simple 3D drawing example with openFrameworks.

Simple 3D drawing

For simple 3D drawing in openFrameworks, follow these steps:

1. Add the `ofEnableDepthTest()` function call in the beginning of the `testApp::draw()` function to enable z-buffering. If you omit it, all the graphics objects will be rendered without respect to their z coordinate in correspondence with the graphical primitives' rendering order.

2. Draw primitives as follows:

    ○ The `ofLine( x1, y1, z1, x2, y2, z2 )` function draws a line segment between points (x1, y1, z1) and (x2, y2, z2). There is an overloaded version of the function, `ofLine( p1, p2 )`, where p1 and p2 have type `ofPoint`. Use the `ofSetColor()` and `ofSetLineWidth()` functions to adjust its rendering properties of color and line width.

In *Chapter 2, Drawing in 2D*, we used the `ofPoint` class to represent 2D points using its fields x and y. Actually, `ofPoint` has a third field z, which, by default, is equal to zero. So `ofPoint` can represent points in 3D. Just declare `ofPoint` p and work with values p.x, p.y, and p.z.

    ○ The `ofTriangle( p1, p2, p3 )` function draws a triangle with vertices in points p1, p2, and p3. Use the `ofSetColor()`, `ofFill()`, `ofSetLineWidth()`, and `ofNoFill()` functions to adjust its rendering properties.

○ The ofRect(x, y, z, w, h) function draws a rectangle with the top-left corner at (x, y, z) and the width w and height h, oriented parallel to the screen plane. If you need to get a rotated rectangle, you need to rotate the coordinate system using the ofRotate() function.

To draw arbitrary polygons—for example, quadrangles—use the following method:

```
ofBeginShape();              //Begin shape
ofVertex( x1, y1, z1 );      //The first vertex
ofVertex( x2, y2, z2 );      //The second vertex
//...
ofVertex( xn, yn, zn );      //The last vertex
ofEndShape();                //End shape
```

If ofFill() was called before drawing, the shape will be drawn filled and closed. If ofNoFill() was called before drawing, just an unclosed polygon will be drawn.

3. Translate, scale, and rotate the rendered objects by manipulating the coordinate system:

○ The ofTranslate(x, y, z) function translates the coordinate system by vector (x, y, z)

○ The ofScale(x, y, z) function scales the coordinate system by factors (x, y, z)

○ The ofRotate(angle, x, y, z) function rotates the coordinate system along vector (x, y, z) by angle degrees

As in a 2D case, use ofPushMatrix() and ofPopMatrix() to store and retrieve the current coordinate system in a matrix stack.

Now we will illustrate these steps in an example.

The triangles cloud example

Let's draw 1500 random triangles, located at an equal distance from the center of the coordinates. This will look like a triangle cloud in the shape of a sphere. To make the visualization more interesting, colorize the triangles with random colors from black to red and add constant rotation to the cloud.

 This is example 07-3D/01-TrianglesCloud.

The example is based on the `emptyExample` project in openFrameworks. In the `testApp.h` file, inside the `testApp` class declaration, add arrays `vertices` and `colors` to hold the vertices and the colors of the triangles and variables `nTri` and `nVert` corresponding to the number of triangles and their vertices:

```
vector<ofPoint> vertices;
vector<ofColor> colors;
int nTri;        //The number of triangles
int nVert;       //The number of the vertices equals nTri * 3
```

The `setup()` function fills the arrays for the triangles' vertices and colors. The vertices of the first triangle are stored in `vertices[0]`, `vertices[1]`, and `vertices[2]`. The vertices of the second triangle are stored in `vertices[3]`, `vertices[4]`, `vertices[5]`, and so on. In general, the vertices of the triangle with index i (where i is in range from 0 to N-1) are stored in the `vertices` with the indices `i * 3`, `i * 3 + 1`, and `i * 3 + 2`.

```
void testApp::setup() {
  nTri = 1500;         //The number of the triangles
  nVert= nTri * 3;     //The number of the vertices

  float Rad = 250;     //The sphere's radius
  float rad = 25;      //Maximal triangle's "radius"
                       //(formally, it's the maximal coordinates'
                       //deviation from the triangle's center)

  //Fill the vertices array
  vertices.resize( nVert );        //Set the array size
  for (int i=0; i<nTri; i++) {     //Scan all the triangles
    //Generate the center of the triangle
    //as a random point on the sphere

    //Take the random point from
    //cube [-1,1]x[-1,1]x[-1,1]
    ofPoint center( ofRandom( -1, 1 ),
          ofRandom( -1, 1 ),
          ofRandom( -1, 1 ) );
    center.normalize(); //Normalize vector's length to 1
    center *= Rad;       //Now the center vector has
                         //length Rad

    //Generate the triangle's vertices
    //as the center plus random point from
    //[-rad, rad]x[-rad, rad]x[-rad, rad]
    for (int j=0; j<3; j++) {
      vertices[ i*3 + j ] =
```

```
                    center + ofPoint( ofRandom( -rad, rad ),
                              ofRandom( -rad, rad ),
                              ofRandom( -rad, rad ) );
        }
    }

    //Fill the array of triangles' colors
    colors.resize( nTri );
    for (int i=0; i<nTri; i++) {
        //Take a random color from black to red
        colors[i] = ofColor( ofRandom( 0, 255 ), 0, 0 );
    }
}
```

The update() function is empty here, and the draw() function enables z-buffering, which rotates the coordinate system based on time, and draws the triangles with the specified colors.

```
void testApp::draw(){
    ofEnableDepthTest();    //Enable z-buffering

    //Set a gradient background from white to gray
    //for adding an illusion of visual depth to the scene
    ofBackgroundGradient( ofColor( 255 ), ofColor( 128 ) );

    ofPushMatrix();    //Store the coordinate system

    //Move the coordinate center to screen's center
    ofTranslate( ofGetWidth()/2, ofGetHeight()/2, 0 );

    //Calculate the rotation angle
    float time = ofGetElapsedTimef();    //Get time in seconds
    float angle = time * 10; //Compute angle. We rotate at speed
                        //10 degrees per second
    ofRotate( angle, 0, 1, 0 );     //Rotate the coordinate system
                        //along y-axe
    //Draw the triangles
    for (int i=0; i<nTri; i++) {
        ofSetColor( colors[i] );         //Set color
        ofTriangle( vertices[ i*3 ],
                vertices[ i*3 + 1 ],
                vertices[ i*3 + 2 ] ); //Draw triangle
    }

    ofPopMatrix();    //Restore the coordinate system
}
```

Run the code and you will see a sphere-like rotating cloud of triangles as shown in the following screenshot:

To draw the background, we use the `ofBackgroundGradient( color1, color2, type )` function. It creates the gradient filling of type `type` for the entire application's screen, with colors interpolated from `color1` to `color2`. The possible values of `type` are as follows:

- `OF_GRADIENT_CIRCULAR` – This type gives a circular color gradient with the center being the center of screen. This is the default value.
- `OF_GRADIENT_LINEAR` – This type gives you a top-to-bottom gradient.
- `OF_GRADIENT_BAR` – This type gives you a center-to-top and a center-to-bottom gradient.

Note that each triangle moves and rotates on the screen but its color always remains unchanged. The reason for this is that we don't use light and normals, which control how a graphics primitive is lit and shaded.

The simplest way to add lighting and normals is using the ofMesh class, which we will consider now.

Using ofMesh

The ofMesh class is a powerful class that is used for representing, modifying, and rendering 3D objects. By default, it draws triangle meshes, but it can also be used for drawing curves and points.

The ofMesh class performs rendering of many thousands and even millions of triangles by one OpenGL call, at the highest possible speed. Even though using ofMesh will at first seem slightly more complicated than using ofTriangle(), it will give you more flexibility in creating and modifying 3D objects in return. So it is highly recommended that you use ofMesh for 3D in all cases, except the very beginning or for learning 3D. You can use ofMesh not only for 3D but for 2D graphics as well.

openFrameworks has one more class, named ofVBOMesh, that is used for working with meshes. The class name means "mesh based on **Vertex Buffer Object (VBO)**". This class is similar to ofMesh, but it renders significantly faster when the vertices of the mesh are not changing. See details of its usage and performance in comparison with ofMesh in openFrameworks example examples/gl/vboExample.

To draw a surface consisting of a number of triangles, follow these steps:

This is example 07-3D/02-PyramidMesh. It is based on the emptyExample project in openFrameworks.

1. Declare an object mesh of type ofMesh in the testApp class declaration:

    ofMesh mesh;

2. Add the vertices of the surface triangles to the mesh using the mesh.addVertex(p) function. Note that if a vertex belongs to several triangles, you should specify these vertices just once. This feature is very useful for changing the surface; you change the position of just one vertex, and all the triangles will be drawn correctly.

Vertices are added to the end of a special array of vertices in the mesh and are later referenced by indices in this array. So the first vertex has the index 0, the second vertex has the index 1, and so on. For example, to draw a pyramid, we specify its four vertices as follows:

```
//Pyramid's base vertices with indices 0, 1, 2
mesh.addVertex( ofPoint( -200, -100, -50 ) );
mesh.addVertex( ofPoint( 200, -100, -50 ) );
mesh.addVertex( ofPoint( 0, 200, 0 ) );

//Pyramid's top vertex with index 3
mesh.addVertex( ofPoint( 0, 0, 50 ) );
```

3. Add the triangles by specifying the indices of the vertices for each triangle using the mesh.addTriangle(index1, index2, index3) function. Be careful to order this in the clockwise direction for correct lighting. In our pyramid example, we specify just three of its four triangles, so that you can see the interior of the object.

```
//Vertices with indices 3, 2, 0
mesh.addTriangle( 3, 2, 0 );

//Vertices with indices 3, 1, 2
mesh.addTriangle( 3, 1, 2 );

//Vertices with indices 3, 0, 1
mesh.addTriangle( 3, 0, 1 );
```

4. Draw a mesh in the testApp::draw() function using the mesh.draw() function. You may need coordinate system transformations for moving and rotating the object. For example, a rotating pyramid can be drawn with the following code in testApp::draw():

```
ofEnableDepthTest();    //Enable z-buffering

//Set a background
ofBackgroundGradient( ofColor( 255 ), ofColor( 128 ) );

ofPushMatrix();    //Store the coordinate system

//Move coordinate center to screen's center
ofTranslate( ofGetWidth()/2, ofGetHeight()/2, 0 );

//Rotate the coordinate system
float time = ofGetElapsedTimef(); //Get time in seconds
float angle = time * 30;          //Rotate angle
```

```
ofRotate( angle, 0, 1, 1 );

ofSetColor( 0, 128, 0 );    //Set a dark green color
mesh.draw();                //Draw the mesh

ofPopMatrix();              //Restore the coordinate system
```

When you run this code, you will see the pyramid is uniformly colored a dark green color. It looks like some animated 2D polygon and it is hard to make out that this is really a 3D pyramid surface. To see the mesh as a 3D object, you need to enable lighting for the scene and add normals information to the mesh. Let's do it.

Enabling lighting and setting normals

Lighting is needed for different parts of the surface to have different shading, depending on their orientation to the viewer. Such shading makes the surfaces look much more interesting than if just rendered with a uniform color because it emphasizes the 3D curvature of the surfaces. openFrameworks has an `ofLight` class for controlling light sources.

This is example `07-3D/03-PyramidLighting`. This example is a good starting point for drawing smooth surfaces using the `setNormals()` function.

It is a continuation of example `07-3D/02-PyramidMesh`.

To use one light source with default parameters, add the following line in the `testApp` class declaration:

```
ofLight light;
```

Add the following line in the `testApp::setup()` function to enable it:

```
light.enable();     //Enabling light source
```

For the light to interact with the mesh properly, you need to set up normal vectors for all the vertices using the `mesh.addNormal( normal )` function. Each normal vector should have unit length and direction perpendicular to the surface in the vertex. Information about the normals gives openFrameworks information about the correct lighting of the surface. Across the chapter, we will use the `setNormals()` function for normals computing, which we will discuss.

Computing normals using the setNormals() function

To compute normals for a mesh consisting of triangles, you can use the following function:

```
//Universal function which sets normals for the triangle mesh
void setNormals( ofMesh &mesh ){

    //The number of the vertices
    int nV = mesh.getNumVertices();

    //The number of the triangles
    int nT = mesh.getNumIndices() / 3;

    vector<ofPoint> norm( nV ); //Array for the normals

    //Scan all the triangles. For each triangle add its
    //normal to norm's vectors of triangle's vertices
    for (int t=0; t<nT; t++) {
        //Get indices of the triangle t
        int i1 = mesh.getIndex( 3 * t );
        int i2 = mesh.getIndex( 3 * t + 1 );
        int i3 = mesh.getIndex( 3 * t + 2 );

        //Get vertices of the triangle
        const ofPoint &v1 = mesh.getVertex( i1 );
        const ofPoint &v2 = mesh.getVertex( i2 );
        const ofPoint &v3 = mesh.getVertex( i3 );

        //Compute the triangle's normal
        ofPoint dir = ( (v2 - v1).crossed( v3 - v1 ) ).normalized();

        //Accumulate it to norm array for i1, i2, i3
        norm[ i1 ] += dir;
        norm[ i2 ] += dir;
        norm[ i3 ] += dir;
    }

    //Normalize the normal's length
    for (int i=0; i<nV; i++) {
        norm[i].normalize();
    }

    //Set the normals to mesh
    mesh.clearNormals();
    mesh.addNormals( norm );
}
```

To use it in your project, insert this function at the end of the `testApp.cpp` file, and add its declaration in the `testApp.h` file (outside the `testApp` class):

```
//Universal function which sets normals for the triangle mesh
void setNormals( ofMesh &mesh );
```

Now you can call `setNormals( mesh )` and the normals will be computed. You need to call the `setNormals( mesh )` function after each modification of vertices of `mesh` for the normals to be up-to-date.

 Scaling using `ofScale()` while drawing affects not only the object's vertices but the normals vectors too, and it can make shading improper. So when using normals, just avoid scaling or recalculating the normals so that they have unit length even after the usage of `ofScale()`.

With lighting and normals, the pyramid looks a little more like a 3D object, which changes its shade depending on its orientation:

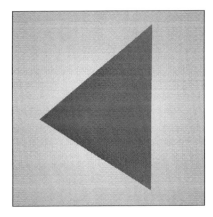

Note that the lightness of all the surface triangles mainly depends on the orientation of the central ("top") vertex of the pyramid. The reason is that shading of each triangle is computed by interpolating the normals of its vertices, and in our case, the normal of the central vertex is perpendicular to the pyramid's base. Such an approach works well for drawing smooth surfaces; see the *The oscillating plane example* section. Although in our case of pyramid, it can look a little bit unnatural.

To obtain the most natural visualization of the pyramid with sharp edges, we need to draw triangles independently without formally creating any common vertices.

Drawing sharp edges

The simplest way to achieve sharp edges is to add the vertices for all the triangles in mesh and not use the addTriangle() function at all and then call the mesh. setupIndicesAuto() function, which sets indices automatically such that vertices (0, 1, 2) are used for drawing the first triangle, vertices (4, 5, 6) for the second triangle, and so on.

> This is example 07-3D/04-PyramidSharpEdges. This example is a good starting point for drawing sharp 3D objects.
>
> It is based on example 07-3D/03-PyramidLighting.

In the example with the pyramid, replace all the lines with addVertex() and addTriangle() with the following lines:

```
//Pyramid's base vertices
ofPoint v0 = ofPoint( -200, -100, 0 );
ofPoint v1 = ofPoint( 200, -100, 0 );
ofPoint v2 = ofPoint( 0, 200, 0 );
//Pyramid's top vertex
ofPoint v3 = ofPoint( 0, 0, 100 );
//Add triangles by its vertices
mesh.addVertex( v3 ); mesh.addVertex( v2 ); mesh.addVertex( v0 );
mesh.addVertex( v3 ); mesh.addVertex( v1 ); mesh.addVertex( v2 );
mesh.addVertex( v3 ); mesh.addVertex( v0 ); mesh.addVertex( v1 );
mesh.setupIndicesAuto();     //Set up indices
```

As a result, you will see a pyramid with sharp edges as shown in the following screenshot:

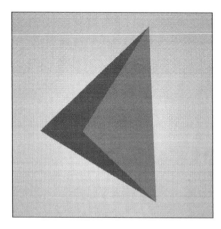

We have considered a basic workflow with meshes. Now we will consider other useful capabilities of the ofMesh class.

Drawing line segments and points

Instead of mesh.draw(), you can use the following functions:

- The mesh.drawWireframe() function draws only surface edges without the interiors of the triangles. Such a mode of drawing is called **wireframe drawing**; it is very useful for debugging, and of course, can be used as an effect.

- The mesh.drawVertices() function draws only vertices of the mesh. It is useful for debugging and also as an effect.

Also, to represent not only triangular surfaces but also objects consisting of line segments or points, use the mesh.setMode(mode) function, where mode has type ofPrimitiveMode enumeration. To see all the possible values for mode, check its definition. We will mention only three values:

- OF_PRIMITIVE_TRIANGLES is a default value, which draws a mesh as triangles. We had considered how to use this mode in the pyramid examples mentioned earlier.

- OF_PRIMITIVE_LINES draws a mesh as a number of line segments.

- OF_PRIMITIVE_POINTS draws a mesh as a number of points.

Let's consider the last two modes in detail.

Drawing line segments

Calling mesh.setMode(OF_PRIMITIVE_LINES) switches mesh to a mode in which it draws line segments. After calling this function, add all vertices of segments using mesh.addVertex(p), and for each segment, it adds the indices of the vertices using the following code:

```
mesh.addIndex( i1 );    //Index of segment's first vertex
mesh.addIndex( i2 );    //Index of segment's second vertex
```

For example, to draw a tripod, create the mesh using the following code:

```
mesh.setMode( OF_PRIMITIVE_LINES );
mesh.addVertex( ofPoint( 0, 0, 0 ) );              //Vertex 0
mesh.addVertex( ofPoint( -100, -100, 0 ) );        //Vertex 1
mesh.addVertex( ofPoint( 100, -100, 0 ) );         //Vertex 2
```

```
mesh.addVertex( ofPoint( 0, 100, 0 ) );          //Vertex 3

mesh.addIndex( 0 ); mesh.addIndex( 1 ); //Segment 0
mesh.addIndex( 0 ); mesh.addIndex( 2 ); //Segment 1
mesh.addIndex( 0 ); mesh.addIndex( 3 ); //Segment 2
```

Note that for correct lighting you need to specify normals, which normally cannot be defined for lines. So the best idea is to disable lighting using the ofDisableLighting() function before drawing and then enabling it again using the ofEnableLighting() function:

```
ofDisableLighting();          //Disable lighting
mesh.draw();                  //Draw lines
ofEnableLighting();           //Enable lighting
```

Drawing points

Calling mesh.setMode(OF_PRIMITIVE_POINTS) switches mesh to a mode in which it draws its vertices as points.

Additionally, call glPointSize(size) to specify point size in pixels, and call glEnable(GL_POINT_SMOOTH) to draw circular points (instead of square points as on some graphics cards). For example, add the following lines after specifying tripod vertices in the previous example:

```
mesh.setMode( OF_PRIMITIVE_POINTS );
glPointSize( 10 );
glEnable( GL_POINT_SMOOTH );
```

Once you run the code, you will see four circles, corresponding to the tripod's vertices.

Coloring the vertices

It is possible to specify the colors of the vertices. In this case, you must provide a color for all the vertices using the mesh.addColor(color) function; for example, mesh.addColor(ofColor(255, 0, 0)). Note that in this case, the ofSetColor() function will not affect the drawing of the mesh. Remember: you should call this function as many times as you call the mesh.addVertex() function.

Texturing

You can wrap any image or texture on the surface using the `mesh.addTexCoord(texPoint )` function. Here `texPoint` is of the `ofPoint` type. It is a 2D point that should lie in range *[0, w]* × *[0, h]*, where *w* × *h* is the size of the image that you want to use as a texture. Remember that you should call this function as many times as you call the `mesh.addVertex()` function so that all the vertices will have texture coordinates.

During rendering each primitive of the mesh (whether triangle, line, or point depends on the mesh's mode), the texture coordinates of each rendered pixel will be calculated by OpenGL as interpolation of texture coordinates of the primitive's vertices. Resulting texture coordinates for the pixel are used for the pixel's color computing. In other words, the final pixel color is computed using three values: the color given by the texture, the color of the last `ofSetColor()` calling, and the shading information obtained from the light and normals data. To change the algorithm of computing pixel color and the use of fragment shaders, see *Chapter 8, Using Shaders*.

For example, let's wrap the `sunflower.png` image onto the pyramid.

 This is example `07-3D/05-PyramidTextured`. It is a continuation of example `07-3D/04-PyramidSharpEdges`.

Copy the image into the `bin/data` folder of the project, and declare the `ofImage` image in the `testApp` class declaration. Then add the following lines in `testApp::setup()`:

```
//Set up a texture coordinates for all the vertices
mesh.addTexCoord( ofPoint( 100, 100 ) );   //v3
mesh.addTexCoord( ofPoint( 10, 300 ) );    //v2
mesh.addTexCoord( ofPoint( 10, 10 ) );     //v0

mesh.addTexCoord( ofPoint( 100, 100 ) );   //v3
mesh.addTexCoord( ofPoint( 300, 10 ) );    //v1
mesh.addTexCoord( ofPoint( 10, 300 ) );    //v2

mesh.addTexCoord( ofPoint( 100, 100 ) );   //v3
mesh.addTexCoord( ofPoint( 10, 10 ) );     //v0
mesh.addTexCoord( ofPoint( 300, 10 ) );    //v1
//Load an image
image.loadImage( "sunflower.png" );
```

Finally, in `testApp::draw()`, find the following lines:

```
ofSetColor( 0, 128, 0 );   //Set a dark green color
mesh.draw();
```

Replace the preceding lines with the following:

```
ofSetColor( 255, 255, 255 );   //Set white color
image.bind();                  //Use image's texture for drawing
mesh.draw();                   //Draw mesh
image.unbind();                //End using image's texture
```

After running the preceding code, you will see the pyramid with a wrapped texture as shown in the following screenshot:

Working with vertices

There are a number of functions for accessing the vertices and their properties:

- The `getNumVertices()` function returns the number of vertices.

- The `getVertex( i )` function returns the position of the vertex with index `i`.

- The `setVertex( i, p )` function sets the position of vertex `i` to `p`. Note that this function can change the vertex but it cannot add a new vertex. So if `i` is greater or equal to `mesh.getNumVertices()`, you need to add a vertex (or vertices) using the `mesh.addVertex( p )` function as described in the *Using ofMesh* section.

- The `removeVertex( i )` function deletes the vertex with index `i`. Be very careful when using this function; after deleting a vertex, you should probably also delete the corresponding normal, color, and texture coordinate, and change the indices of the triangles to keep its coherence.

- The `clearVertices()` function deletes all the vertices. See corresponding cautions for `removeVertex()`.

- The `clear()` function clears the mesh, including its vertices, normals, and all other arrays.

After changing vertices, you will most probably need to update the normals using the `setNormals( mesh )` function, as described in the *Computing normals using the setNormals() function* section.

There are similar functions for controlling normals, colors, texture coordinates, and indices; for example, functions `getNumNormals()`, `getNumColors()`, `getNumTexCoords()`, and `getNumIndices()` return number of normals, colors, texture coordinates, and indices respectively.

Let's see a simple example of modifying the positions of the vertices.

The oscillating plane example

This example demonstrates how to create a flat plane from triangles and then oscillate its vertices to obtain a dynamic surface. Also, the color of vertices will depend on the oscillation amplitude.

[This is example `07-3D/06-OscillatingPlane`.]

The example is based on the `emptyExample` project in openFrameworks. Begin with adding the declaration and definition of the `setNormals()` function, as described in the *Computing normals using the setNormals() function* section. Then in the `testApp.h` file, in the `testApp` class declaration, add definitions of `mesh` and `light`:

```
ofMesh mesh;        //Mesh
ofLight light;      //Light
```

In the beginning of the `testApp.cpp` file, add constants with vertex grid size:

```
int W = 100;        //Grid size
int H = 100;
```

The `setup()` function adds vertices and triangles to the mesh and enables lighting:

```
void testApp::setup(){
  //Set up vertices and colors
  for (int y=0; y<H; y++) {
    for (int x=0; x<W; x++) {
      mesh.addVertex(
              ofPoint( (x - W/2) * 6, (y - H/2) * 6, 0 ) );
      mesh.addColor( ofColor( 0, 0, 0 ) );
    }
  }
  //Set up triangles' indices
  for (int y=0; y<H-1; y++) {
    for (int x=0; x<W-1; x++) {
      int i1 = x + W * y;
      int i2 = x+1 + W * y;
      int i3 = x + W * (y+1);
      int i4 = x+1 + W * (y+1);
      mesh.addTriangle( i1, i2, i3 );
      mesh.addTriangle( i2, i4, i3 );
    }
  }
  setNormals( mesh );   //Set normals
  light.enable();       //Enable lighting
}
```

The `update()` function changes the z coordinate of each vertex using Perlin noise (refer to *Appendix B, Perlin Noise*) and also sets its color between the range blue to white:

```
void testApp::update(){
  float time = ofGetElapsedTimef();        //Get time
  //Change vertices
  for (int y=0; y<H; y++) {
    for (int x=0; x<W; x++) {
      int i = x + W * y;          //Vertex index
      ofPoint p = mesh.getVertex( i );
      //Get Perlin noise value
      float value =
          ofNoise( x * 0.05, y * 0.05, time * 0.5 );
      //Change z-coordinate of vertex
```

```
            p.z = value * 100;
            mesh.setVertex( i, p );
            //Change color of vertex
            mesh.setColor( i,
                        ofColor( value*255, value * 255, 255 ) );
        }
    }
    setNormals( mesh );   //Update the normals
}
```

The `draw()` function draws the surface and slowly rotates it:

```
void testApp::draw(){
  ofEnableDepthTest();      //Enable z-buffering

  //Set a gradient background from white to gray
  ofBackgroundGradient( ofColor( 255 ), ofColor( 128 ) );

  ofPushMatrix();              //Store the coordinate system

  //Move the coordinate center to screen's center
  ofTranslate( ofGetWidth()/2, ofGetHeight()/2, 0 );

  //Calculate the rotation angle
  float time = ofGetElapsedTimef();   //Get time in seconds
  float angle = time * 20;   //Compute angle. We rotate at speed
                              //20 degrees per second
  ofRotate( 30, 1, 0, 0 );             //Rotate coordinate system
  ofRotate( angle, 0, 0, 1 );

  //Draw mesh
  //Here ofSetColor() does not affects the result of drawing,
  //because the mesh has its own vertices' colors
  mesh.draw();

  ofPopMatrix();      //Restore the coordinate system
}
```

Run the example and you will see a pulsating surface that slowly rotates on the screen:

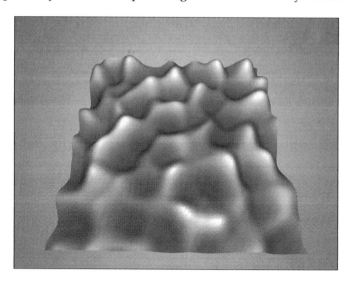

Now replace in the `testApp::draw()` function in the line `mesh.draw();` by the following line:

```
mesh.drawWireframe();
```

Now, run the project and you will see the wireframe structure of the surface.

Until now you knew how to create simple animated smooth surfaces and disconnected clouds of primitives. Let's consider an advanced example of constructing a smooth surface that grows and twists in space.

The twisting knot example

In this example we will create a tube-like surface, that is formed from a number of deformed circles. At each `update()` call, we will generate one circle and connect it with the previous circle by adding triangles to the surface. At each step the circle will slowly move, rotate, and deform in space. As result, we will see a growing and twisting 3D knot.

 This is example `07-3D/07-TwistingKnot`.

The example is based on the `emptyExample` project in openFrameworks. Begin with adding declaration and definition of the `setNormals()` function, as is described in the *Computing normals using the setNormals() function* section. Then in the `testApp.h` file, in the `testApp` class declaration, add definitions of the `mesh`, `light`, and `addRandomCircle()` function:

```
ofMesh mesh;            //Mesh
ofLight light;          //Light
void addRandomCircle( ofMesh &mesh ); //Main function which
        //moves circle and adds triangles to the object
```

In the beginning of the `testApp.cpp` file, add the constants and the variables for the circle that will be used for knot generation:

```
//The circle parameters
float Rad = 25;                 //Radius of circle
float circleStep = 3;           //Step size for circle motion
int circleN = 40;               //Number of points on the circle

//Current circle state
ofPoint pos;                    //Circle center
ofPoint axeX, axyY, axyZ;       //Circle's coordinate system
```

The `setup()` function sets the initial values of the circle's position and also enables lighting with `light`, using its default settings:

```
void testApp::setup(){
  pos = ofPoint( 0, 0, 0 );   //Start from center of coordinate
  axeX = ofPoint( 1, 0, 0 );  //Set initial coordinate system
  axyY = ofPoint( 0, 1, 0 );
  axyZ = ofPoint( 0, 0, 1 );
  light.enable();             //Enable lighting
  ofSetFrameRate( 60 );       //Set the rate of screen redrawing
}
```

The `update()` function just calls the `addRandomCircle()` function, which adds one more circle to the knot:

```
void testApp::update(){
  addRandomCircle( mesh );
}
```

The `draw()` function draws the mesh on the screen. Note that we use the `mesh.getCentroid()` function, which returns the center of mass of mesh's vertex array. In other words, we apply it for the shift coordinate system `ofTranslate( -mesh.getCentroid() )`, which helps us to draw our object positioned in the center :

```
void testApp::draw(){
    ofEnableDepthTest();       //Enable z-buffering

    //Set a gradient background from white to gray
    ofBackgroundGradient( ofColor( 255 ), ofColor( 128 ) );

    ofPushMatrix();  //Store the coordinate system
    //Move the coordinate center to screen's center
    ofTranslate( ofGetWidth()/2, ofGetHeight()/2, 0 );

    //Calculate the rotation angle
    float time = ofGetElapsedTimef(); //Get time in seconds
    float angle = time * 20;          //Compute the angle.
                      //We rotate at speed 20 degrees per second
    ofRotate( angle, 0, 1, 0 );        //Rotate the coordinate system
                                       //along y-axe
    //Shift the coordinate center so the mesh
    //will be drawn in the screen center
    ofTranslate( -mesh.getCentroid() );

    //Draw the mesh
    //Here ofSetColor() does not affects the result of drawing,
    //because the mesh has its own vertices' colors
    mesh.draw();

    ofPopMatrix();  //Restore the coordinate system
}
```

The most important function in the example is `addRandomCircle()`. It pseudorandomly moves the circle, adds new vertices from the circle to the object's vertex array, and adds corresponding triangles to the object. It also sets colors for the new vertices.

```
void testApp::addRandomCircle( ofMesh &mesh ){
    float time = ofGetElapsedTimef();       //Time

    //Parameters - twisting and rotating angles and color
    float twistAngle = 5.0 * ofSignedNoise( time * 0.3 + 332.4 );
    float rotateAngle = 1.5;
```

```
ofFloatColor color( ofNoise( time * 0.05 ),
                     ofNoise( time * 0.1 ),
                     ofNoise( time * 0.15 ));
color.setSaturation( 1.0 );   //Make the color maximally
                              //colorful

//Rotate the coordinate system of the circle
axeX.rotate( twistAngle, axyZ );
axyY.rotate( twistAngle, axyZ );

axeX.rotate( rotateAngle, axyY );
axyZ.rotate( rotateAngle, axyY );

//Move the circle on a step
ofPoint move = axyZ * circleStep;
pos += move;

//Add vertices
for (int i=0; i<circleN; i++) {
    float angle = float(i) / circleN * TWO_PI;
    float x = Rad * cos( angle );
    float y = Rad * sin( angle );
    //We would like to distort this point
    //to make the knot's surface embossed
    float distort = ofNoise( x * 0.2, y * 0.2,
                             time * 0.2 + 30 );
    distort = ofMap( distort, 0.2, 0.8, 0.8, 1.2 );
    x *= distort;
    y *= distort;

    ofPoint p = axeX * x + axyY * y + pos;
    mesh.addVertex( p );
    mesh.addColor( color );
}

//Add the triangles
int base = mesh.getNumVertices() - 2 * circleN;
if ( base >= 0 ) {   //Check if it is not the first step
                     //and we really need to add the triangles
    for (int i=0; i<circleN; i++) {
        int a = base + i;
        int b = base + (i + 1) % circleN;
        int c = circleN  + a;
        int d = circleN  + b;
```

```
            mesh.addTriangle( a, b, d ); //Clock-wise
            mesh.addTriangle( a, d, c );
        }
        //Update the normals
        setNormals( mesh );
    }
}
```

Run the example and you will see a growing and twisting knot, as shown in the following screenshot:

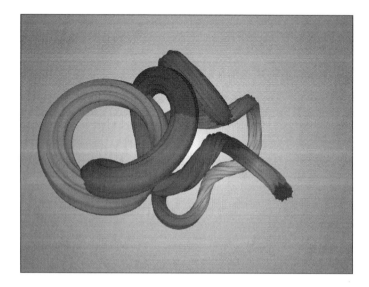

Note that we control the rate of `testApp::update()` callings (and hence the `addRandomCircle()` rate) using the `ofSetFrameRate( 60 )` call in `testApp::setup()`. If you change the rate, say to `ofSetFrameRate( 30 )`, you will obtain a differently shaped knot. To make the resultant shape independent of frame rate, you should make the `circleStep` parameter dependent on the time between current and previous frames.

 At each `update()` call, the application constantly adds new vertices and triangles to the object. Then it recalculates all the normals, though many of the triangles did not change. So application performance will degrade with time because the `setNormals()` function will take more and more computing power. To solve this problem, you can optimize the `setNormals()` function so it does not recalculate the unchanged normals and does not check the old triangles at all.

Additional topics

In this chapter we mainly considered representing and drawing 3D objects using openFrameworks. For further learning, we suggest studying the following topics:

- Working with the `ofLight` class to control lights, that is, the type of light (spot light and point light), its position, light direction, and color parameters. See openFrameworks examples `examples/3d/normalsExample` and `examples/3d/advanced3dExample`.

- Working with the `ofCamera` and `ofEasyCam` classes to control the camera, that is, the position of the observer of the 3D scene. The camera lets you move easily through the virtual 3D world and also change perspective parameters. See openFrameworks examples `examples/3d/cameraRibbonExample` and `examples/3d/easyCamExample`.

- Using 3D model files with the `.3ds` and `.dae` extensions. You can load and draw such files as static or animated objects. Note that you can use 3D file models as a source of vertex data for further manipulation and processing. See openFrameworks examples `examples/3d/modelNoiseExample`, `examples/addons/3DModelLoaderExample`, and `examples/addons/assimpExample`.

- Rendering volumetric data using the **marching cubes** algorithm. This technique allows rendering isolines of an arbitrary function defined in some volume. It opens the possibility of drawing complex surfaces with constantly changing shape and number of connected components, such as metaballs. To use this algorithm, download and install the `ofxMarchingCubes` addon from `ofxaddons.com` and see its example. For more details on installing addons see *Appendix A, Working with Addons*.

Summary

In this chapter we learned how to represent, modify, and draw 3D objects using the `ofMesh` class and also how to perform simple 3D drawing with the `ofTriangle()` function. We looked at examples of drawing a sphere-shaped cloud of trianlges, a oscillating surface, and a twisting 3D knot.

In the next chapter, we will cover how to use shaders to process images and 3D object geometry.

8

Using Shaders

Shader is a small program that allows you to unleash the computation power of GPUs. This power exceeds the computation capabilities of the most powerful CPUs. So using shaders is crucial for creating competitive and astonishing projects. This chapter will cover the basics on using shaders in openFrameworks for creating 2D video effects and 3D object deformations. We will cover the following topics:

- Structure of a shader's code
- An example of a simple fragment shader
- Creating video effects with fragment shaders
- Deforming objects with a vertex shader
- Using a geometry shader

Basics of shaders

Shaders are small programs executed on a **Graphics Processing Unit (GPU)**, which is located on the video card. Shaders work when OpenGL renders something on the screen (or in the screen buffer), and they modify the geometry and pixels of the rendered objects. They work very fast and perform advanced processing of images and complex 3D scenes at faster rates, which is impossible using today's CPUs. This is the reason that shaders are widely used for interactive rendering and VJing.

Shaders are written using **Graphics Library Shading Language (GLSL)**, which is actually a C++ language, and are extended with vector and matrix types and mathematical operations. Some of the C++ features, such as working with memory (pointers, references, and the `new` operator) and classes, are not included in GLSL.

Formally, GLSL is a subset of the C language with some extensions, including constructor-like functions for initializing vectors and other types. As a result, the GLSL style of programming, in general, is very similar to C++.

When shaders are used in openFrameworks, the shaders' codes are stored in the text files in the `data` folder of the project. Unlike an ordinary C++ program, shaders' code is compiled at runtime, just when it's needed. So you can change the shaders' code and restart your project without recompiling the openFrameworks' project.

No special GLSL compiler is needed because it is embedded in all the modern video card drivers. So shaders are universal; once written, they can be used in many interactive software platforms such as openFrameworks, Processing, Cinder, Quartz Composer, Touch Designer, and vvvv.

You can run and edit simple shaders right in your browser using online shader sandboxes such as `http://glsl.heroku.com`. They contain galleries with examples of great shaders which you can learn and use in your projects. For example, try `http://glsl.heroku.com/e#8801.0`.

Working with shaders in openFrameworks is simple with the class `ofShader`. It lets you load and compile the shaders, enable the shaders and set their parameters, and finally disable the shaders.

Types of shaders

There are several types of shaders. Each of them works in a particular part of the rendering pipeline. You can use only one shader of a given type at a particular moment. Nevertheless, you can use many different shaders of the same type by switching between them.

In this chapter, we will consider only three types of shaders, which are the most popular and are used in most applications:

- A **vertex** shader processes each vertex of the rendered object and changes its properties, such as position, normal, color, and some custom attributes. It can be used for geometric transformations of 3D objects. See the *Deforming objects with a vertex shader* section for details.

- A **geometry** shader gets the list of vertices of a primitive to be rendered (for example, the three vertices of a triangle), and generates a new list of vertices, forming one or several primitives that will actually be rendered instead of the one that was input. For example, it can replace each rendered triangle with a bunch of lines that form a "furry" surface. See the *Using a geometry shader* section for details.

- A **fragment** shader processes the color and depth of a pixel which is ready to be rendered to the screen or screen buffer. A fragment shader can be used for implementing postprocessing effects, and also for more complex image processing and generation. See the *Creating video effects with fragment shaders* section for details.

See the full list of the different types of shaders in *Chapter 2, Overview of OpenGL Shading* of the *OpenGL Shading Language Specification* document. Currently, the latest specification can be downloaded at http://www.opengl.org/registry/doc/GLSLangSpec.4.30.6.pdf. Check newer versions and other documents at http://www.opengl.org/documentation/glsl.

Though all the shaders are written in one GLSL language, different types of shaders have different built-in input and output variables and special commands in their syntax.

Shaders work in a particular order, that is, first the vertex shader, then the geometry shader, and finally the fragment shader. If you want to use the vertex or fragment shader, you need to specify and enable both of them. If you want to use the geometry shader, you need to specify and enable all three types of shaders. This is not a problem because when you are interested in one particular type of shader, you can use "dummy" shaders for the other shader types.

When to use shaders

When deciding whether you should use the shaders technology in your openFrameworks project or not, take into account the following considerations:

- If you need to make a vibrant real-time visualization, including the transforming and pulsating of 3D objects or images, then using shaders for the effects is most probably the best choice.

- If you have some shader code and want to try it in your project, you can often embed the shader without it being changed but sometimes, a little modification is needed in the shader's code.

- If you have a working project and are manipulating the project with 2D graphics or 3D objects' geometry using CPU, and you notice that it works too slowly, then you can move a part of the graphics computations to shaders. Then the CPU usage will decrease, and the overall application performance will (often radically) improve.

- If you need to perform massive nongraphics computations, such as simulating the physics of the million particles, you still can do it with shaders. For such a purpose, you need a way for retaining shaders' processing results:

  ○ To retain data from the vertex and geometry shaders, use OpenGL's **Transform Feedback** feature (see details in OpenGL Wiki at `http://www.opengl.org/wiki/Transform_Feedback`)

  ○ To retain data from a fragment shader, perform rendering in an offscreen buffer (see details in the *Using FBO for offscreen drawing* section in *Chapter 2, Drawing in 2D*)

Alternatively, instead of vertex, geometry or fragment shaders, you can use **compute** shaders, which let you perform universal computations and output their results in your custom arrays.

 For extremely complex computations; instead of shaders, a better option would be to use powerful GPGPU technologies such as OpenCL and NVIDIA CUDA.

Anyway, shaders and other GPU-programming technologies are the dominant topics in modern computing and supercomputing in the near future. So we highly recommend learning them.

Now let's consider the structure of the simplest fragment and vertex shaders and some basics of GLSL language. (A geometry shader has a similar structure, and so is not discussed in this section. See the *Using a geometry shader* section for details.)

Structure of a shader's code

The shader's text is a C++ file and contains the void main() function. This function works on GPU and is called once for processing every object (vertex, primitive, or pixel, depending on the shader's type). The main() function has no parameters. All the necessary parameters such as coordinates, colors, and textures are held by built-in GLSL variables such as gl_Color and gl_Position. Also, you can use your own custom parameters passed from your CPU code, such as float time (see the *Passing a float parameter to a shader* section).

The simplest code for the fragment shader will look as follows:

```
#version 120
void main() {
  gl_FragColor = vec4( 1.0, 0.0, 0.0, 1.0 );
}
```

This shader will render everything in the red color. Namely, if you enable the shader and then draw lines, images, and any other objects, then OpenGL will call the shader's main() function for each drawn pixel, and the shader will set the pixel color to red. Let's study the shader's code in detail.

The first line #version 120 is a compiler directive, which means that we want to use the GLSL Version 1.2 in the shader. Though this is quite an old version of the language, it is currently used in all the openFrameworks examples and in all our examples in the chapter. The reason is that Version 1.2 is the last version that contains many built-in variables, which simplify shader interfacing. (Most of these variables were removed in the latest GLSL versions. Though this makes shaders more flexible, it seems a little hard to begin the study of shaders with a very high level of flexibility.)

The rest of the code is the main() function. The body of the function consists of a single line which sets the gl_FragColor variable to value vec4(1.0, 0.0, 0.0, 1.0). Actually, gl_FragColor is a built-in variable, which holds an output color of the pixel processed by a fragment shader. The mission of any fragment shader is to set a value to this gl_FragColor variable inside its main() function. In this example, we set it to a constant value. For more realistic shaders, the output color depends on the pixel position gl_FragCoord, current drawing color, textures, normals, lighting information and other parameters.

The list of built-in GLSL variables can be found at:
http://www.opengl.org/sdk/docs/manglsl/xhtml/
index.html#Built-in%20Variables

Notation vec4(1.0, 0.0, 0.0, 1.0) returns the object of type vec4. This is a vector with four float components. In our example, vec4 holds the color and its components are red, green, blue, and alpha respectively. In GLSL, color components have a meaningful range from 0.0 to 1.0, so vec4(1.0, 0.0, 0.0, 1.0) means the opaque red color.

Besides vec4, there are types vec2 and vec3, which hold the float values with two and three components respectively. All these types are implemented in hardware and work very fast.

There are several ways for accessing the vector components in GLSL, similar to working with union in C++. Namely, if you have a vec4 v object, you can access its four components in the following ways:

- As an ordinal array: v[0], v[1], v[2], and v[3]
- As a color: v.r, v.g, v.b, and v.a
- As coordinates: v.x, v.y, v.z, and v.w

The fourth coordinate v.w comes from projective coordinates' notation and most often is set to 1.0.

- As texture coordinates: v.s, v.t, v.p, and v.q

In GLSL, you can use a notation called **swizzle**. This technique allows the usage of any combination of letters of the same type to access several vector components at once:
- v.xyz means the vec3 vector (v.x, v.y, v.z)
- v.bg means the vec2 vector (v.b, v.g)
- v.xy = vec2(0.0, 100.0); and vec3 u = v.xxx; are correct GLSL operations

See details on GLSL types and swizzle at http://www.opengl.org/wiki/GLSL_Type.

There is an exhaustive list of the built-in mathematical functions, which work with numbers and vectors, such as sin(x), distance(v, u), and dot(u, v). You can find the list of functions in the full language specification at http://www.opengl.org/documentation/glsl/.

In order to make the fragment shader work, you need to enable a vertex shader too. The simplest vertex shader just transforms the input vertex position gl_Vertex to output the vertex position gl_Position using a built-in matrix gl_ModelViewProjectionMatrix. This matrix translates the internal coordinate system of an object into screen coordinates. The simplest vertex shader's code is as follows:

```
#version 120
void main() {
  gl_Position = gl_ModelViewProjectionMatrix * gl_Vertex;
}
```

The preceding shaders' examples only illustrate the shaders' structure and are too trivial to be useful. Now, we will consider a really useful example of using the shaders in an openFrameworks project.

A simple fragment shader example

Consider a complete example of using the fragment shader in an openFrameworks project. It will be a base for other fragment shaders' examples. The shader here is pretty simple. It just inverts the colors of all the drawn pixels.

This is example 08-Shaders/01-ShaderInverting.

This example is based on the emptyExample project in openFrameworks.

Creating the fragment shader

In the bin/data folder, create a new text file shaderFrag.c that contains the fragment shader's code as follows:

```
#version 120
#extension GL_ARB_texture_rectangle : enable
#extension GL_EXT_gpu_shader4 : enable

uniform sampler2DRect texture0;

void main(){
  //Getting coordinates of the current pixel in texture
  vec2 pos = gl_TexCoord[0].xy;

  //Getting the pixel color from the texture texture0 in pos
```

```
vec4 color = texture2DRect(texture0, pos);

//Changing the color - invert red, green, blue components
color.r = 1.0 - color.r;
color.g = 1.0 - color.g;
color.b = 1.0 - color.b;

//Output the color of shader
gl_FragColor = color;
}
```

We will use the .c extension for the shaders files in this chapter, because it seems especially convenient to open these files with proper highlighting with your programming IDE. Note, the native openFrameworks example shaders files have extensions .frag, .vert, and .geom, and sometimes, shaders have the extension .glsl. Actually, you can choose any convenient extension.

The first line of the code specifies Version GLSL 1.2; see the *Structure of a shader's code* section for details. The second and third lines enable some GLSL features that existed in the newest GLSL versions but were not included in GLSL 1.2. So it lets us use modern language capabilities inside GLSL 1.2.

The line uniform sampler2DRect texture0; is something very special. The line declares that the shader wants to use some texture, which you bound during rendering in openFrameworks. Such a binding occurs implicitly when you draw an image on the screen. If you do not need to draw the image, but want to bind the image for using in a shader, do it by calling image.getTextureReference().bind().

If you need to use several images, you should declare them in a similar way and explicitly bind them to the shader; see the *Processing several images* section.

The body of the shader's main() function begins with getting the current texture coordinates from the built-in gl_TexCoord[0] variable. This variable holds the texture coordinate of texture0 for the current pixel for which the shader is called.

Then, using the built-in texture2DRect() function, we get the color from the texture0 in the position pos. Note, the texture coordinates can be a non-integer value, and GLSL interpolates the texture color properly.

Finally, we change the color parameter by inverting its red, green, and blue components. The last line of the main() function's body sets the resulted color to the built-in gl_FragColor variable, meaning that this color will be drawn in the processed pixel.

The vertex shader

In order to work with the fragment shader, we need a vertex shader. In the `bin/data` folder, create a new text file `shaderVert.c`, which contains the "dummy" vertex shader's code:

```
#version 120
#extension GL_ARB_texture_rectangle : enable
#extension GL_EXT_gpu_shader4 : enable

void main() {
  gl_Position = gl_ModelViewProjectionMatrix * gl_Vertex;
  gl_TexCoord[0] = gl_MultiTexCoord0;
  gl_FrontColor = gl_Color;
}
```

It begins with the same three lines that specify the GLSL 1.2 Version and extensions. The body of the shader's `main()` function does nothing special and just passes all the needed information to the fragment shader. Namely, the first line `gl_Position = gl_ModelViewProjectionMatrix * gl_Vertex;` translates the current processed vertex position to the screen coordinate system (see the *Structure of a shader's code* section). As you will see in the following example, we will draw just one image (`fbo`) with the shader, so the vertex shader will process just four vertices of the image's corners.

The second line of the function sets the built-in vertex attribute `gl_TexCoord[0]` equal to the texture coordinate of the bound image, held in the built-in variable `gl_MultiTexCoord0`. This value will be interpolated to the `gl_TexCoord[0]` value of each pixel incoming to the fragment shader.

Such an interpolation is one of the most important things in the shaders' technology, so let's look at it more closely. In our case, we will draw an image on the screen with shaders. Drawing an image technically means that openFrameworks renders a textured rectangle using OpenGL. The rectangle is drawn by specifying the four vertices' coordinates and texture coordinates and binding the corresponding image texture. The vertex shader processes these four vertices, and OpenGL rasterizes the rectangle as a number of pixels. Then each pixel is processed by our fragment shader and the texture coordinates for each pixel `gl_TexCoord[0]` are the result of interpolation of texture coordinates of vertices in correspondence to the relation between the pixel's position and the position of the four vertices.

In a similar way, you can use other attributes such as normals and colors, and even create your own custom attribute. You set values of an attribute at each vertex, and while rendering the object's primitive, OpenGL will automatically interpolate these values at each rendered pixel. So you can use the interpolated value of the attribute in the given pixel for some computations in the fragment shader. The detailed illustration of this is outside the scope of this book.

> The last line of the vertex shader `gl_FrontColor = gl_Color` is not necessary for this example, but can be effective for your future use of the shader. `gl_Color` is a built-in variable that is equal to the color you set by calling the `ofSetColor()` function in openFrameworks code. `gl_FrontColor` is a built-in variable that assigns a color for the **frontal faces** of 3D and 2D objects. We draw 2D images using these frontal sides, so this value is passed to the fragment shader as a built-in `gl_Color` variable. So you can make the result of the fragment shader responsive to `ofSetColor()` callings by changing its last line `gl_FragColor = color` to `gl_FragColor = color * gl_Color`.

Embedding shaders in our project

The shaders are ready. Let's embed these shaders in the project.

In the `testApp.h` file, in the `testApp` class declaration, add the following lines:

```
ofShader shader;        //Shader
ofFbo fbo;              //Buffer for intermediate drawing
ofImage image;         //Sunflower image
```

The main line here is `ofShader shader`, which declares the `shader` object for managing work with shaders. It can hold the vertex, fragment, and geometry shaders at once. This is very useful because these shaders cannot work alone.

If you need to use several sets of shaders, you need to declare new `ofShader` objects for each of them, as shown in the following code:

```
ofShader shader2, shader3; //, ...
```

We will use the `fbo` object as an intermediate buffer for rendering all that we want to see on the screen (see the *Using FBO for offscreen drawing* section in *Chapter 2, Drawing in 2D*). Then we will enable `shader` and draw `fbo` on the screen. Because shader is enabled, the drawing will be passed through shaders that are contained in the `shader`. So the four corners of the image will be processed by a vertex shader, and all drawn pixels will be processed by a fragment shader.

Such a technique of rendering the screen in the buffer and then passing the buffer through a fragment shader is widely used for applying postprocessing effects to the whole screen.

The `setup()` function loads the vertex and fragment shaders' texts into the `shader` object, allocates `fbo`, and also loads `image`, which we will use for test drawing.

```
void testApp::setup(){
  shader.load( "shaderVert.c", "shaderFrag.c" );

  fbo.allocate( ofGetWidth(), ofGetHeight() );
  image.loadImage( "sunflower.png" );
}
```

 The `shader.load()` call not only loads the shaders' texts but also compiles them.

During compilation, all the errors will be printed on the console. If some error occurs, the shader will not work. So don't forget to check the console while working with shaders.

The `update()` function is empty here. The `draw()` function consists of two parts — drawing a background and image to the `fbo` buffer and drawing `fbo` to the screen through `shader`:

```
void testApp::draw(){
  //1. Drawing into fbo buffer
  fbo.begin();          //Start drawing into buffer

  //Draw something here just like it is drawn on the screen
  ofBackgroundGradient( ofColor( 255 ), ofColor( 128 ) );
  ofSetColor( 255, 255, 255 );
  image.draw( 351, 221 );

  fbo.end();            //End drawing into buffer

  //2. Drawing to screen through the shader
  shader.begin();       //Enable the shader

  //Draw fbo image
  ofSetColor( 255, 255, 255 );
  fbo.draw( 0, 0 );

  shader.end();         //Disable the shader
}
```

Note that we enable and disable the shader by calling `shader.begin()` and `shader.end()`. The `shader` works only when it is enabled.

 You cannot enable several of `Shader` objects simultaneously. If you need to perform image processing with many shaders, do it using a processing chain that is made from several of `Shader` and of `Fbo` objects.

The project is ready. Before running it, copy the `sunflower.png` file into the `bin/data` folder of your project. When you run the code, you will see the inverted sunflower image as shown in the following screenshot:

Comment the following lines of the fragment shader as follows:

```
color.r = 1.0 - color.r;
color.g = 1.0 - color.g;
color.b = 1.0 - color.b;
```

When you do so, you will see the original, unprocessed image. Now change these lines to the following line:

```
color.rg = color.gr;
```

Once you do so, you will see the red and green components of the image. We will continue investigating using fragment shaders for postprocessing and video effects, but let's first talk a little about debugging shaders.

Debugging shaders

The newest GLSL versions have debugging capabilities, and there are number of utilities for debugging shaders. But most of the C++ IDEs cannot debug shaders the way we deal with ordinary C++ programs, using breakpoints and watches.

So the easiest way for working and debugging shaders is the following:

1. Start your project that will use shaders from the working sketch.

2. If you change the shader's code, do not add any new modifications until it compiles and runs correctly.

3. During the shader code modification, check the console messages, because the shader's errors are printed there.

4. To debug the shader, you cannot print anything using `cout`. But you can render some intermediate shader values on the screen by representing the values as pixel colors. For example, if you are interested in some q variable, which takes values in [0, 100], then add the line `gl_FragColor = vec4( q*0.01, 0.0, 0.0, 1.0 )` at the end of the fragment shader's `main()` function and you will see its distribution in red.

Creating video effects with fragment shaders

In this section, we will extend the knowledge of shaders and will see how to pass parameters from your C++ code, how to use Perlin noise, and how to process several images. The examples will be about the fragment shaders, but all the principles extend to the vertex and geometry shaders.

Passing a float parameter to a shader

In order to make the shader interactive, we need a way to pass in it some parameters, such as time, mouse position, and some arrays. To add a parameter, you need to add its declaration in the shader's code using the `uniform` keyword. For example, to declare the `time` parameter, use the following line:

```
uniform float time;
```

To specify the parameter's value in openFrameworks, you need to add the following line after the `shader.enable()` calling:

```
shader.setUniform1f( "time", time );
```

The 1f suffix in the setUniform1f() function name means that you pass one float value to the shader. The first parameter "time" indicates the parameter name as it's declared in the shader. The second parameter time is a float variable holding the time value:

```
float time = ofGetElapsedTimef();
```

Let's illustrate this in a simple example.

A simple geometrical distortion example

This example uses a fragment shader for distorting the geometry of an image. It transforms the image by shifting its horizontal lines by a sine wave, which also changes with time.

> This example is similar to the example, which is described in the *A simple geometrical distortion example* section in *Chapter 4, Images and Textures*. However, it is based on the shaders technology. So it works much faster and the resultant image has no **aliasing** effect.

This is example 08-Shaders/02-ShaderHorizDistortion. The project is based on the example given in the *A simple fragment shader example* section.

The fragment shader's code is as follows:

```
#version 120
#extension GL_ARB_texture_rectangle : enable
#extension GL_EXT_gpu_shader4 : enable

uniform sampler2DRect texture0;

uniform float time; //Parameter which we will pass from OF

void main(){
  //Getting the coordinates of the current pixel in texture
  vec2 pos = gl_TexCoord[0].st;

  //Changing pos by sinewave
  float amp = sin( pos.y * 0.03 );
  pos.x += sin( time * 2.0 ) * amp * 50.0; //Shifting x-coordinate

  //Getting pixel color from texture tex0 in position pos
  vec4 color = texture2DRect( texture0, pos );
  //Output of shader
  gl_FragColor = color;
}
```

This shader sets the color obtained by shifting the original position `pos` along the x axis to its output value `gl_FragColor`. The value of shifting depends on `time` as `sin( time * 2.0 )` and on the y coordinate as `sin( pos.y * 0.03 )`.

In the openFrameworks' project, add the following lines to the `draw()` function's body, just after the `shader.begin()` line:

```
float time = ofGetElapsedTimef();
shader.setUniform1f( "time", time );
```

This code will set the `time` variable equal to the number of seconds from the application's start, and set it to the shader's `time` parameter.

Running the project, you will see a waving sunflower image as shown in the following screenshot:

Play with different distortion functions. For example, find the following line in `shaderFrag.c`:

```
float amp = sin( pos.y * 0.03 );
```

Replace the preceding line by the following line:

```
float amp = sin( pos.x * 0.03 );
```

Passing the float array to the shader

Sometimes it is necessary to pass to the shader not just a single float value but an array of floats. To do this, just declare the array in the shader's code as follows:

```
#define N (256)
uniform float myArray[N];
```

Now bind the array from the openFrameworks project' code:

```
shader.setUniform1fv( "myArray", myArray, 256 );
```

In the preceding line of code, `myArray` is a float array with `256` elements.

> In this example, we declared an array with 256 elements just for certainty. You can use any other arrays' size.

Using Perlin noise in shaders

It is a good idea to use Perlin noise in shaders (see *Appendix B, Perlin Noise*, for details on Perlin noise). Though the GLSL language specification has built-in functions `noise1`, `noise2()`, `noise3()`, and `noise4()` for Perlin noise computing, most of the video cards return a zero value when calling these. So we need to implement it by ourselves. Fortunately, there are several ready-to-use Perlin and simplex noise implementations for GLSL, which are open for use.

We will use Perlin and simplex noise developed by *Ashima Arts* and *Stefan Gustavson* in the `webgl-noise` library located at `https://github.com/ashima/webgl-noise`. This library is distributed along with the MIT license. Download and unpack the library, and then copy and paste the necessary functions right into your shader's code. Don't forget to include information about the license as requested in the library's description. Let's illustrate the usage of Perlin noise in an example.

A liquify distortion example

Let's implement a fragment shader, which will shift each pixel using Perlin noise. The resultant effect will be liquid-like waving of the input image.

> This is example `08-Shaders/03-ShaderLiquify`.

The project is based on the `08-Shaders/02-ShaderHorizDistortion` example, which was explained in the *A simple geometrical distortion example* section.

Change the fragment shader's text by the following code:

```
#version 120
#extension GL_ARB_texture_rectangle : enable
#extension GL_EXT_gpu_shader4 : enable
uniform sampler2DRect texture0;
uniform float time;

//Classic Perlin noise function declaration
float cnoise( vec3 P );

void main(){
  vec2 pos = gl_TexCoord[0].xy;

  //Shift pos using Perlin noise
  vec2 shift;
  shift.x = cnoise( vec3( pos*0.02, time * 0.5 + 17.0 ) )*30.0;
  shift.y = cnoise( vec3( pos*0.02, time * 0.5 + 12.0 ) )*30.0;
  pos += shift;

  vec4 color = texture2DRect( texture0, pos );
  //Output of the shader
  gl_FragColor = color;
}
//Insert src/classicnoise3D.glsl file contents here
//---------
```

Also, you need to add the code definition of the `cnoise()` function by pasting the contents of the `src/classicnoise3D.glsl` file located in the `webgl-noise` library, at the end of the code.

 We decided to put the definition of the `cnoise()` function at the end of the shader for the convenience of editing our own code.

The declared `cnoise()` function computes the Perlin noise as a function of three parameters. We use it for computing the `shift` vector, which pseudo-randomly depends on the current position `pos` and `time`. (See *Appendix B, Perlin Noise*, for details). Then, we shift `pos` and get the resulting color from this shifted position.

Run the example, and you will see the liquid-like waving of the sunflower image as shown in the following screenshot:

Processing several images

For some effects such as masking, the fragment shader should read colors from more than one image. To use several images, in the shader's code you should declare additional uniform sampler2DRect parameters:

```
uniform sampler2DRect texture1;     //Second image
uniform sampler2DRect texture2;     //Third image
//and so on
```

In openFrameworks' project code, you should link your images' textures to this shader's parameters, right after the shader.enable() calling:

```
shader.setUniformTexture( "texture1",image2.getTextureReference(),
                          1 );
shader.setUniformTexture( "texture2",image3.getTextureReference(),
                          2 );
//and so on
```

Here, the first parameter means the shaders' uniform parameter name, the second is texture, and the third is OpenGL texture identifier, which should be more than 0, because the identifier 0 is used for default binding to texture0 in the shader (see the *Structure of a shader's code* section for details on texture0).

A masking example

Let's demonstrate the processing of several images by creating a fragment shader that masks the drawing image with some predefined mask.

 This is example `08-Shaders/04-ShaderMasking`.

The project is based on the `08-Shaders/02-ShaderHorizDistortion` example, which was explained in the *A simple geometrical distortion example* section.

Create the fragment shader with the following code:

```
#version 120
#extension GL_ARB_texture_rectangle : enable
#extension GL_EXT_gpu_shader4 : enable

uniform sampler2DRect texture0;
uniform sampler2DRect texture1;      //Second texture

void main(){
  vec2 pos = gl_TexCoord[0].xy;
  vec4 color0 = texture2DRect( texture0, pos );
  vec4 color1 = texture2DRect( texture1, pos );
  //Compute resulted color
  vec4 color;
  color.rgb = color0.rgb;
  color.a = color1.r;
  //Output of the shader
  gl_FragColor = color;
}
```

This shader assumes that both images have the same size, and uses the red component of the `texture1` pixel for setting the alpha value of the output color. To use the shader, make a grayscale mask, enable `shader`, bind the mask to `texture1`, and then draw your `fbo` image. The pixels, corresponding to the black pixels in the mask, will have zero alpha in the output picture, and so will be invisible.

See the full example code in `08-Shaders/04-ShaderMasking`, where we use this shader for masking the sunflower image with the rotating triangle. The following screenshot shows the original image, the mask, and the result of applying the shader:

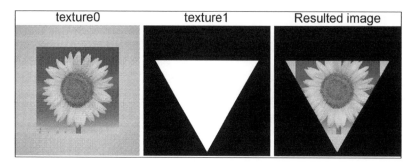

An audio-reactive project example

This is the end of the *Creating video effects with fragment shaders* section. Let's consider the concluding example, which combines music and images for obtaining audio-reactive visualization using a shader.

 This is example `08-Shaders/05-ShaderAudioReactive`.

This example plays music and computes the spectrum array `spectrum` of the current sound (see the *Getting spectral data from sound* section in *Chapter 6, Working with Sounds*). This array is converted into an image `spectrumImage`, which is passed to the shader as `texture2`. Finally, the shader uses `texture2` for affecting the process of masking two input images `texture0` and `texture1`.

As a result, we obtain an animated picture which gleams and pulsates accordingly with the music beats:

You might ask why we pass the sound spectrum into the shader as a texture but not as a float array. The reason is simple; using the float array will result in steps in an output image, so some interpolation is needed for getting a smooth result. Fortunately, GLSL performs smooth interpolation of textures, so we just represent spectrum array as texture and delegate interpolating to GLSL.

Until now, we have considered the basic capabilities of processing 2D images with fragment shaders. Now let's look at the example of using a vertex shader for deforming 3D objects.

Deforming objects with a vertex shader

A vertex shader processes each vertex of drawing objects and can change their built-in attributes such as position, color, normal, and can also change any custom attributes. Here, we consider the example of the vertex shader that just moves vertices according to a rule with the help of parameters that are controlled by the mouse position.

This is example `08-Shaders/06-VertexDeformation`.

This example is based on the example given in the *The triangles cloud example* section of *Chapter 2, Drawing in 3D*. The original example draws a rotated sphere-shaped cloud of random triangles.

Vertex shader

In the `bin/data` folder, create a new text file `shaderVert.c` containing the following code:

```
#version 120
#extension GL_ARB_texture_rectangle : enable
#extension GL_EXT_gpu_shader4 : enable

uniform float phase = 0.0;   //Phase for "sin" function
uniform float distortAmount = 0.25; //Amount of distortion

void main() {
  //Get original position of the vertex
```

```
    vec3 v = gl_Vertex.xyz;

    //Compute value of distortion for current vertex
    float distort = distortAmount * sin( phase + 0.015 * v.y );

    //Move the position
    v.x /= 1.0 + distort;
    v.y /= 1.0 + distort;
    v.z /= 1.0 + distort;

    //Set output vertex position
    vec4 posHomog = vec4( v, 1.0 );
    gl_Position = gl_ModelViewProjectionMatrix * posHomog;

    //Set output texture coordinate and color in a standard way
    gl_TexCoord[0] = gl_MultiTexCoord0;
    gl_FrontColor = gl_Color;
}
```

This shader has two parameters, `phase` and `distortAmount`, which affect the phase of a sine wave and the amount of distortion respectively. The `main()` function transforms `gl_Vertex` using the `phase` and `distortAmount` parameters, and finally writes the result to `gl_Position` (see details on these variables in the *Structure of a shader's code* section).

The most notable thing here is the relation between variables `gl_Vertex` and `gl_Position` having type `vec4`, and variable v having type `vec3`. The variables of type `vec4` are 3D vectors in homogeneous coordinates, where the last coordinate just sets the scaling (which is most often equal to `1.0`). In the example, we wish to perform computations in ordinary 3D space, so we can truncate the last coordinate of `gl_Vertex` and obtain v. We then perform all computations with v, and finally just append to v the fourth coordinate (equal to `1.0`) to obtain `vec4 posHomog`, which is used for the final computation of `gl_Position`.

The last two lines of the `main()` function are as follows:

```
gl_TexCoord[0] = gl_MultiTexCoord0;
gl_FrontColor = gl_Color;
```

The lines the set texture coordinate (not needed in the example, but can be effective for future use of the shader) and front color to the a standard values. See the *A simple fragment shader example* section for details on these.

Fragment shader

In the `bin/data` folder, create a new text file `shaderFrag.c`, which contains the following code:

```
#version 120
#extension GL_ARB_texture_rectangle : enable
#extension GL_EXT_gpu_shader4 : enable

void main(){
  gl_FragColor = gl_Color;
}
```

This is a dummy fragment shader, which just writes the output color equal to the `gl_Color` value (which is equal to the interpolated `gl_FrontColor` value from the vertex shader).

Using vertex shader in our project

In the `testApp.h` file, in the `testApp` class declaration, add the shader object declaration as follows:

```
ofShader shader;   //Shader
```

At the end of the `setup()` function declaration, add the following line for loading shaders:

```
shader.load( "shaderVert.c", "shaderFrag.c" );
```

Change the empty `update()` function with the following code:

```
float time0 = 0;
float phase = 0;
float distortAmount = 0;

void testApp::update(){
  //Compute dt
  float time = ofGetElapsedTimef();
  float dt = ofClamp( time - time0, 0, 0.1 );
  time0 = time;

  float speed = ofMap( mouseY, 0, ofGetHeight(), 0, 5 );
  phase += speed * dt;
  distortAmount = ofMap( mouseX, 0, ofGetWidth(), 0, 1.0 );
}
```

This function computes time step `dt` as a time difference between the current time and time of previous calling of the `update()` function (see details in the *Implementing a particle in the project* section in *Chapter 3, Building a Simple Particle System*). Next it computes the `phase` and `distortAmount` parameters depending on the mouse position. Note that the phase value changes steadily over time, so our shape distortion will change with time.

In `draw()`, add the following lines before the `//Draw the triangles` line:

```
shader.begin();         //Enable the shader
shader.setUniform1f("phase", phase );
shader.setUniform1f("distortAmount", distortAmount );
```

This code enables the shader and sets its parameters.

Finally, add the line for disabling the shader just before the `ofPopMatrix();` line:

```
shader.end();   //Disable the shader
```

Run the project and move the mouse. You will see how the sphere-like cloud will deform depending on the mouse position. Namely, the mouse x-position sets the amount of distortion and the mouse y-position sets the speed of wave-like fluctuations:

Now we will consider the example of using a geometry shader.

Using a geometry shader

In the rendering pipeline, a geometry shader works between the vertex shader and the fragment shader. It processes the groups of vertices that are organized in primitives. The possible primitives are point (one vertex), line (two vertices), and triangle (three vertices). Also, there are two new primitives, **line with adjacent** and **triangle with adjacent**, which represent the line and the triangle with some additional vertices providing adjacency information needed for computing the normals.

The geometry shader gets access to the input positions of the primitive's vertices using a built-in array gl_PositionIn, which holds values of type vec4. These positions are equal to the output values gl_Position generated by the vertex shader.

During its work, processing of the geometry shader should generate a number of output vertices by setting some values to gl_Position, gl_FrontColor, and other variables (similar to the vertex shader), and finally calling the EmitVertex() function. This function tells OpenGL that the geometry shader has finished forming values for the next vertex and rendered it.

The type of primitives rendered by the geometry shader is often different from its input primitives' type. The output type can be a point, a line strip, or a triangle strip. The last two types are strips, and so they can contain a different number of vertices. To denote whether the geometry shader finished the strip primitive, it should call the EndPrimitive() function. Then OpenGL finishes rendering the last primitive and is ready to render a new one.

The "classical usage" of the geometry shader is in smoothing curves and surfaces by subdividing (dividing each line segment or triangle on several primitives of the same type). We will consider an example of more experimental usage of the geometry shader.

The furry carpet example

Let's make a shader that replaces each passed line with a bunch of lines such that these vertices' positions will be distorted using Perlin noise. We obtain a "furry" collection of lines. Additionally, we set the color of each generated line as an average color of a random image along this line. Finally, we will obtain a colored 2D "furry carpet" with a picture resembling the original image.

 This is example 08-Shaders/07-GeometryFurryCarpet.

The example is based on the example given in the *A simple fragment shader example* section. See the entire source code of the project in `08-Shaders/07-GeometryFurryCarpet`. Here we note just the example's key points:

A new file, `shaderGeom.c`, which contains the geometry shader is added there. It takes the vertices' positions, and the input lines are as follows:

```
vec2 p0 = gl_PositionIn[0].xy;
vec2 p1 = gl_PositionIn[1].xy;
```

In the next step it generates 50 lines. Namely, it distorts the positions `p0` and `p1` by Perlin noise and obtains distorted positions `q0` and `q1`. At the next stage, the shader computes the average color of the input image along the line segment [`q0`, `q1`]. Finally, it emits two corresponding vertices.

In the example the line of vertex shader code, which `computes` the output vertex position (`gl_Position = gl_ModelViewProjectionMatrix * gl_Vertex;`) is replaced by trivially passing original position of the output:

```
gl_Position = gl_Vertex;
```

The reason is that the geometry shader needs an unchanged vertex position for computing, and finally makes a transformation with `gl_ModelViewProjectionMatrix` by itself.

The body of the fragment shader's `main()` function consists of just one line, which only passes the input color:

```
gl_FragColor = gl_Color;
```

In the openFrameworks's project, one line of the `setup()` function which loads the shader is replaced with the following code:

```
shader.setGeometryInputType(GL_LINES);
shader.setGeometryOutputType(GL_LINE_STRIP);
shader.setGeometryOutputCount(128);
shader.load( "shaderVert.c", "shaderFrag.c", "shaderGeom.c" );
```

The first three lines set the geometry shader's parameters—its input and output primitive types—and also the maximum possible number of output vertices. You need to specify such parameters for the geometry shader before loading this. The `shader.load()` function here contains three parameters with filenames for the vertex, fragment, and geometry shader.

Instead of using the `sunflower.png` image, we are using the version with a transparent background, `sunflower-transp.png`.

Finally, in the `draw()` function, we enable `shader` and draw a number of vertical lines. So each line passes through the vertex, geometry, and fragment shaders. During processing by the geometry shader, the line is replaced with 50 lines that are actually rendered on the screen. The important point here is that we do some optimization, and do not render lines that lie in the transparent background.

Running the project, you will see a slow moving carpet resembling the original sunflower image, as shown in the following screenshot:

Additional topics

In this chapter, we introduced very basic topics on shaders with the main focus on 2D image processing. For further knowledge of shaders, we suggest the following topics:

- 3D objects lighting using vertex and fragment shaders
- Working with attributes, which is a powerful way for propagating various types of information from a vertex shader to a fragment shader.
- Ping-Pong FBO method, which is used for some computations with the fragment shader, for example, particle physics simulation. See the corresponding openFrameworks example in the `examples/gl/gpuParticleSystemExample` folder.

Summary

In this chapter, we covered the shaders, one of the most progressing areas of computer graphics. We looked at examples of using the fragment, vertex, and geometry shaders and ways to pass float numbers, float arrays, and images into the shader. Also, we learned how to use Perlin noise in shaders.

This is the last topic on the media capabilities of openFrameworks. In the next chapter, we will consider how to use a computer vision based on the OpenCV library in openFrameworks projects.

9
Computer Vision with OpenCV

In this chapter, we will learn how to use computer vision algorithms for performing advanced video analysis and processing using the ofxOpenCv addon and the OpenCV library. You will learn how to work with the addon's class of images and perform filtering, geometrical transformations of images, and find contours of the objects in the image. Finally, we will consider how to use native OpenCV functions in an example and also learn to use optical flow. We will cover the following topics:

- Using ofxOpenCv
- Motion detection
- Image filtering
- Geometrical transformations of images
- Searching for objects in an image
- Optical flow
- Video morphing

Understanding computer vision and OpenCV

Computer vision is a wide scientific field between mathematics and computer sciences. Its primary goal is to build automatic methods for understanding the content of images. This goal is difficult to achieve; however, we already have a lot of great algorithms, including image enhancement and correction, object detection, tracking and recognition, stereo vision, and automatic machine learning.

You will find that many of the algorithms such as image filtering and object tracking are common for computer vision and video processing. The reason is that some basic procedures are common while dealing with images. The difference is in the goal. The goal of computer vision is automatic analysis of images from the cameras used for controlling machines; for example, robots, or interactive installations. The goal of video processing is in creating video and video effects for spectators to watch.

If you want to use existing computer vision methods, a good choice is **Open Computer Vision (OpenCV)** library. It contains hundreds of classic and newest algorithms for image processing and analysis. Currently, the library is going through the standardization stage by Khronos Group (`khronos.org`), and it will be standard like **OpenGL** and **OpenCL** soon.

> Though OpenCV works with stereo vision and has functions for transforming 3D point clouds, it's mainly focused on working with two-dimensional images obtained from cameras. So, for processing and analyzing 3D point clouds that are obtained from depth cameras, you should use your own algorithms. Also, you can use the PCL library, which is a special library for working with 3D point clouds. However, note that this is outside the scope of this book.

> OpenCV has distinct functions for working with CPU and GPU. We will only consider the CPU functions because these are simpler to learn. Always remember that OpenCV functions are highly optimized so they always work faster than your own pixel-by-pixel algorithms. However, CPU functions are not fast enough for processing big images such as Full HD frames in real time. For such purposes, you need to use GPU. If you need just image processing with some video effects, you may use the shaders technology without OpenCV at all because using shaders is normally simpler and more universal. However, when real computer vision stuff is needed, then use OpenCV's GPU functions.

The way to start linking OpenCV to the openFrameworks project is to use the ofxOpenCv addon. It also adds a number of classes which simplify the common tasks of image processing and tracking. Most of this chapter will be devoted to ofxOpenCv and only the last section *Using OpenCV functions* will be devoted to using OpenCV functions directly.

 Normally, the ofxOpenCv addon is quite fresh and stable, but it's not the latest version of OpenCV. If for some reason you need the latest one, download OpenCV from its site and link it to your project. Note, this procedure demands some experience of working with libraries.

Using ofxOpenCv

The most straightforward way to use the ofxOpenCv addon in your project is to start a new project based on the example of the ofxOpenCv usage. To do so, copy the `examples/addons/opencvExample` folder to the folder with your projects (for example, `apps/myApps`) and rename it (for example, to `myCompVision`).

The second way is to generate a new project using the Project Generator wizard included in openFrameworks. It lets you select which addons to link to the project and then creates a new empty project that includes the required addons. In our case, you need to include ofxOpenCv. See *Appendix A, Working with Addons*, for more details.

When the project has been copied or generated, you need to include the addon's header into your `testApp.h` file, just after the `#include "ofMain.h"` line:

```
#include "ofMain.h"
#include "ofxOpenCv.h"
```

The ofxOpenCv addon is a collection of classes. The classes' names begin with `ofxCV`. There are two groups of classes: the image classes and the algorithm classes.

Image classes contain images of different types and additionally have a set of functions for image processing performed by OpenCV:

- The `ofxCvColorImage` class represents the three-channel (red, green, and blue) color images with color components of the type `unsigned char`. These images are obtained from cameras.

- The `ofxCvGrayscaleImage` class represents grayscale, one-channel images with pixel values of the type `unsigned char`. These images are used for internal processing such as thresholding and contour finding, and as a class for working with **binary images** that contain only two pixel values (0 and 255).

- The ofxCvFloatImage class represents grayscale, one-channel images with pixel values of the type float. It is used in situations when accurate calculations are needed; for example, special filters for smoothing and Fourier transform.

- The ofxCvShortImage class represents grayscale, one-channel images with pixel values of the type unsigned short int. So the range of the pixel value is from 0 to 65,535. Such images are obtained from depth cameras where the pixel value means the corresponding distance in millimeters.

- The ofxCvImage class is a base class for all the preceding image classes. It contains declarations of most of the functions for image processing so you can explore them. Note, you should not declare objects of this class directly because it has a number of **abstract functions**, that is, functions which are declared but not defined. So, calling this class with an object of the class ofxCvImage causes an execution error.

 Currently, there are no implemented three-channel float-type and unsigned short-type images, and no four-channel (red, green, blue, and alpha) image types.

Algorithm classes implement a couple of computer vision algorithms, which are as follows:

- The ofxCvContourFinder class finds bounding contours that connect the white regions in the input binary image. Such a class can be used for searching objects. See details in the *Using class ofxCvContourFinder for finding contours* section.

- The ofxCvHaarFinder class implements the **Viola-Jones** method of searching objects on the image using **Haar-like features** and a machine learning method calling **Boosting**. This method works especially well for searching frontal human faces of different sizes on an image. See openFrameworks example of searching faces in examples/addons/opencvHaarFinderExample.

Now we will take a look at the image classes and image processing in greater detail.

Working with ofxCv images

The main object of computer vision is the image. So before diving into image processing and analysis, we should learn how to work with OpenCV-related images freely. We will consider images of classes ofxCvColorImage, ofxCvGrayscaleImage, ofxCvFloatImage, and ofxCvShortImage. These class names have the prefix ofxCv, so we will call them **ofxCv images**. To be precise, we will assume that we have these image objects:

```
ofxCvColorImage image, image2;                //Color images
ofxCvGrayscaleImage grayImage, grayImage2;    //Grayscale images
ofxCvFloatImage floatImage;                   //Float-type image
ofxCvShortImage shortImage;   //Image with "unsigned short" pixels
```

It is convenient to group functions and operations into several groups.

Image initializing

You always need to initialize an image before using it for the first time. Let us look at a few functions used to initialize images:

- The allocate(w, h) function initializes the image with width w and height h pixels; for example, image.allocate(320, 240) creates an image with size 320 × 240 pixels.

 Note, the values of pixels can be nonzero values after initialization, so if you need to set its initial values, use the set (value) function (see the description given at the end of this section).

- The = operator copies images of equal or different types and performs the necessary pixel conversions; for example:
    - image2 = image; copies image to image2. Note that there is no need to initialize image2 using image2.allocate(w, h) because = initializes it automatically.
    - grayImage = image; converts a color image to a grayscale image
    - floatImage = grayScale; converts a grayscale image to a float image

The important thing here is initialization. If destination image was not initialized, the = operator performs the required initialization automatically. However, if the image was initialized, it must have a size equal to the size of the source image. In opposite cases, you should clear the image using the clear() function, or set a prerequisite size using the resize() function.

> During image type conversion, the range of pixel values is transforming correspondingly with the range of the image class. The range for ofxCvColorImage and ofxCvGrayscaleImage is from 0 to 255, while that for ofxCvFloatImage is segment [0, 1], and the range for ofxCvShortImage is from 0 to 65535.
>
> For example, during the floatImage = grayImage operation, the assigned pixel values of floatImage are equal to the pixel values of grayImage image multiplied by 1.0 / 255.0. So, the pixel values of floatImage will lie in [0, 1]. Similarly, during the grayImage = shortImage operation, the assigned pixel values of grayImage are equal to the pixel values of the shortImage image multiplied by 255.0 / 65535.0.
>
> You can change the range of ofxCvFloatImage to any value using the setNativeScale(vMin, vMax) function; for example, floatImage.setNativeScale(0.0, 255.0) sets the range to [0, 255].

- The setFromPixels(data, w, h) function sets image dimensions to w × h pixels and sets its pixel values to the values from an unsigned char array data. Note that the size of the data array should be equal to w × h × 3 for ofxCvColorImage and w × h for other types. There is an alternative form, setFromPixels(pixels), with pixels having the type ofPixels; for example, if you are getting video frames from a camera using the object ofVideoGrabber grabber (see the *Processing a live video from camera* section in *Chapter 5, Working with Videos*), you can initialize an image in the following way:

```
image.setFromPixels( grabber.getPixelsRef() );
```

- For float images, there is an overloaded function for setting its pixels from an array of floats which is known as setFromPixels(dataFloat, w, h) where dataFloat is the array of floats.

- In order to check whether the image was allocated, use the `bAllocated` member, which has the type `bool` as shown in the following code:

```
if ( image.bAllocated ) {
  //...
}
```

There are two functions that are close to the initialization stage:

- The `set( value )` function sets all the image pixels to the `value` value. For color images, there is also a function `set( valueRed, valueGreen, valueBlue )`, that sets each pixel of red, green, and blue color components to `valueRed`, `valueGreen`, and `valueBlue` respectively.

- The `clear()` function clears all the memory allocated for an image. Usually, you don't need to use this function because it is called automatically by the image's destructor.

Algebraic operations with images

Algebraic operations apply mathematical operations such as addition and subtraction to each pixel of the images. The following are a few algebraic functions:

- The `+=`, `-=`, and `*=` operations with an operand of the ofxCV image type are operations that are applicable for images of an equal size and type. The operations do the corresponding operation on the corresponding pixels of the both images; for example, `image += image2` adds `image2` to `image`.

> Currently the `*=` operation divides the operand on 255.0 for all images except `ofxCvFloatImage`.

- The `+=` , `-=`, `*=`, and `/=` operations with the float operand argument `value` perform addition, subtraction, multiplication, and division respectively on all pixel values in the image with the value specified in the `value` variable; for example, `image += 1` adds 1 to the image's pixel values. The `*=` and `/=` operations are currently only available for float images of the class `ofxCvFloatImage`.

Currently, the `*=` operation truncates negative pixel values to zero. So do not use this operation when you need to work with negative pixel values during intermediate operations. So, instead of `floatImage *= value`, call the `multiplyByScalar( floatImage, value )` function, where the function's code is as follows:

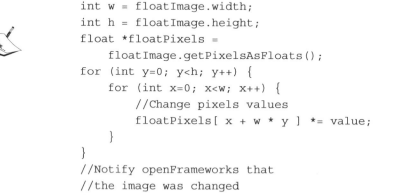

```
void multiplyByScalar( ofxCvFloatImage &floatImage,
                       float value ){
    int w = floatImage.width;
    int h = floatImage.height;
    float *floatPixels =
        floatImage.getPixelsAsFloats();
    for (int y=0; y<h; y++) {
        for (int x=0; x<w; x++) {
            //Change pixels values
            floatPixels[ x + w * y ] *= value;
        }
    }
    //Notify openFrameworks that
    //the image was changed
    floatImage.flagImageChanged();
}
```

- The `grayImage.absDiff( grayImage2 )` function calculates the absolute difference value between the corresponding pixels of `grayImage` and `grayImage2` and writes the result to `grayImage`. There is an overloaded `grayImage.absDiff( grayImageA, grayImageB )` function, which puts the result of the absolute difference between `grayImageA` and `grayImageB` to `grayImage`. Though this is not formally an algebraic operation, it is obviously related to them. The function is useful for marking the regions where the two given images differ. Note, the `absDiff` function is currently available for grayscale images only.

All the image types except `ofxCvFloatImage` have a limited range of pixel values (see the discussion of ranges in the preceding information box for the operator `=`). In the case when the result of any operation goes beyond the range, the **saturation arithmetic** is applied, that is, the value is truncated to the range. For example, for an image of type `ofxCvGrayscaleImage`, the values 300 and -10 will be truncated to 255 and 0 respectively. Hence, if you perform advanced mathematical calculations with images, it is a good idea to convert input images to `ofxCvFloatImage` first, then perform calculations, and finally convert the final result to the required type.

Drawing functions

The drawing functions are similar to the corresponding functions of the ofImage class for openFrameworks' images, discussed in *Chapter 4, Images and Textures*. The following are a few drawing functions:

- The draw(x, y, w, h) function draws the image to the screen. Note, for images of classes ofxCvFloatImage and ofxCvShortImage, the pixel values are mapped from the corresponding ranges [0, 1] and 0 to 65,535 to the range 0 to 255 for screen output. The range for a float image can be changed using the setNativeScale(vMin, vMax) function. There are overloaded versions: draw(x, y), draw(point), and draw(rect) with point of type ofPoint and rect of type ofRectangle.

- The setAnchorPercent(xPct, yPct), setAnchorPoint(x, y), and resetAnchor() functions let us control the origin of the output image, just like in ofImage.

- The setUseTexture(use) function with use of the type bool enables or disables using texture for the image. This texture is automatically recalculated only before the image drawing. If the image is used only for internal calculations and will never be shown on the screen, call setUseTexture(false) for saving the video memory.

- The getTextureReference() function returns the reference on the ofTexture object of the image. If you change the image and need its texture, you need to call updateTexture() before getting the texture reference.

Access to pixels

For implementing custom image processing functions or using OpenCV functions not implemented in the ofxOpenCv addon, you need to have access to the pixel values and OpenCV image inside the ofxCv image. There are number of functions for dealing with it:

- The width and height values can be used for getting the current size of the image.

- The getPixels() function returns an array of unsigned char values, corresponding with the image's values. For ofxCvFloatImage and ofxCvShortImage images, the pixel's values are mapped to 0 to 255 range, as in the draw() function described earlier.

- The getPixelsRef() function returns a reference to a pixel array of the current frame represented by a class ofPixels.

[Note that currently the name of the function differs from the name of the corresponding function in the ofImage class where it is called getPixelRef().]

- The getPixelsAsFloats() and getFloatPixelsRef() functions respectively return an array of floats and reference to ofFloatPixels for images of class ofxCvFloatImage.

- The getShortPixelsRef() function returns a reference to ofShortPixels for images of class ofxCvShortImage.

- The getCvImage() function returns a pointer to an object of type IplImage. This is an OpenCV type used for holding an image. The function is used for applying any OpenCV operations to the images directly. Normally, you will use this function for those OpenCV capabilities that are not implemented in the ofxOpenCv addon.

- If you make some modification in the pixel values of the image or its IplImage object, you need to call flagImageChanged() to notify the ofxOpenCv addon that the image was changed. If you need a texture reference to the image, you should call updateTexture(). Note, when calling image.draw(), the texture updates automatically, if needed.

Working with color planes and color spaces conversion

There are a number of functions for manipulating color planes. They are as follows:

- The image.setFromGrayscalePlanarImages(planeR, planeG, planeB) function creates a color image with color planes from three ofxCvGrayscaleImage images, planeR, planeG, and planeB. These images planeR, planeG, and planeB should be allocated before calling setFromGrayscalePlanarImages().

- The image.convertToGrayscalePlanarImages(planeR, planeG, planeB) function does the opposite. It splits an image into its color planes, and writes them to planeR, planeG, and planeB. Note, currently image should be allocated before calling convertToGrayscalePlanarImages().

- The image.convertToGrayscalePlanarImage(grayImage, index) function extracts the color plane number index from an image and writes it into grayImage. Here index = 0, 1, and 2 corresponds to red, green and blue color components respectively, and grayImage does not need to be allocated before calling convertToGrayscalePlanarImage().

The class `ofxCvColorImage` has two functions for converting between **RGB (Red, Green, Blue)** and **HSV (Hue, Saturation, Value)** color spaces: `convertRgbToHsv()` and `convertHsvToRgb()`.

Now we will consider an example of using ofxCv images for a simple motion detector.

Motion detection from movies

Let's consider a live video from the camera or a video from a movie, and consider the absolute difference between its two successive frames, which is computed using the function `grayImage.absDiff( grayImage2 )`, considered in the *Algebraic operations with images* section. The regions in this difference image, corresponding to the moving objects, will have higher values than the static regions. So, for getting pixels with high values, it is possible to detect the regions of motion in the video. This information can be used for controlling the behavior of your application; for example, if you have a particle system, the motion areas can be used as places of particles' emitting or as areas of particles' attraction. Then, people walking in front of your camera will see how their silhouette controls the particles on the screen.

This method of using difference image is simple and has been successfully used in a number of interactive projects for more than thirty years now. However, if you consider two successive difference images, they will most likely have very few common pixels with high values. The reason is that difference image emphasizes the changed pixels of successive frames, or in another words, "motion border", which changes each frame. So difference image is not stable in time. To regularize it, it is a good idea to accumulate the differences in an image buffer that slowly decreases its values.

The following example illustrates the calculation of absolute differences and accumulation of them in the buffer using ofxCv images of the ofxOpenCv addon.

This is example `09-OpenCV/01-MotionDetection`.

Use the Project Generator for creating an empty project with the linked ofxOpenCv addon (see the *Using ofxOpenCv* section). Then, copy the `handsTrees.mov` movies into the `bin/data` folder of the project.

Include the addon's header into the `testApp.h` file, just after the `#include "ofMain.h"` line:

```
#include "ofMain.h"
#include "ofxOpenCv.h"
```

Also, add the following lines in the `testApp` class declaration:

```
ofVideoPlayer video;          //Declare the video player object

ofxCvColorImage image;        //The current video frame

//The current and the previous video frames as grayscale images
ofxCvGrayscaleImage grayImage, grayImagePrev;

ofxCvGrayscaleImage diff;     //Absolute difference of the frames
ofxCvFloatImage diffFloat;    //Amplified difference images
ofxCvFloatImage bufferFloat;  //Buffer image
```

Now let's assemble `testApp.cpp`. The `testApp::setup()` function loads and starts the video as follows:

```
void testApp::setup(){
  video.loadMovie( "handsTrees.mov" );  //Load the video file
  video.play();                         //Start the video to play
}
```

The `testApp::update()` function reads video frames and processes them by calculating the absolute difference `diff`, amplifying it for better visibility in `diffFloat`, and then updating the accumulate buffer `bufferFloat`. Note, we check the fact that an image is initialized using the `bAllocated` value:

```
void testApp::update(){
  video.update();  //Decode the new frame if needed
  //Do computing only if the new frame was obtained
  if ( video.isFrameNew() ) {
      //Store the previous frame, if it exists till now
      if ( grayImage.bAllocated ) {
          grayImagePrev = grayImage;
      }

      //Getting a new frame
      image.setFromPixels( video.getPixelsRef() );
      grayImage = image;  //Convert to grayscale image

      //Do processing if grayImagePrev is inited
      if ( grayImagePrev.bAllocated ) {
          //Get absolute difference
          diff.absDiff( grayImage, grayImagePrev );

          //We want to amplify the difference to obtain
          //better visibility of motion
```

```
        //We do it by multiplication. But to do it, we
        //need to convert diff to float image first
        diffFloat = diff;    //Convert to float image
        diffFloat *= 5.0;    //Amplify the pixel values

        //Update the accumulation buffer
        if ( !bufferFloat.bAllocated ) {
            //If the buffer is not initialized, then
            //just set it equal to diffFloat
            bufferFloat = diffFloat;
        }
        else {
            //Slow damping the buffer to zero
            bufferFloat *= 0.85;
            //Add current difference image to the buffer
            bufferFloat += diffFloat;
        }
    }
  }
}
```

Finally, the `testApp::draw()` function draws four images (from left to right and from top to bottom). These four images are as follows:

- The current frame as the grayscale image `grayImage`.
- The `diffFloat` image, which is the absolute difference of the current and the previous frames amplified for better visibility.
- The accumulated buffer image `bufferFloat`.
- Finally, it draws the motion areas as black pixels on a white image. The pixels of motion calculate right in the `draw()` function. The pixel is regarded as a motion pixel if its value in `bufferFloat` exceeds the threshold value `0.9`.

 You can calculate motion areas in the `update()` function, use it for controlling particles, and so on. We do it in the `draw` function just for the code's simplicity.

Let's take a look at the code:

```
void testApp::draw(){
    ofBackground( 255, 255, 255 );  //Set the background color

    //Draw only if diffFloat image is ready.
    //It happens when the second frame from the video is obtained
```

```
if ( diffFloat.bAllocated ) {
    //Get image dimensions
    int w = grayImage.width;
    int h = grayImage.height;

    //Set color for images drawing
    ofSetColor( 255, 255, 255 );

    //Draw images grayImage,  diffFloat, bufferFloat
    grayImage.draw( 0, 0, w/2, h/2 );
    diffFloat.draw( w/2 + 10, 0, w/2, h/2 );
    bufferFloat.draw( 0, h/2 + 10, w/2, h/2 );

    //Draw the image motion areas

    //Shift and scale the coordinate system
    ofPushMatrix();
    ofTranslate( w/2+10, h/2+10 );
    ofScale( 0.5, 0.5 );

    //Draw bounding rectangle
    ofSetColor(0, 0, 0);
    ofNoFill();
    ofRect( -1, -1, w+2, h+2 );

    //Get bufferFloat pixels
    float *pixels = bufferFloat.getPixelsAsFloats();
    //Scan all pixels
    for (int y=0; y<h; y++) {
        for (int x=0; x<w; x++) {
            //Get the pixel value
            float value = pixels[ x + w * y ];
            //If value exceed threshold, then draw pixel
            if ( value >= 0.9 ) {
                ofRect( x, y, 1, 1 );
                //Rectangle with size 1x1 means pixel
                //Note, this is slow function,
                //we use it here just for simplicity
            }
        }
    }
    ofPopMatrix();   //Restore the coordinate system
}
}
```

Run the example. You will see an animation consisting of four images on the screen: the current movie frame in grayscale, absolute difference of the current and the previous frame, the accumulated buffer, and finally, the motion areas shown in black color:

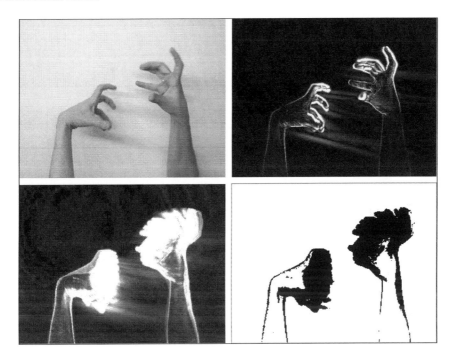

 The video in the example has a frame size of 640 x 480 pixels so its processing consumes a lot of CPU resources. So, run the example in the **Release** mode for smooth video playing.

You can observe that all the operations in the example can be done using pixel-by-pixel processing, described in *Chapter 5, Working with Videos*. So, why use complicated stuff like OpenCV? The answer is that although the example is very simple, when you do more complicated image processing and then use pixel-by-pixel programming, it makes the code cumbersome. When using OpenCV, you can do most of the image operations with a single line of code. Also, OpenCV uses various optimizations, so using it usually improves the performance of your project.

Now we will consider the control parameters of the motion detection algorithm.

Discussing the algorithm's parameters

There are three parameters of the motion detection algorithm:

- The amplification parameter `5.0` is in the following line of the `update()` function:

```
diffFloat *= 5.0;   //Amplify pixel values
```

  Change the parameter to `1.0` and `10.0` to see the decrease and increase in the brightness of the second image. (Note that the parameter affects the third and fourth image as well).

- The buffer damping parameter `0.85` is in the following line of the `update()` function:

```
bufferFloat *= 0.85;
```

  Increase or decrease the parameter for slower or faster damping correspondingly; for example, change the parameter value to `0.8` and `0.95` to see results on the third image. (Note, the parameter affects the fourth image too).

- The threshold parameter `0.9` for motion area detection is in the following line of the `draw()` function:

```
if ( value >= 0.9 ) {
```

  Increasing or decreasing the value leads to a corresponding decrease or increase in the sensitivity of the algorithm, that is, the detected area becomes larger or smaller correspondingly. Try to change the parameter to `0.3` and `2.0` and see the result on the fourth image.

The second and third images on the screen are the result of drawing float-valued images `diffFloat` and `bufferFloat`. As we discussed earlier, pixel values of these images are mapped from the range [0, 1] to 0 to 255 while drawing. So, all the pixel values greater than 1.0 are rendered in white color. In our case, pixels of the `bufferFloat` image can have values greater than 1.0, so its image on the screen is clamped in the sense of color representation. To reduce the color clamping on the screen, decrease the amplification parameter.

Motion detection from live video

It is easy to change the previous example to search motion areas in a live video from a camera. That is, find the following line in `testApp.h`:

```
ofVideoPlayer video;   //Declare the video player object
```

Replace the preceding line with the following:

```
ofVideoGrabber video;   //Video grabber from the camera
```

Now, find the following lines in testApp.cpp in the testApp::setup() function:

```
video.loadMovie( "handsTrees.mov" );   //Load the video file
video.play();                          //Start the video to play
```

Replace the preceding lines with the following:

```
video.initGrabber( 640, 480 ); //Start the video grabber
```

 For details on capturing images from cameras, see the *Processing a live video from the camera* section in *Chapter 5, Working with Videos*.

When you run the example with a live video, you will possibly find that the motion has not tracked so well as in the prerecorded video handsTrees.mov. In this case, you need to adjust the algorithm's parameters, see the *Discussing the algorithm's parameters* section.

We have considered the algorithm of motion detection, which is great for learning the basics of computer vision and making simple interactive installations. Though, it has a drawback in that you need to adjust its parameters depending on the light conditions. Also, the result of detection depends on the colors of the objects.

There are several ways to avoid this problem:

- Add an additional automatic algorithm for adjusting parameters.
- Use another advanced background detection algorithm. OpenCV has some implemented algorithms. See OpenCV example c/bgfg_segm.cpp (you can find the example in OpenCV's Github repository). Currently, this algorithm is not integrated in openFrameworks, so you need to adopt the code in your project on your own.
- Use optical flow analysis for detecting motion areas, see the *Optical flow* section.
- Use a depth camera. This is the most robust and simple solution (but it only works indoors because of the limitations of cheap depth cameras). A depth camera will provide you with a depth information in each pixel. Hence, you will be able to detect the motion of physical objects as areas with fast depth change. See *Chapter 10, Using Depth Cameras*, for details.

Now we will consider the methods of image filtering, which include smoothing and other essential image processing operations.

Image filtering

Image filtering means the processing of images using a **filter**. The term **filter** in computer vision usually means pixel values modification, which for the given pixel depends only on the pixel values in the neighborhood of the pixel and is independent of the pixel's position. The simplest filters are **pixel operations**, which transform each pixel value using a rule; for example, the multiplication of each image's pixel with some scalar value. So, `+= value`, `-= value`, `*= value` and `set( value )` functions, discussed in the *Working with ofxCv images* section, are pixel operations.

The ofxCv images contain the following filtering functions and pixel operations:

- The `blur( winSize )` function is a smoothing filter that averages the pixel values in a square window around the given pixel with size `winSize` × `winSize` pixels. Here, `winSize` must be an odd integer (that is `winSize` is equal to `2*rad+1` for some integer rad). Increasing the `winSize` parameter leads to more smoothing. This filter is very fast and gives a smoothing result of moderate quality.

- The `blurGaussian( winSize )` function is a smoothing filter that uses the Gaussian weight function for averaging. The window size is `winSize` × `winSize` pixels and `winSize` must be an odd integer. This filter is more accurate than `blur` (because `blur` adds artifacts such as **moire** due to its square averaging). However, `blurGaussian()` is more CPU-expensive.

  If you wish to compare the results of `blur` and `blurGaussian()`, you should use different window sizes. The size in `blurGaussian()` should be greater than `blur()` by at least twice; for example, `blur( 11 )` and `blurGaussian( 21 )`.

- The `erode()` function is a minimizing filter that sets the minimal value to a pixel from a square window of 3 × 3 pixels. This operation is called **morphological erosion**. It is often used for binary images where it is used for removing small noisy white areas.

- The `dilate()` function is a maximizing filter that sets the maximal value to a pixel from a square window of 3 × 3 pixels. This operation is called **morphological dilation**. It is often used for binary images where it is used for filling small holes in the white areas.

- The `convertToRange( minValue, maxValue )` pixel operation maps pixel values from the range of the image class to the [`minValue`, `maxValue`] range. It is very useful for any linear transformation of pixel values; for example, `floatImage.convertToRange( 0.5, 1.5 )` maps the pixel values from the range [0, 1] to the range [`0.5, 1.5`] so it acts on pixel values by formula *value = 0.5 + value * (1.5 - 0.5).*

- The `invert()` function is a pixel operation that inverts every bit of the pixel value. It is useful for images of the type `ofxCvGrayscaleImage` where it acts by the formula value that equals `255-value`, and so it transforms the pixel value from 0 to 255 and 255 to 0. Such an operation can be done using `grayImage.convertToRange( 255, 0 )` but `invert()` works faster.

- The `ofxCvGrayscaleImage` class has a very important pixel operation of thresholding `threshold( threshValue )`. It sets the pixel value to 255 for each pixel if its value is not less than `threshValue` or 0. Otherwise, there is the second optional parameter in the function, `doInvert` of the type `bool`. When it is `true`, that is `threshold( threshValue, true )`, the result is inverted.

- Use of the `threshold()` function is a crucial step in many computer vision processing algorithms because it converts a grayscale halftone image to a binary image. These binary images are then used for detecting, recognizing, and measuring objects such as human fingers and objects on a table. The reason for this is that binary images are simple objects used for performing shape analysis, area and perimeter calculation, and other things. See the example in the *An example for searching bright objects in video* section.

Now we will consider examples of using filtering.

The image filtering example

Gaussian smoothing is probably the most used filter in computer vision because this filter optimally suppresses random noise in the image for the corresponding filter window size. Additionally, because smoothing gives a smoothed image, it is better suited for further processing such as binarization.

We will consider an example that demonstrates a smoothing effect using the Gaussian filter. You will see and compare the thresholded original image and the thresholded smoothed image.

 This is example `09-OpenCV/02-ImageFiltering`.

Use the Project Generator wizard for creating an empty project with the linked ofxOpenCv addon (see the *Using ofxOpenCv* section). Then, copy the sunflower.png image into bin/data of the project.

In the testApp.h file, add a line that includes the addon's header just after the #include "ofMain.h" line:

```
#include "ofMain.h"
#include "ofxOpenCv.h"
```

Add the following members to the testApp class declaration:

```
ofxCvColorImage image;              //Original image
ofxCvGrayscaleImage grayImage;      //Grayscaled original image
ofxCvGrayscaleImage filtered;       //Image used for filtering
```

In testApp.cpp, the setup() function loads an image from the file, copies it to the color image image, and creates its grayscaled copy grayImage. Note that for loading the image from the file, we use a temporary object imageOf as follows:

```
void testApp::setup(){
  ofImage imageOf;  //Temporary image for loading from the file
  imageOf.loadImage( "sunflower.png" );  //Load image from
                                          //the file

  //Set image pixels
  image.setFromPixels( imageOf.getPixelsRef() );

  //Convert to a grayscale image
  grayImage = image;
}
```

To obtain a shorter code, we perform the all image processing steps right in draw() and directly draw its results on the screen using just one filtered image. A more accurate approach is to declare a separate image for each image we want draw, and then process it once in update(). Also, in the example, the input image has not changed so we can do the processing right in setup(). So, the update() function is empty here, and the draw() function does all the image processing:

```
void testApp::draw(){
  ofBackground( 128, 128, 128 ); //Set the background color

  //Get image dimensions
  int w = image.width;
  int h = image.height;
```

```
    ofSetColor( 255, 255, 255 );  //Set a color for images drawing

    //Draw original image
    grayImage.draw( 0, 0, w, h );

    //Thresholding original image
    filtered = grayImage;          //Copy the image
    filtered.threshold( 128 );     //Thresholding original image
                                   //using thresold 128
    filtered.draw( w+10, 0, w, h );  //Draw

    //Smoothing original image
    filtered = grayImage;              //Copy the image
    filtered.blurGaussian( 9 );        //Gaussian blurring
                                       //with window size 9x9
    filtered.draw( 0, h+10, w, h );  //Draw

    //Thresholding smoothed image
    filtered.threshold( 128 );         //Thresholding smoothed image
                                       //using thresold 128
    filtered.draw( w+10, h+10, w, h );  //Draw
}
```

Run the example and you will see four images:

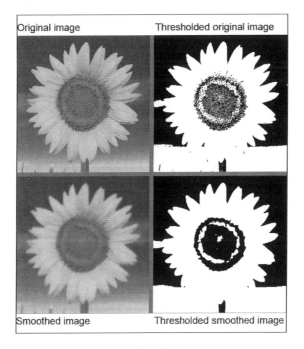

Note that the *Thresholded smoothed image* has more smooth contours.

Here are two parameters of the algorithm:

- The size of the smoothing window that is equal to 9 as shown in the following line:

```
filtered.blurGaussian( 9 );
```

- The threshold value that is equal to 128 as outlined in the following two lines:

```
filtered.threshold( 128 ); //Thresholding original image
...
filtered.threshold( 128 ); //Thresholding smoothed image
```

Adjust these parameters and watch how the smoothness of the contours and the overall number of white pixels change. Now we will consider geometrical transformation of images.

Geometrical transformations of images

Here we consider the different kinds of geometrical transformations that change the position of the image's pixel. OpenCV does operations such as image resizing and warping using interpolation that suppress the **aliasing effect**. Hence, using OpenCV operations is more preferable than custom pixel-by-pixel implementation, except when you implement your own transformation algorithm with antialiasing (which can be tricky), or maybe when you need the aliasing effect. The following is a list of geometrical transformations that are applicable to ofxCv images:

- The resize(w, h) function changes the image size to w × h pixels. For example:

```
image2 = image;
image2.resize( image2.width * 0.5, image2.height * 0.5 );
```

This code transforms image to image2 with a size that equals 50 percent of the size of image. Such a procedure decreases the number of pixels four times, so the speed of processing increases 4 times. However, object localization accuracy in x and y axes decreases only twice.

So, input image decimation lets you adjust the balance between the speed and the accuracy of your computer vision algorithm. Hence, if your algorithm works too slowly and the accuracy is not very important, try to decimate the input image.

- The `scaleIntoMe( mom, interpolationMethod )` function is an advanced resizing function. It scales the content of the `mom` image into the image calling the function and additionally lets you choose an interpolation method by using the `interpolationMethod` parameter. Its possible values are:

  - `CV_INTER_LINEAR` – This method is used for the bilinear interpolation of pixel values. This method is fast and moderately qualitative. It is used by default in all other functions that deal with resizing and warping.

  - `CV_INTER_AREA` – This method is used for interpolation using the pixel area relation. It gives the highest quality when it performs image decimation, though it works slower than `CV_INTER_LINEAR`. Note, it does not work well for image zooming, just as `CV_INTER_NN`.

  - `CV_INTER_NN` – This method is used for resizing using the "nearest neighbor" rule. It just selects the nearest pixel and hence does not perform interpolation at all. It is the fastest method but gives poor quality. It is useful for the pixelization effect.

  - `CV_INTER_CUBIC` – This method uses cubic splines for interpolation. It works well for image zooming. Compared to `CV_INTER_LINEAR`, it gives sharper edges and is slower.

  Note, you need to allocate the image before calling `scaleIntoMe()`.

- The `scale( scaleX, scaleY )` function resizes the content of the image proportionally to `scaleX` and `scaleY`. If both parameters are equal to `1.0`, the image will not change.

- The `mirror( flipY, flipX )` function flips the image vertically or horizontally if `flipY` or `flipX` equals `true` respectively.

- The `translate( shiftX, shiftY )` function shifts the image at `shiftX` along the x axis and at `shiftY` along the y axis where `shiftX` and `shiftY` are of the type `float`. This function works with subpixel quality. Free space in the image is filled with black color.

- The `rotate( angle, centerX, centerY )` function rotates the image counterclockwise at `angle` (measured in degrees) and around the position (`centerX`, `centerY`). All the parameters are `float`. For example, if you need to rotate image at 45 degrees around its center, use the following function calling:

  ```
  image.rotate( 45, image.width/2, image.height/2 );
  ```

  Free space in the image is filled with black color.

- The `transform( angle, centerX, centerY, scaleX, scaleY, moveX, moveY )` function is used for making several transformations such as scaling the image, rotating it, and then moving it.

- The `undistort( radialDistX, radialDistY, tangentDistX, tangentDistY, focalX, focalY, centerX, centerY )` function is a crucial function for correcting camera distortions such as fish-eye. The **camera calibration** technique is outside the scope of this book. But you can play with parameters for obtaining "rubber" image distortions; for example, if you wish to apply such transformations to the `sunflower.png` image, try the following function calls:

```
image.undistort( 0, 1, 0, 0, 200, 200, w/2, h/2 );
image.undistort( 0, 1, 0.0, 0.2, 200, 200, w/2, h/2 );
image.undistort( -0.5, 1, 0.2, 0.1, 2000, 150, w/2, h/2 );
```

  After applying the preceding transformations, you will obtain the following results:

- The `warpPerspective( A, B, C, D )` function performs perspective transform in such a way that points A, B, C, and D map to the corresponding corners of the image, that is, top-left, top-right, bottom-right, and bottom-left respectively. The points A, B, C, and D are of the `ofPoint` type. This function is exceptionally useful for correcting images of rectangular flat surfaces that were obtained from a tilted camera. See the example in the *Perspective distortion removing example* section.

- The `warpIntoMe( mom, srcPoints, dstPoints )` function is an advanced version of the `warpPerspective()` function. It performs perspective warping of the `mom` image into the image by calling this function so that points `srcPoints` map to points `dstPoints`. Here `srcPoints` and `dstPoints` are point arrays that are `ofPoint src[4]` and `dst[4]` respectively.

- The `remap( mapX, mapY )` function lets you perform arbitrary image warping with float images `mapX` and `mapY` so that the resulted value for pixel (x, y) is taken from the pixel with coordinates (`mapX( x, y )`, `mapY( x, y )`). Note, `mapX` and `mapY` are pointers to OpenCV images of the type `IplImage*`. This function is useful for various nonlinear image deformations. See the *Video morphing example* section for more details.

Perspective distortion removing example

Perspective distortion is a geometrical distortion of an object's shape when captured by the camera so that the straight or parallel lines on the object become curvilinear or nonparallel lines in an image. If you want to remove this distortion using strict mathematical modeling, you need to specify the camera's optical characteristics and information about the object's points in three dimensions, although it can be hard.

Fortunately, we often just need to restore the image on a flat rectangular surface in space. This happens while creating interactive floors and tables using color or depth camera. For resolving this, it is enough to specify the coordinates of the four surface corners in the image and then perform perspective warping using `warpPerspective()`.

This method works well for cameras with optics close to the ideal pinhole model. However, if your camera has a wide angle (with the fish-eye effect), the resulted image will not be an ideal rectangle. To obtain better results, you need to undistort the image first using the `undistort()` function.

Let's consider an example that shows us how to do perspective distortion removing.

 This is example `09-OpenCV/03-PerspectiveRemoving`.

Consider a camera-captured image `table.png`, which contains a sheet of paper. We want to restore the picture printed on the paper. The image has a size of 1024×768 pixels, and the coordinates of the paper's corners are A (192, 286), B (742, 188), C (950, 489), and D (215, 665) as shown in the following screenshot:

Assume that this image is loaded to the `image` object. To restore the picture printed on the paper, call the following function:

```
image.warpPerspective(
    ofPoint( 192, 286 ),
    ofPoint( 742, 188 ),
    ofPoint( 950, 489 ),
    ofPoint( 215, 665 ) );
```

The resulting image is shown here:

You can see that the picture is restored quite well except the black area at the top of the image, which appears because the sheet of paper does not lie perfectly smoothly.

Note, the resulted image has proportions different from the original paper's picture. The used sheet of paper has the size A4 (297 × 210 mm), so it has size proportions 3:2, whereas the `image` object has the size 1024 × 768 pixels, so the proportions are 4:3. To obtain the image with correct proportions, you need to use `image2.warpIntoMe()` instead of `image.warpPerspective()` and specify the size of `image2` proportional to 297 × 210; for example, 297 × 210 or 594 × 420 pixels.

We have finished explaining basic image processing using the classes of ofxCv images. Now, we will consider applying this for solving a particularly important task of detecting objects on the image, and we will see how to use the `ofxCvContourFinder` class for this.

Searching for objects in an image

In order to make your project or installation respond to user actions by using the data from camera, often you need to search, recognize, and track objects on the live video from camera. In this section, we will only cover searching objects.

There are several methods to search a specific object in an image:

- **Template matching** is used for searching objects of a fixed shape. The image is scanned using a referenced "ideal" template of the interested object for finding the best match.

- **Contour analysis** (other name is **geometrical matching**) is used for searching objects captured by the camera on a simple background (such as details on the conveyor line). It's based on computing and analyzing the edges of the objects on the image for searching the edge's configurations and matching the interested objects.

  This method can work with complex and overlapped objects but is sensitive to a number of conditions; for example, object should have distinctive edges and there should not be too many edges in the whole image.

- **Algorithms based on machine learning** are used for searching complex objects in complex and outdoor scenes. The algorithms use a number of image features (the sum of pixel values over some rectangles or the local statistics of edges orientations) together with machine learning algorithms (**Boosting** or **SVM**).

  This is the most advanced and robust technique today. Most famous algorithms are the **Viola-Jones** algorithm for searching frontal human faces and the **HOG-method** (**Histogram of Orientated Gradients**) for searching pedestrians, cars, bicycles, animals, and other outdoor objects.

We will consider a simple example of object searching with **contour analysis**. Here we will not search specific objects but will find all the bright objects in the image and find the centers of these objects. To achieve this, we will find contours and call the pixels inside each distinct contour, *the object*. Finding contours is provided by a functionality of the ofxCvContourFinder class, which we will discuss now.

Using the ofxCvContourFinder class for finding contours

The ofxCvContourFinder class is used for searching contours and bounding connected white regions in a binary image. These regions here are called **blobs**. The typical usage of ofxCvContourFinder is as follows:

1. Declare the ofxCvContourFinder contourFinder; object.

2. Find the contours using the following line of code:

   ```
   contourFinder.findContours( mask, minArea, maxArea,
   maxNumber, findHoles );
   ```

   Here mask is a binary image. The parameters minArea and maxArea set the range of the pixels' number in the blobs to reject too small or too large blobs.

   Also, maxNumber is an upper limit of the number of resulted blobs and the findHoles value specifies searching the holes mode. If it is false, black holes in blobs are simply ignored, else the holes are regarded as blobs too.

   For example, contourFinder.findContours(mask, 10, 10000, 20, false); searches for not more than 20 white blobs containing 10 to 10000 pixels and the holes are ignored.

3. Use the found contours via the `contourFinder.blobs` array. The number of blobs is given by `contourFinder.blobs.size()`. Each `contourFinder.blobs[i]` blob has the following members:

   ° `area` – The number of pixels in the blob

   ° `length` – The perimeter of the blob's contour

   ° `boundingRect` – The bounding rectangle of the blob

   ° `centroid` – The point of the blob's center of mass

   ° `hole` – A boolean value that is equal to `true` if the blob is not a blob but the hole of some other blob

   ° `pts` – The point array of the blob's contour

   ° `nPts` – The number of points in the contour

 Note that the list of blobs is calculated independently for each frame, so you should not assume that blobs with same the index i mean the same blob on successive video frames. If you need to retain blobs identifiers, you should implement it in your own algorithm; for example, you can assign the IDs of the blobs in the current frame by getting the ID of the nearest blob in the previous frame.

4. Draw contours using the `contourFinder.draw( x, y, w, h )` function. Note that the function uses its internal colors for drawing and draws the blob's contour line and bounding box.

An example for searching bright objects in video

Let's consider an example realizing the full processing of the input image `image` to the list of objects' center's `obj`.

 This is example `09-OpenCV/04-SearchingObjects`.

Use the project Generator wizard for creating an empty project with the linked ofxOpenCv addon (see the *Using ofxOpenCv* section). Then, copy the `fruits.mov` movie into `bin/data` of the project, and copy sources of the example to the `src` folder.

Here, we will consider just the part of the code related to searching for objects.

Assume that the scene has a dark background and the objects are brighter than the background. Then, the processing steps inside the `update()` function will be the following:

1. Get the frame from a camera or movie video and convert it into the `ofxCvColorImage` image as follows:

   ```
   image.setFromPixels( video.getPixelsRef() );
   ```

2. Decimate the image size for speeding up the process. We use a special image `imageDecimated` for storing the decimated image, and allocate it at the first iteration as follows:

   ```
   if ( !imageDecimated.bAllocated ) {
     imageDecimated.allocate( image.width * 0.5,
                              image.height * 0.5 );
   }
   imageDecimated.scaleIntoMe( image, CV_INTER_NN );
   ```

3. Convert the image to a grayscale image `ofxCvGrayscaleImage grayImage`:

   ```
   grayImage = imageDecimated;
   ```

4. Perform smoothing for noise suppressing as follows:

   ```
   blurred = grayImage;
   blurred.blurGaussian( 9 );
   ```

5. Store the first frame of the movie to the background image. We will assume that this frame is the "true background image":

   ```
   if ( !background.bAllocated ) {
     background = blurred;
   }
   ```

6. Find the difference between the current blurred image and the stored background image. Note, we use the difference but not the absolute difference (`absDiff()`) because we assume that objects are brighter than the background.

   ```
   diff = blurred;
   diff -= background;
   ```

7. Perform thresholding for obtaining a binary image where the white regions correspond to the bright objects on the original image.

   ```
   mask = diff;
   mask.threshold( 40 );
   ```

   Here the value `40` is the threshold parameter and should be adjusted for good results while using videos other than the one in example.

8. Find the contours of the objects using the `contourFinder` object of type `ofxCvContourFinder`.

   ```
   contourFinder.findContours( mask, 10, 10000, 20, false );
   ```

   This function searches no more than `20` white blobs containing `10` to `10000` pixels, and the holes are ignored.

9. Collect all the blob's centers to an array of the points `obj`, namely, `vector<ofPoint> obj`. For shortening the code, we use the reference to the blob list `blobs`:

   ```
   vector<ofxCvBlob>  &blobs = contourFinder.blobs;
   int n = blobs.size();      //Get number of blobs
   obj.resize( n );           //Resize obj array
   for (int i=0; i<n; i++) {
     obj[i] = blobs[i].centroid;  //Fill obj array
   }
   ```

10. Draw the original image on the screen and mark the objects found.

Compile and run the project. You will see an animation with four images showing the processing video with rolling fruits. The first image is a frame from the video, which is decimated by 50 percent. The second image is the difference `diff` between the smoothed and background images. The third image is a thresholded image `mask` with contours drawn over it. Finally, the last image is the original (decimated) frame with crosses marking the found objects.

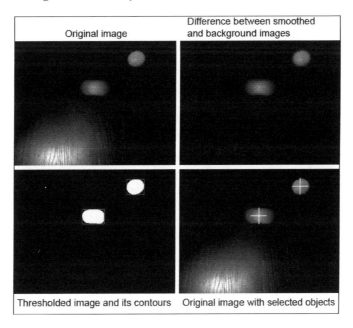

Note that the difference image does not contain the bright spot that existed at the bottom-left corner of the original image, because this spot is included in the background image and hence was subtracted.

Press 2 and you will see an example of using the centers of the objects `obj` for generating images.

This is the original image with some white lines drawn over it. These lines depict the isolines of some function f(x,y), which depend on the `obj` array. Each object's center `obj[i]` adds to the function cone with the center `obj[i]`. See a detailed description of this function in `generateImg()` function in the full example's code. For returning to the processing screen, press 1.

In this example, we were interested in searching all the objects irrespective of their shape. Nevertheless, such a simple example can be used in a wide range of projects for detecting objects such as bright spots. In particular, it is useful in the following situations:

- **Interactive installation with sticks**: You are preparing some lighting objects such as sticks with LEDs on their ends and giving them to users. The users flutter the sticks in front of the installation's camera and the installation responds accordingly.

- **Interactive pool installation**: It's based on using an infrared light source (such as an IR projector) and a camera that senses IR light of the corresponding wavelength (it can be a camera such as Sony PS3-Eye, equipped with a special IR filter). So, the infrared light illuminates the pool table with balls. The infrared camera detects the pool balls' coordinates, and your installation draws some visuals using this data back to the table using a projector. This method works because the IR light and the visible light of the projector do not interfere.

- **Interactive floor installation**: Here the infrared light illuminates the floor, the infrared camera detects objects as humans walking on the floor, and the projector draws the corresponding game's events on the floor.

Note that for accurately detecting the fact that a foot is standing on the floor, it is often better to use depth cameras; see how to do this in the *Creating interactive surface* section in *Chapter 10, Using Depth Cameras*. Though depth cameras are much simpler to adjust and use, they have limitations in their tracking range. So three or more depth cameras are needed for tracking areas of size 10×10 meters. And when using ordinary cameras, just one or two cameras can be enough.

Although the ofxOpenCv addon provides a handy interface for basic filtering and geometrical transformations of images, it is a very small part of OpenCV. So now we will learn how to use other OpenCV functions in your projects.

Using OpenCV functions

OpenCV is a really huge library with hundreds of functions, including optical flow computing, feature detection and matching, and machine learning. Most of these functions are currently not wrapped in the addon ofxOpenCv. You can use these capabilities by calling the OpenCV functions directly, by performing the following steps:

1. First, in the `testApp.h` file, add the following line after the line `#include "ofxOpenCv.h"`, which instructs the compiler to use the OpenCV's namespace:

   ```
   using namespace cv;
   ```

2. Now you can declare OpenCV's images, which are objects of the type `Mat`:

   ```
   Mat imageCV;
   ```

3. For converting the `ofxCv` image `image` into `imageCV`, call the following function:

```
imageCV = Mat( image.getCvImage() );
```

Note, this is fast operation that does not involve copying of data. `imageCV` and `image` will share the same memory region with pixel values. So, we would suggest only using `imageCV` for reading and not for changing.

 We do not suggest the use of the `setNativeScale()` function for images that will be converted to `Mat` objects and back because there can be some undesirable pixel values range conversion.

4. If you need to change the `Mat` object, you can copy it. Remember, the operator `=` applied for `Mat` objects does not copy pixel values. So, for copying those you need to use the direct command:

```
Mat imageCV2;
imageCV2 = imageCV.clone();   //Copy imageCV to imageCV2
//Processing imageCV2...
```

5. If you want to show `Mat` object on the screen, use the `imshow()` function:

```
imshow( "Image", imageCV );
```

The image will be shown in a separate window with the title "Image". This is very useful for debugging purposes. However, when debugging is finished, you can comment these functions because `imshow()` is a CPU-consuming operation.

To use this function, you should add the line `#include "highgui.h"` after all other inclusions at the top of the `testApp.cpp` file.

6. For converting the result of OpenCV back to ofxCv image, use the following code:

```
IplImage iplImage( imageCV2 );
image = &iplImage;            //Copy result to image
```

The last operation makes a copy so you can change `imageCV2` further without affecting `image`. Note, the `image` type of pixel values and number of channels should be the same as in `imageCV2`.

Warning

Currently, the described operation `image = &iplImage` raises an error when `image` is not allocated. This is caused by a small bug in the addon's code. To fix this, open `addons/ofxOpenCv/src/ofxCvImage.cpp` and find the following function definition:

```
void ofxCvImage::operator = ( const IplImage* mom )
```

In this function body, find the line with this command:

```
if( mom->nChannels == cvImage->nChannels && mom->depth
== cvImage->depth )
```

Replace the preceding line with the following line:

```
if( !bAllocated || mom->nChannels == cvImage-
>nChannels && mom->depth == cvImage->depth )
```

We will demonstrate all these steps in example of using optical flow.

Optical flow

Optical flow is a **vector field** that characterizes the motion of objects between two successive frames. Simply put, it is a two-channel image where the first and second channels mean the x and y axes of the pixels shift respectively. There are many algorithms for optical flow computing. Most algorithms assume that the motion between frames is relatively small.

The applications of optical flow in interactive applications includes:

- Detecting areas of motion for tracking the user's activity. This method of motion detection is stable with ordinary nondepth cameras because it is invariant to the changing light conditions. Also, it is possible to use an average motion vector for controlling particles and other objects.

- Segmenting the image using directions of optical flow for finding and using the contours of the moving objects further.

- Using optical flow for interpolating between frames of a video. It lets you implement effects such as the famous **Flo-Mo** video effect. In general, this is the way for automating video morphing between arbitrary pairs of images. See the *Video morphing example* section.

- Implementing a video effect similar to the **datamoshing** effect by applying the optical flow data obtained from one video for shifting pixels of another video or still image. The key idea behind this is considered in the end of this section.

Consider an example of using optical flow for video morphing and warping.

Video morphing example

Let's take two images of the same size, calculate the optical flow between these, and use this data for warping the first image to the second image in correspondence with the morphing parameter morphValue in the range [0, 1]. The value 0 means no warping and value 1 means warping on the entire range of optical flow.

This is example 09-OpenCV/05-VideoMorphing.

Before running the example, fix a small bug in ofxOpenCv, as described in the information box in the *Using OpenCV functions* section.

Use the Project Generator wizard for creating an empty project with the linked ofxOpenCv addon (see the *Using ofxOpenCv* section). Then, copy images checkerBoard.png, hands1.png, and hands2.png into bin/data of the project, and copy sources of the example to the src folder.

Here, we will consider just the main parts of the code related to computing optical flow and video morphing.

Declare images in the testApp class declaration as follows:

```
ofxCvColorImage color1, color2; //First and second original images
ofxCvGrayscaleImage gray1, gray2;  //Decimated grayscaled images
ofxCvFloatImage flowX, flowY;      //Resulted optical flow
                                   //in x and y axes
```

At the beginning of the testApp::setup() function, implement loading and decimating of images. Decimating is needed for a faster computing optical flow:

```
ofImage imageOf1, imageOf2;  //Load openFrameworks' images
imageOf1.loadImage("hands1.png");
imageOf2.loadImage("hands2.png");

color1.setFromPixels( imageOf1 );  //Convert to ofxCv images
color2.setFromPixels( imageOf2 );

float decimate = 0.3;              //Decimate images to 30%
ofxCvColorImage imageDecimated1;
imageDecimated1.allocate( color1.width * decimate,
                          color1.height * decimate );

//High-quality resize
imageDecimated1.scaleIntoMe( color1, CV_INTER_AREA );
```

```
gray1 = imageDecimated1;

ofxCvColorImage imageDecimated2;
imageDecimated2.allocate( color2.width * decimate,
                          color2.height * decimate );
//High-quality resize
imageDecimated2.scaleIntoMe( color2, CV_INTER_AREA );
gray2 = imageDecimated2;
```

Now continue the `testApp::setup()` function body, and compute optical flow using the **Farneback**'s method. Currently, it is the most stable optical flow algorithm in OpenCV. The resulting optical flow `flow` is held as a two-channel image, so we split it into two separate images `flowX` and `flowY`, that we declared earlier:

```
Mat img1( gray1.getCvImage() );    //Create OpenCV images
Mat img2( gray2.getCvImage() );
Mat flow;                          //Image for flow
//Computing optical flow
calcOpticalFlowFarneback( img1, img2, flow,
                          0.7, 3, 11, 5, 5, 1.1, 0 );
//Split flow into separate images
vector<Mat> flowPlanes;
split( flow, flowPlanes );
//Copy float planes to ofxCv images flowX and flowY
IplImage iplX( flowPlanes[0] );
flowX = &iplX;
IplImage iplY( flowPlanes[1] );
flowY = &iplY;
```

For improving the sensitivity of detecting larger motions between images, it is desirable to smooth the images before computing optical flow, especially when input images are binary or have hard edges.

In `testApp::draw()`, we draw the original images and then draw optical flow as blue lines. For this purpose, we use optical flow values:

```
float *flowXPixels = flowX.getPixelsAsFloats();
float *flowYPixels = flowY.getPixelsAsFloats();
```

Now let's check the optical flow. Run the project.

> If you run the project, it might crash with an error in line `flowX = &iplX` if you didn't fix the small bug in ofxOpenCv yet. Fix it as it described in information box in the *Using OpenCV functions* section.

At the top of the screen, you will first see an image with an overlaid optical flow, and the second image just for reference:

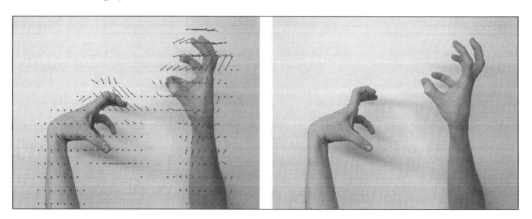

Note that in general, the optical flow is computed correctly. Now let's continue our consideration and see how to morph using the computed optical flow.

Using optical flow for morphing

Morphing will be implemented as warping using the remap() function, discussed in the *Geometrical transformations of images* section. So, we need to construct ofxCvFloatImage images mapX and mapY, which point how to do warping in the x and y axes. For this purpose, we will use optical flow and the morphing value morphValue:

```
mapX.allocate( w, h );      //w and h is size of gray1 image
mapY.allocate( w, h );
//Get pointers to pixels data
float *flowXPixels = flowX.getPixelsAsFloats();
float *flowYPixels = flowY.getPixelsAsFloats();
float *mapXPixels = mapX.getPixelsAsFloats();
float *mapYPixels = mapY.getPixelsAsFloats();
for (int y=0; y<h; y++) {
  for (int x=0; x<w; x++) {
      int i = x + w * y;        //index
      mapXPixels[ i ] = x + flowXPixels[ i ] * morphValue;
      mapYPixels[ i ] = y + flowYPixels[ i ] * morphValue;
  }
}
//Notify that pixels values were changed
mapX.flagImageChanged();
mapY.flagImageChanged();
```

Now we can perform warping. The most important thing here is that our mapping (mapX, mapY) is direct, whereas the remap() function uses inverse mapping. So, we inverse it using our own function inverseMapping(mapX, mapY), see the function definition in the project's code. Now for warping, we just need to resize the mappings to the original images' size and perform remap() as follows:

```
//bigMapX and bigMapY have type ofxCvFloatImage
int W = color1.width;
int H = color1.height;
bigMapX.allocate( W, H );
bigMapY.allocate( W, H );
bigMapX.scaleIntoMe( mapX, CV_INTER_LINEAR );
bigMapY.scaleIntoMe( mapY, CV_INTER_LINEAR );
multiplyByScalar( bigMapX, 1.0 * W / w );
multiplyByScalar( bigMapY, 1.0 * H / h );

//Do warping
morph = color1;
morph.remap( bigMapX.getCvImage(), bigMapY.getCvImage() );
```

Let's see how it works. Run the project and look at the bottom of the screen. You will see the result of morphing between the first and second images. Move the mouse from left to right to change the morphing parameter. You will see how the hands on the first image continuously change their shape to the shape of the hands from the second image:

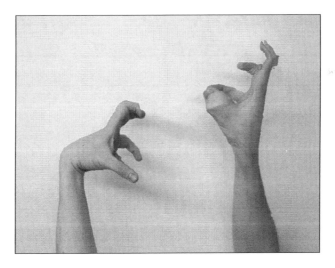

The morphing result is quite good. But you can see some undesirable effects in the resultant image. There are several reasons for this: decimation of images before optical flow computing, mistakes in the resultant optical flow, and roughness of the `inverseMapping()` function. However, this method is automatic, so it can be used in interactive projects for creating strange and interesting effects.

> In our example, we have morphed just the geometry of the first image to match the shape of the second image. For morphing the colors of objects, you need to morph the second image too, and then blend the colors using the `morphValue` parameter.

Applying morphing to another image

Having computed optical flow, you can use it for morphing any other image, not necessarily the first input image. This is really a very interesting effect—you will see how morphing reveals the structure of the original moving hands in this arbitrary image. Try it in our example by pressing 2. For returning to the original morphing view, press 1. You will see the result of morphing for a checkerboard image:

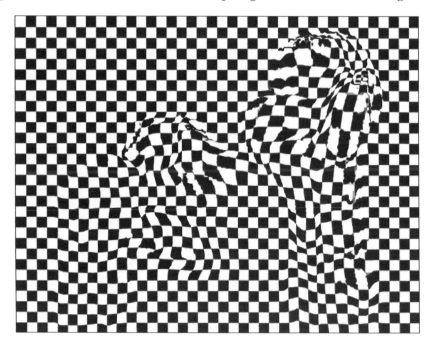

In this example, we are applying optical flow for shifting pixels on the fixed checkerboard image. However, you can apply this transformation to a warped image obtained at the last warping step. Then you will see the "smudge" of the original image, which looks like the datamoshing effect widely used in "glitch" videos.

Summary

In this chapter, we learned how to use the ofxOpenCv addon for finding motion areas in the video, and how to correct perspective distortions for restoring images of planar rectangular surfaces. Also, we saw how to detect bright objects in the image and mark their centers. Finally, we learned to use native OpenCV functions for computing optical flow. We also covered how to use optical flow for video morphing.

In the next chapter, we will consider how to use depth cameras. Compared to ordinary cameras, depth cameras let you analyze real scenes easily and with more stability.

10
Using Depth Cameras

A depth camera measures the distance from its sensor to objects and provides us with information about the 3D scene it sees. Using this information, it is easy to analyze and recognize 3D objects in the scene, including humans and their body parts. So today, depth cameras are the most used sensors for providing touchless interactions in most of the interactive projects. In this chapter, we will learn how to use depth cameras in openFrameworks projects using the ofxOpenNI addon. Also, we will consider the example of using depth images for making a flat surface such as a wall, a table, or a floor interactive.

The topics covered are as follows:

- Depth camera basics
- Installing the ofxOpenNI addon
- ofxOpenNI examples
- Creating interactive surface

Depth camera basics

The depth camera is a camera device that captures depth images. The value of a depth image pixel is not equal to light's brightness, or color, but equal to a distance from the camera to the corresponding part of the object. The main types of such cameras are the following:

- **Time-of-flight camera**: It emits a laser beam and waits for this signal to come back. By measuring the time between emission and receipt of the beam, and using the known speed of light, it computes the distance to an object. Such cameras work in light and dark environments and have high accuracy. One class of such cameras is relatively slow and is used for exact geo-measuring and 3D scanning of big areas. Another class of these cameras, such as Panasonic D-Imager, works in real time and is widely used for interactive applications at indoor and outdoor scenes.

- **Passive stereo camera**: It consists of two or more visible-light cameras, which are a little separated in space and precisely aligned. The cameras capture frames, and then calculate stereo correspondence between their pixels for estimating the distance to the objects using the **parallax** effect. Stereo cameras are used in a big variety of applications such as outdoor robotics and surgery assistance. They capture objects in the visible light, so they work in all the scenes with good lighting. Due to the nature of stereo correspondence, the measuring accuracy of such cameras decreases with distance.

- **Active infrared stereo camera**: It uses a low energy infrared laser for projecting a pseudo random dots pattern on objects and then capturing it with an infrared camera.

 The human eye does not see the infrared light, so you never see the dots without an equipment, for example a camera on your mobile phone.

A depth image is computed using stereo correspondence between the projected pattern and the captured image. The measuring accuracy of such cameras decreases with distance like in the passive case. They work perfectly in indoor locations in light and dark environments.

Because of using the low energy lasers, such cameras do not work in outdoor environment with direct sunlight. Also, they poorly see transparent objects such as glasses, and light sources such as lamps.

Today, they are the cheapest cameras, used for entertainment and gesture-controlled applications, and also for many kinds of robotics and interactive experiments.

In this chapter, we will consider only the active infrared stereo cameras. They work in indoor space, have advanced SDK (OpenNI), and cost about $200. Time-of-flight real-time cameras and passive stereo cameras can be considered more powerful, because they can work in outdoor space, but currently their price starts from $1800.

It is expected that Microsoft Kinect 2 will be a cheap time-of-flight camera

Active infrared stereo cameras

There are several depth camera lines from different vendors: Microsoft Kinect, Asus Xtion, and PrimeSense Carmine, and each vendor, in its turn, has several camera models. Most of the cameras used today have the following characteristics:

- Stable ranging distance is from 80 cm to 4 m (also, some cameras can work in the near mode, ranging from 40 cm).

- The output depth image resolution is 640×480 pixels at 30 FPS. The accuracy of depth measuring depends on the distance to the object, but the average value is 2 cm.

- The field of view is 57 degrees, so it sees a horizontal object with a length of 1 m from a distance of 1 m.

- Additionally, the camera can include an ordinary color web-camera and microphones for audio capturing.

The most notable differences between cameras are in connectivity and size. Microsoft Kinect connects to USB 2.0 and USB 3.0, but is quite big. Asus Xtion and PrimeSense Carmine are smaller and hence are more convenient for mounting, but currently have some issues when connecting to USB 3.0.

The depth images from these cameras can be used for 3D scene analysis, including human body recognition and analysis of hand gestures. These capabilities are implemented in the open cross-platform library **OpenNI** developed by not-for-profit consortium OpenNI (Open Natural Interface), `http://www.openni.org`.

OpenNI, and particularly its subpart called **NiTE**, is centered on analyzing and recognizing humans' postures and gestures. If you need any other 3D-objects' processing capabilities, such as searching specific objects like spheres and cylinders, or stitching data from multiple depth images, you should additionally use the **PCL** library. This is an open library for working with 3D point clouds, obtained from depth images.

Appearance of new depth cameras is expected in the near future. We believe that the major principles discussed in the chapter will be applicable to these cameras too.

The simplest way of using OpenNI in the openFrameworks project is by linking the ofxOpenNI addon. Let's discuss how to install the addon and explain its examples.

Let's note, openFrameworks has core addon ofxKinect for working with Microsoft Kinect cameras. Currently it does not use OpenNI. This addon is good for the projects which use depth image or 3D point cloud obtained from camera. For details, see the openFrameworks' example `examples/addons/kinectExample`. In this chapter we will use OpenNI-based solution (implemented in the ofxOpenNI addon), because it has additional capabilities like tracking users and recognizing gestures, and works with all depth cameras models.

Installing the ofxOpenNI addon

The ofxOpenNI addon was originally developed by Matthew Gingold. The addon wraps the basic OpenNI capabilities, including the following:

- Getting a depth image
- Getting a color image if the web camera is included in your depth camera model
- Tracking the hands (namely, the wrist position) for use in gesture applications
- Tracking human bodies, getting their silhouettes and skeleton point positions

Also, it supports several depth cameras simultaneously.

Currently, ofxOpenNI is a non-core addon, so you need to download and install it yourself. To do it, perform the following steps:

1. Download the ofxOpenNI addon from the site `http://ofxaddons.com`.

 Currently, the addon's page with the download button **Download ZIP** is located at `https://github.com/gameoverhack/ofxOpenNI`.

2. Unzip the file, rename the folder to `ofxOpenNI`, and move it to the `addons` folder of your openFrameworks installation.

3. Read the *Drivers & getting the examples to work* section of the README file included in the addon's folder. It contains detailed step-by-step information on installing required components, including OpenNI and camera drivers for your operating system (Windows, Mac OS X, or Linux). It also contains information on running the examples.

 Current version of addon is written for openFrameworks 0.7.4. It works with openFrameworks 0.8.0 in Mac OS X seamlessly, but does not work in Windows, and probably has issues with Linux. So if at the time of reading this, the addon is still not updated for using with openFrameworks 0.8.0, you need to use it with the older version of openFrameworks, 0.7.4. Download it from the **older releases** page at `http://www.openframeworks.cc/download/older.html`.

Currently, the addon is not supported by the Project Generator wizard, which is used for creating new openFrameworks projects. So the simplest way of creating your project with ofxOpenNI is by using its examples as starting sketches. If you need to use another core or non-core addon in the project, then add it manually. See *Appendix A, Working with Addons* for details.

Let's consider ofxOpenNI's capabilities by looking at examples included in it.

ofxOpenNI examples

The addon includes a number of examples, exploring basic depth camera and OpenNI capabilities. The examples are short, self-explanatory, and well commented. There are three groups of examples: working with depth images, tracking hands, and tracking users. Let's discuss them.

Currently, the ofxOpenNI addon holds examples in an "almost ready form". You need to construct the desired example by copying the source files and libraries in one folder. It's not very comfortable but is quite simple. Please see the *Drivers & getting the examples to work* section of the README file inside the addon's folder for details.

When you compile an ofxOpenNI example under Mac OS X for the first time, you can get the following compiler error:

`The specified SDK "Current OS X" does not appear to have all of the necessary headers installed...`

To fix the error, you need to install the `Command Line Tools` package in Xcode. Namely, go to the Xcode menu, click on **Preferences...**, and go to the **Downloads** pane. Select the **Command Line Tools** item and click on the **Install** button.

Working with examples of depth images

There are two examples that demonstrate grabbing and visualizing of depth images. The following examples can be used as starting points for the projects, which require just raw depth images or 3D point clouds, without hands or user's body tracking:

- The `ImageAndDepth-Simple` example draws depth and color images on the screen. All the work with the depth camera is done using the `openNIDevice` object having the type `ofxOpenNI`.

If you press the *I* key, the infrared images will be shown instead of the color images. Using this capability, you can use the depth camera just like the infrared camera. By closing the laser hole and adding an infrared light source with the corresponding wavelength, you can build an infrared-based sensing solution.

- The `ImageAndDepthMultDevice-Medium` example shows the depth and color images like in the previous example, but here both the images are pixel-to-pixel aligned. Using this, you can, for example, use depth data for creating a mask for the color image for removing the background and a depth-based chroma-keying effect. Such an alignment is enabled by the `openNIDevice.setRegister( true )` function. For comparing the aligned and non-aligned modes, press the *T* key. Also, this example works with all the depth cameras connected to your computer and shows all of them on the screen.

> Because of big data rates, you should connect each depth camera to a different USB hub. Most of the computers have just two hubs. For connecting the third camera, you need to buy an additional PCI-e USB hub.

Hand-tracking examples

The following two examples show how to detect and track hands. You can use them as a starting point for your own interactive drawing projects:

> Note that currently the hand tracking examples stop tracking new hands after about 30 hands are tracked. So use hand tracking via ofxOpenNI just for testing and learning, and in more serious projects, use the corresponding OpenNI functions directly, without the addon.

- The `HandTracking-Simple` example shows how to enable and use hand detection and tracking. It searches for wrists in the depth image and marks them with red rectangles. Actually, the OpenNI algorithm does not use human skeleton tracking for searching hands, but just searches for them in depth map singularities, which can be hand wrists, and then tracks their movement. So you can deceive the algorithm by exposing some moving things in front of the camera.

  The tracked hand is retrieved in the example using the `ofxOpenNIHand` object by the following line:

  ```
  ofxOpenNIHand &hand = openNIDevice.getTrackedHand(i);
  ```

  Then its coordinate on the screen is obtained as a hand.

  ```
  ofPoint &handPosition = hand.getPosition();
  ```

The x and y point coordinates of `handPosition` are pixel coordinates of the hand in the depth image, and the z coordinate is a distance between the camera and the hand in millimeters.

 If you need a 3D position of the hand in millimeters relative to the camera, use the `hand.getWorldPosition()` function that returns the `ofPoint` object.

- The `HandTracking-Medium` example tracks hands, and also cuts some portion of the depth image around each tracked hand and draws it in separate images in the bottom part of the screen.

User tracking examples

User tracking is the most advanced feature of OpenNI, which is used in many interactive wall installations. It is demonstrated in the following examples:

 Note that currently the user tracking examples track only the first user and then don't detect new users. So use the user tracking capability via ofxOpenNI just for testing and learning, and in more serious projects, use the corresponding OpenNI functions directly, without the addon.

- The `UserAndCloud-Simple` example shows how to enable a user's body tracking and draw the user's silhouette and his/her 3D skeleton. When OpenNI detects some object as the user's body, which has the size of a human body, the object moves and is separated from the other objects in the depth image. After such a detection, the 3D model of the human body consisting of a number of joined cylinders is fitted to the found object. So we obtain a 3D skeleton, representing the body as a number of points (head, torso, shoulders, elbows, hands, hips, knees, and feet).

- The `UserAndCloud-Medium` example shows the 3D point-cloud of the tracked user body in 3D, which is colored using the data from the color camera.

There is one more example, `ONIRecording-Simple`. It demonstrates how to record and play `ONI` files and store data from the depth cameras. Such files simplify the testing of algorithms: you can prepare test recordings and then tune algorithms using them instead of the real depth cameras.

Now consider the example of using depth data for tracking objects on flat surfaces.

Creating interactive surface

A depth image can be used for detecting the presence of an object on any rectangular flat surface, such as a rectangular part of a wall, a table, or a floor. Coupled with a projector or a TV panel, it lets us create an interactive system, sensitive to hands or feet, which move near the surface without touching.

The easiest way to make such a projector-camera interactive system is the following:

1. If you are using a projector for creating a surface, fix it and turn it on to obtain a picture on a wall, table, or floor. If you are using a TV panel, turn it on.

2. Direct the depth camera to see the whole picture from the projector or TV and fix the camera's position. There is no need to place the camera in a way that the whole image occupies exactly all of the camera's image frame, because at the next step, we will mark this area's corners and later use the marks for cropping.

3. Mark the corners of the surface on the color image for using these for cropping. In the following image, you can see the image in a color camera, which captures the surface. The surface here is a part of a wall with a projected picture. The room is darkened, so the color camera sees the area outside the projection picture as black. The surface's corners are marked manually by the user and shown in red circles:

See a similar topic in the *Perspective distortion removing example* section in *Chapter 9, Computer Vision with OpenCV.*

4. Note that because of the projector showing the screen of the program, you see an infinite "picture in picture" effect.

5. Capture and store the depth image of the clean surface, without any objects near it. We will call it the **background depth image**.

6. Now we can regularly capture depth images and subtract these values from the background depth image. The pixels with positive values in the difference image indicate that some object had appeared between the background and the camera. If we crop the difference image using the corners obtained in step 2, we will obtain a rectangular image, geometrically corresponding to the original surface. Its pixel values give us the distribution of distances of all the objects over the surface. We can use this height distribution for some interactivity purposes, such as interactive wall, table, or floor.

Let's demonstrate this technology in the example of the drawing application, which draws colors on the surface with dependence on the distance from the surface to the object. This project turns your surface (the surface with the projector's picture or TV panel) into a drawing surface, responding to your hands at a distance, without touching.

This is example 10-DepthCameras/SurfacePainting.

For playing with the project, you need a depth camera, containing both depth and color sensors. If you have a depth camera with just a depth sensor, you need to change the project's code by yourself to calibrate it without the color camera's image.

The example is based on the ImageAndDepth-Simple example of ofxOpenNI.

In the testApp.h file, add the following declarations in the testApp class declaration:

```
int W, H;                   //Screen size
vector<ofPoint> corners;    //Marked corners of the surface
ofShortPixels backgroundDepth;//Background depth image

ofPixels outPixels;         //Pixels array holding current drawing
ofImage outImage;           //Output image built from outPixels

bool calibrating;   //Working mode selector - calibrate or draw
ofPoint shift;      //Point used for drawing shifted color image
```

Keep the `openNIDevice` object declaration without changing it.

The `calibrating` variable is the mode selector. If its value is `true`, the application works in the calibration mode, where the user marks corners using a mouse. If its value is `false`, the application works in the drawing mode, turning the projected image into a drawing surface.

The `setup()` function sets up the depth camera, enables its depth and color images and the alignment between them, and starts the depth camera to capture. It also allocates pixels for user drawing, and finally turns on the full screen mode. The body of the function is the following:

```
//Depth camera setup
openNIDevice.setup();
openNIDevice.addDepthGenerator();
openNIDevice.addImageGenerator();
openNIDevice.setRegister(true);    //Enable alignment
                                   //of depth and color images
openNIDevice.start();              //Start depth camera to capture

//Set up drawing variables
W = 1024;                          //Desired screen size
H = 768;
outPixels.allocate( W, H, OF_IMAGE_GRAYSCALE );
calibrating = true;                //Set calibrating mode at start
shift = ofPoint( 100, 200 );       //The value of shifting
                                   //camera's image from the corner
                                   //of the screen

//Set full screen mode
ofSetWindowShape( W, H );
ofSetFullscreen( true );
```

The `update()` function updates the depth camera for obtaining its new images, and then analyzes the depth data, only if we are in the drawing mode and the user has specified all the four calibrating corners. The result of the analysis is written to the `outPixels` values. Finally, it loads the `outPixels` data into the `outImage` image for drawing it on the screen. The body of the function is the following:

```
openNIDevice.update();    //Update depth camera
if ( !calibrating && corners.size() == 4 ) {
  //Analyze depth

  //Get current depth image
```

```
ofShortPixels &input = openNIDevice.getDepthRawPixels();

//Process pixels
int w = input.getWidth();
int h = input.getHeight();
int minV = 30;     //Minimal distance in mm
int maxV = 150;    //Maximal distance in mm
for (int Y=0; Y<H; Y++) {
  for (int X=0; X<W; X++) {
    //Process pixel (X, Y)
    //See code below
  }
}
outImage.setFromPixels( outPixels );
}
```

The two parameters, `minV` and `maxV`, set the range in millimeters around the surface. We will analyze the objects lying on the distance in this range from the surface.

For compactness, we omit the computing part in the `update()` function, after the `//Process pixel (X, Y)` line. Now let's see the remaining code and discuss it. For processing the pixel (X, Y) in screen coordinates, it computes the uniform values a and b lying in [0, 1], and then computes the pixel (x, y) in depth image coordinates using bilinear interpolation of corners with weights (a, b). It is assumed that the corners are ordered clock-wise starting from the top-left corner:

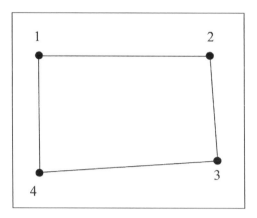

The code for this (X, Y) → (x, y) transformation is as follows:

```
//Transform screen coordinates (X, Y)
//to depth image coordinates (x, y)
float a = float(X) / W;
float b = float(Y) / H;
```

```
ofPoint p =
  (1-a) * (1-b) * corners[0]
  + a * (1-b) * corners[1]
  + a * b * corners[2]
  + (1-a) * b * corners[3];

int x = int( p.x );
int y = int( p.y );
```

Similar transformation of a whole image can be made using OpenCV functions. See the additional discussion of this method in the *Perspective distortion removing* example in *Chapter 9, ComputerVision with OpenCV*. There we use another transformation (perspective transformation), but the resulting images are very similar. The advantages of the OpenCV method is that the resulting image is anti-aliased and works faster. In this chapter, we use pixel-by-pixel computing for simplicity.

Also, you can do all the depth analysis using shaders. It will work even faster than OpenCV.

Having (x, y) coordinates, we check if it actually lies in the depth image, and then get depth values `inputZ` and `backgroundZ` from the current depth image and the background depth image correspondingly. Though the original depth values are stored as `unsigned short`, we use the `int` type because we need to subtract the values:

```
if ( x >= 0 && x < w && y >= 0 && y < h ) {
  //Getting depth values
  int inputZ = input.getPixels()[ x + w * y ];
  int backgroundZ = backgroundDepth.getPixels()[ x + w * y ];
```

Now we compute the value of `delta`, which is the difference between `backgroundZ` and `inputZ`. Also, we check if any of these values is zero: it means that the depth camera does not measure the distance in this pixel, so we should not compute the difference:

```
int delta;
//Check for zero values - it means that depth camera
//does not compute distance in the pixel
if ( inputZ != 0 && backgroundZ != 0 ) {
  delta = backgroundZ - inputZ;
}
else {
  delta = -1;
}
```

The computed value of delta is a distance between the object and the surface in millimeters. Now we check if it lies in the range between minV and maxV, and update outPixels correspondingly.

```
//Output value
if ( ofInRange( delta, minV, maxV ) ) {
  int value = ofMap( delta, minV, maxV, 0, 255, true );
  outPixels.getPixels()[ X + W * Y ] = value;
}
}
```

We finished the code of the update() function. Let's consider the draw() function. In the calibrating mode, it draws a white screen with color and depth images, and also draws marked corners on the color image. In the drawing mode, it just draws the current drawing outImage. The body of the function is the following:

```
ofBackground( 255, 255, 255 );   //Set white background

if ( calibrating ) {

  //Draw color and depth image
  ofSetColor( 255, 255, 255 );
  int w = openNIDevice.getWidth();
  int h = openNIDevice.getHeight();
  openNIDevice.drawImage( shift.x, shift.y );
  openNIDevice.drawDepth( shift.x+w+20, shift.y, w/2, h/2 );

  //Draw corners
  ofSetColor( 255, 0, 0 );
  ofFill();
  int n = corners.size();
  for (int i=0; i<n; i++) {
    ofCircle( corners[i] + shift, 10 );
  }
  if ( n == 4 ) {
    for (int i=0; i<n; i++) {
      ofLine( corners[i] + shift,
              corners[(i+1)%n] + shift );
    }
  }
}
```

```
else {
  //Show current drawing
  ofSetColor( 255, 255, 255 );
  outImage.draw( 0, 0 );
}
```

Switching between the calibrating and drawing modes will be carried out by the Space key. Also, while switching to the drawing mode, we will store the current depth image as the background depth image, backgroundDepth. This is implemented in the keyPressed() function by the following code:

```
void testApp::keyPressed(int key){
  if ( key == ' ' ) {
    calibrating = !calibrating;
    if ( !calibrating ) {      //store background
      backgroundDepth =
        openNIDevice.getDepthRawPixels();
    }
  }
}
```

Finally, we add to the body of the mousePressed() function the code for creating the corners when the mouse is clicked:

```
void testApp::mousePressed(int x, int y, int button){
  if ( calibrating && corners.size() < 4 ) {
    corners.push_back( ofPoint( x, y ) - shift );
  }
}
```

Note that we store the corners not as original (x, y) mouse coordinates, but shifted by the value of -shift, because the color image is shifted while rendering correspondingly.

The project is ready.

 Compile the project in the **Release** mode for better performance.

Now let's play with it.

Running the project

Working with the project comprises of the following steps:

1. Enable the projector or TV, and send to it the content of your screen.

2. Run the project. You will see the color and depth images on the white screen. Position the camera so that it can see the whole surface image. Then look at the depth image. It is a drawing smaller than the color image and is only used to ensure that the depth camera sees the surface properly. If the depth image is filled with some solid color—all is ok. But if the depth image has many black pixels, it means that the camera is too close or too far from the surface or the surface material is too dark, transparent, or reflecting. In this case, try to move the camera until you find a better position.

3. Use your mouse to mark four corners on the surface of the color image. It is assumed that the corners are ordered clock-wise starting from the top-left corner, as shown in the previous image. An example of the photo of such a surface with selected corners is presented as follows:

4. Note that this is the photo. The content of the screen is inside the white rectangle, where you can see the marked corners.

5. Go away from the surface and press Space. Then the application stores the current depth image as the background depth image and switches to the drawing mode.

6. Now it's time for you to enter. Go to the surface, and move the hands near it at a distance ranging from 30 mm to 150 mm (the distance range corresponds to the values of `minV` and `maxV`). You will see how your hands draw colors on the surface, resulting in a black and white abstract drawing.

Move the hands slowly, and you will obtain the picture with smoothing colors as shown in the following image:

Now move the hands faster and you will see a more stepping picture:

There are some additional notes on using this application:

- You can walk near the surface without disturbing it, because the application changes the drawing only when an object is at a distance between 30 mm and 150 mm from the surface.

- We use a low distance value equal to 30 mm (the parameter `minV` in code) instead of 0 mm, because the depth camera does not measure distances very accurately. So if you use smaller values for `minV`, it can give more noise in the resulting picture.

- Sometimes, due to small movements of the depth camera, the background image becomes inaccurate. In this case, just press Space twice. The application will switch to the calibration mode and then back to the drawing mode, and store a new background depth image.

- You may note that when you move your hand away from the surface, the tracked position of the hand does not coincide with the real hand properly. The reason is that our simple model does not take into account the relative geometrical positions of the projector and the camera. So our model works properly just near a flat surface.

 For creating a more advanced model that will detect the object's position accurately, you should not use the depth image itself, but a 3D point cloud. See the *Additional topics* section.

You can use this example as a sketch for creating interactive tables and floor games. The starting point for this is replacing the following line in the `update()` function:

```
if ( ofInRange( delta, minV, maxV ) ) {
```

with just {. In this case, the application will show not the drawing, but the current distribution of distances over the surface. This distribution is held in pixel values of `outPixels`. You can use it directly, create mask of moving objects using thresholding algorithm, and so on.

We have finished the main example of the chapter. Now we will discuss the topics suggested for further study.

Additional topics

In this chapter, we worked only with objects in screen coordinates, by just using depth values of depth images. But in many applications, you need to use the 3D point cloud, which represents the depth image points in 3D space—in the world coordinate system centered at the camera. For obtaining a 3D point cloud from the depth image, you should convert all its pixels to 3D points using the `openNIDevice.projectiveToWorld( p )` function. Namely, each pixel (x, y) should be represented as point p, where `p.x = x`, `p.y = y`, and `p.z` is equal to the value of the depth image's pixel (x, y): `p.z = openNIDevice.getDepthRawPixels()[ x + w * y ]`.

The 3D point cloud can be used for:

- Accurately modeling the distance distribution over the flat surface. See the discussion at the end of the *Creating interactive surface* section.

- Making **dynamic video mapping**, which maps a projector image exactly on a moving object such as a performer. To achieve this, you should use geometrical information of relative positions of the projector and depth camera. For details see the ofxCamaraLucida addon available at `http://ofxaddons.com`.

- Stitching data from several depth cameras by combining their point clouds for extending the area of interaction.

 For advanced knowledge on working with 3D clouds, you should see the PCL library, which is an open library focused on working with 3D point clouds.

Other topics to learn are user tracking, hand tracking, and gesture recognition. We suggest that you do this not just by exploring the ofxOpenNI source codes, but also by studying the original OpenNI library.

Summary

In this chapter, we learned how to use the ofxOpenNI addon for working with depth cameras. We explored its examples and built a simple projector-camera interactive system, which can be used as a basis for creating interactive walls, tables, and floors.

In the next chapter, we will consider using networking for creating complex and distributed interactive projects.

11
Networking

Networking provides a way for data exchange between several devices. It is a principal component that allows remote control of some parameters inside applications of mobile and tablet devices, and is also used to make interactive projects working in a synchronized manner on several computers. In this chapter, you will learn how to implement and use OSC and TCP protocols in your openFrameworks projects as follows:

- Networking basics
- Using OSC protocol
- Using TCP protocol for streaming images

Networking basics

Networking comprises a number of hardware and software technologies that provide data exchange among digital devices and even among applications inside a computer. The most popular network model today is called **TCP/IP** (**Transmission Control Protocol/Internet Protocol**). It works using wired (**LAN**—Local Area Network) or wireless (**WLAN**—Wireless LAN) connections. All the modern computers and mobile devices have support of TCP/IP.

Another networking technology is wireless ZigBee networks, widely used in physical computing projects. Connecting just two devices can be considered as the simplest network. Old but still popular technologies for wired connections are USB, serial port (RS-232), RS-485, and I2C (used for micro devices).

In this chapter, we will consider usage of TCP/IP for connecting several devices inside a **local network**. Local network is built and controlled by **network router**. A network router is a special network node working as a separate device or integrated within your laptop.

The network router gives a unique identifier, called **network address**, to each device connected to the network. The address has a form such as `192.168.0.3`, or can be a computer name, such as `My machine`. Each device can refer to itself using the address, `localhost`, or its equivalent, `127.0.0.1`. See the properties of your network adapter to find out the network address of your device. You can also request the network information using the Terminal window, by entering the `ipconfig` command (for Windows) or the `ifconfig` command (for Mac OS X and Linux).

For testing the connection between two computers with known addresses, use the `ping` command, for example, `ping 192.168.0.3`. If the connection is not established, it is probably blocked by your router's or computer's firewall or antivirus. In this case, check their settings.

> Note that the network address can vary when restarting devices and routers. So for long-term working interactive installations, you should fix the computers' addresses in their network adapter's settings, or just use computer names instead of numbered addresses.

For sending some data from one device to another, you should specify the network address of the destination device, and also the **port number**, which is an integer number between 0 and 65535. Some ports are reserved, for example, port `80` is used for HTTP protocol exchange by your browser. In the chapter examples we will use port `12345`.

Ports with high numbers (greater than 10,000) are rarely used by system services, so most probably you can use them. To find out which ports are used in your system, use special software or networking commands from Terminal. For connecting devices, we often use ports `12345`, `12346`, `12347`, and `12348`.

In this chapter we will learn how to use the following two protocols for data transmission:

- **OSC**: Open Sound Control is very simple and fast. It's appropriate for transferring small amounts of information (such as commands for changing parameters and objects' coordinates) at fast rates. It is the main protocol used in interactive installations and physical computing projects. It is supported in all the VJ-related software.

> Initially, OSC was made as a network replacement for **MIDI**, which is a wired protocol for connecting musical instruments. Now OSC is used for controlling a wide range of applications and devices, often not related to music.

- **TCP**: Transmission Control Protocol is capable of easily transferring a large amount of data. It is a universal protocol. In this chapter we will see an example of using it for image streaming.

Let's start with OSC protocol.

Using OSC protocol

OSC is an extremely popular protocol for sending control commands and parameters between devices and applications. It is a protocol in which there is no confirmation of the data exchange success, that is, the sender doesn't know if the receiver received the data, and the receiver does not know if somebody sent something to it. As a result, data can be lost without any notification to the sender and the receiver. Though, in a local network such a situation is very rare and occurs only if you are using extremely fast frame rates for sending data.

OSC is a thin layer on the UDP protocol. For more information, read about UDP specification.

For using OSC capabilities in openFrameworks projects, you need to use the ofxOsc addon. This is a **core addon** included in openFrameworks distribution.

We suggest that the first time you try OSC, play with openFrameworks examples `oscSenderExample` and `oscReceiveExample`, located in openFrameworks's folder `examples/addons`. Run both of them on one PC, and then move the mouse over the `oscSenderExample` window. You will see that `oscReceiveExample` receives mouse coordinates and writes them on its screen.

To use the addon in your project, you have three options:

- Start a new project by copying `oscSenderExample` or `oscReceiveExample` into your projects folder. This way is the simplest and the best for the first trial of OSC.

- Create a new project with Project Generator wizard by specifying the ofxOsc addon. See *Appendix A, Working with Addons* for details.

- Link all the files inside the `addons/ofxOsc` folder to your project and specify their paths. This is the method for adding OSC support to the existing project.

Now you have the project with the linked ofxOsc addon, and can send and receive data using OSC protocol.

Sending data

For sending data with OSC in your project, perform the following steps:

1. Add the `#include "ofxOsc.h"` line in the `testApp.h` file right after the `#include "ofMain.h"` line.

2. Declare the sender object that will send the OSC data by adding the `ofxOscSender sender;` line in the `testApp` class definition.

3. Initialize the sender in the `testApp::setup()` function by using the following line:

   ```
   sender.setup("localhost", 12345 );
   ```

   The first argument of the `sender.setup()` function is a string containing the receiver's address. `localhost` is the address of the computer itself, so, `sender` will send data to some other application running on the same computer. For sending data to another device, you must know its address and specify it, for example, `192.168.0.3`. The second integer argument is the port of the receiver. We use `12345` because it is not normally used by the operating systems for any special purposes.

4. When you need to send some data, create the OSC message as an object of the type `ofxOscMessage`, specify its address, fill it with a parameter or parameters, and finally send the message using `sender.sendMessage()`:

   ```
   ofxOscMessage m;
   m.setAddress( "/volume" );
   m.addFloatArg( 0.4f );
   sender.sendMessage( m );
   ```

   The address of the message is not the receiver's network address. It is just the name of a parameter that can be understood by the receiver. The address begins with / and can contain several / symbols if needed, for example, `/object1/velocity`.

   The message can contain one of the several arguments of the following types: `float`, `int`, and `string`. The arguments are attached to the message sequentially by calling the corresponding functions: `m.addFloatArg()`, `m.addIntArg()`, and `m.addStringArg()`. For example:

   ```
   m.addFloatArg( 0.4f );
   m.addIntArg( 1 );
   m.addStringArg( "start" );
   ```

The most used types of arguments are the float values in the range [0, 1]. They are naturally linked to VJ controllers and other equipments via software platforms such as VDMX and Max/MSP. Also, integer values are used for representing a button state (0 - disabled, 1 - enabled).

You can have several senders sending data to many destinations.

We suggest storing destination address and port numbers in an external `.xml` file placed in the `data` folder of your project. We call this file `settings.xml`. Add the operations for reading the values of the destination address and the port number to the `testApp::setup()` function and use these values as parameters of `sender.setup()`. This method gives you the flexibility to run the project in different network configurations without recompiling it.

Use the ofxXmlSettings addon which works with `.xml` files. Learn how to use it in the openFrameworks example: `examples/addons/xmlSettingsExample`.

Please note the following rules:

- Be careful not to send messages too fast because they can be lost. Normally, sending at 30 or 60 fps works well.

- If you need to send many messages at once, a good idea is to combine them into one bunch using the `ofxOscBundle` object. Just create an object of this type, add to it your `ofxOscMessage` messages, and send it:

```
ofxOscBundle bundle;
bundle.addMessage( m );    //First ofxOscMessage message
bundle.addMessage( m2 );   //Second message
//...
sender.sendBundle( bundle );   //Send bundle
```

- OSC packets are limited in size. The maximum size depends on the operating system and network settings, but normally it is not less than 500 bytes. If the limit value exceeds, your OSC packets can frequently get lost. So do not send messages and bundles containing much information. Note that all the data, including numbers, is stored in an OSC packet in text form.

Receiving data

For receiving data with OSC in your project, perform the following steps:

1. Add the `#include "ofxOsc.h"` line in the `testApp.h` file right after the `#include "ofMain.h"` line.

2. Declare the receiver object which will receive OSC data by adding the `ofxOscReceiver receiver;` line in the `testApp` class definition.

3. Start the receiver in the `testApp::setup()` function by using the following line:

   ```
   receiver.setup( 12345 );
   ```

   The argument of the `receiver.setup()` function is the integer value of port number.

    If you need to use several receivers on one computer, you should specify different ports for each of them.

4. Now you should wait for the messages that are incoming to the `receiver` and parse them. The best practice is to do it in the `testApp::update()` function in a `while` loop:

   ```
   while ( receiver.hasWaitingMessages() ){
     //Get the next message
     ofxOscMessage m;
     receiver.getNextMessage( &m );
     //Parse message, for example:
     if ( m.getAddress() == "/volume" ){
       //Get first argument
       float volume = m.getArgAsFloat( 0 );
       //...
       //Use volume value, for example:
       sound.setVolume( volume )
     }
   };
   ```

   You can get the values of arguments in the message m using the functions `m.getArgAsFloat( index )`, `m.getArgAsInt32( index )`, and `m.getArgAsString( index )`, where `index` is the argument's index, 0 – first, 1- second, and so on. For getting the number of attributes, use the `m.getNumArgs()` function, which returns the value of attributes in `m`.

Let's look at some typical schemes for using your projects with other applications by connecting them using OSC.

Typical schemes of OSC usage

Typical usage of OSC is the following:

- Use Apple iPad or other tabletops for sending commands such as saving screenshots to disk or controlling parameters such as particles' velocity. You need to install on your tabletop an application such as TouchOSC, which will send OSC messages from your device to your openFrameworks' project.

- Use your openFrameworks application as a tracker, which obtains some information from the world (for example, use depth camera for computing coordinates of the user's body parts), and send it to Max/MSP, VDMX, QuartzComposer, TouchDesigner, or Unity3D for generating sounds and visuals.

For more complex schemes, you need to use an OSC-manager application, which routes OSC signals, such as OSCulator.

While OSC is well-supported by all the creative coding and VJ software, it cannot easily transmit big data such as images. So let's consider how to do it with another protocol, for example, the TCP.

Using TCP protocol for streaming images

TCP is the basis for all the Internet protocols, for example, HTTP. This is an error-checking protocol, which guarantees obtaining valid data and notifying errors. This makes it appropriate for sending big volumes of data from computers, not only in your local network, but also around the world.

For working with TCP in openFrameworks, you need to use the ofxNetwork addon.

> We suggest that the first time, you should try TCP with openFrameworks examples: `networkTcpServerExample` and `networkTcpClientExample`, located in openFrameworks's folder `examples/addons`. Run both of them on one PC, and then activate the window of `networkTcpClientExample` and press some keys. You will see that the keys will be sent to `networkTcpServerExample` and printed on its screen.

For linking the ofxNetwork addon, there are three options similar to the ofxOsc addon. Check the beginning of the *Using OSC protocol* section for details.

The scheme of working with TCP is based on the client-server technology. In one application, you need to create and start a server using the `ofxTCPServer server` object. In another application, you need to create a client using the `ofxTCPClient client` object, and establish a connection with the server. After this, you can send string messages and raw data bytes from client to server and from server to client. There can be several clients connecting to one server.

In principle, using the ofxNetwork addon, you can implement your own HTTP or FTP server and do anything such as downloading files from Internet. Though, for serious projects, we strongly recommend not to do this by yourself, because TCP is a very low-level protocol for this. Instead, use some ready-made addons or special libraries for this. Also, openFrameworks core contains several classes, which could be useful for your needs:

- If you need to download images from the Internet, you can use the `image.loadImage( url )` function, where `url` is a string specifying URL of an image. Note that it pauses the application execution until the image is downloaded. So, to download the image without pausing (called **asynchronously**), see the openFrameworks example: `examples/graphics/imageLoaderWebExample`.

- To download arbitrary files, you can use the `ofURLFileLoader` class. We will not consider it in this book.

- To work with HTTP requests and responses, see the functions in the `libs/openFrameworks/utils/ofURLFileLoader.h` file. It's also out side the scope of this book.

We will not consider `ofxTCPServer` and `ofxTCPClient` classes in the detail, but we will include an extremely useful example of using it for streaming images between applications by working on the same or different computers.

The streaming images example

Let's consider an example that demonstrates sending images between applications using TCP. It consists of two projects—the sender and the receiver.

 The example consists of two projects, `networkImageSender` and `networkImageReceiver`. They are located in folders `11-Networking/networkImageSender` and `11-Networking/networkImageReceiver` of the book's examples.

These two example projects are presented by a number of source `.h` and `.cpp` files. Read the beginning of the `testApp.h` files for detailed instructions on how to create openFrameworks projects from these sources.

Compile and run both the projects. The sender will grab camera images and send them to the receiver. Both projects draw current images on the screen, and also show the current frame's ID. Additionally, the receiver shows the frame rate of the images received (it depends not only on networking, but also on the real frame rate of the camera):

The sender and the receiver use the `ofxTCPServer` and `ofxTCPClient` classes for sending and receiving images as uncompressed arrays. See the details of its implementation in the `pbNetwork.h` and `pbNetwork.cpp` files, which are included in each of the example's projects.

You can use this example as a sketch for your own projects when you need to send big amounts of information between applications.

We often use such technology in our interactive installations and performances. We mount two PCs, a **Tracker**, which works with depth cameras, and a **Render**, which renders installation visuals. The Tracker gets data from several depth cameras, sticks them into a bigger depth image, and sends it to the Render via TCP. Such separation of tracking and rendering increases the overall system stability and off-loads the Render from analyzing depth data, so we can do more processing and obtain richer visualization.

Normally you can send 320 × 240 grayscale image at 30 fps using wired connections at 100 MBps. For sending bigger images, use faster network equipments, such as 1 GBps and higher. Note that we never use wireless connections during serious concerts and performances because of possible instability induced by viewers' mobile devices.

> If you need to send images from one application to another on a Mac computer, you do not need to use networking. The best option in this case is to use an open library called **Syphon**, by downloading and installing the ofxSyphon addon. This addon allows the exchange of images between openFrameworks and other applications at OpenGL level, so it works faster than networking.

Summary

In this chapter, we learned how to use OSC and TCP protocols to connect application with other applications and devices. It lets us create complex distributed interactive systems with possibilities far beyond one single openFrameworks project.

This was the final chapter of the book. In the book, we learned some of the basics of interactive multimedia. We hope you continue your investigations, realize your own projects, and break the boundaries of interactive experience!

A
Working with Addons

Addons are plugins of a specific kind for openFrameworks. Addons add new capabilities to openFramework projects, such as working with a network, depth cameras, computer vision, and others. In this chapter, we will learn the basic principles of addons' structure, and working with addons:

- Installing a non-core addon
- Linking addons to a project
- Using Project Generator
- List of selected addons

Addons basics

Though openFrameworks' core has powerful capabilities for processing and generating various kinds of multimedia data, it does not contain everything. For example, the core does not contain support for depth cameras, processing the images using the computer vision library OpenCV, or sending and receiving data via a network.

For using such capabilities in your project, you would link and use any of the C++ or C external libraries that are available on the Internet. But, each library is different so using them in your project is sometimes easy and sometimes not. Fortunately, openFrameworks has a friendly mechanism for plugging libraries to your project. Such a mechanism is called an **addon**.

Most often, an addon is a class that acts as a wrapper for a library. Also, the addon contains the library itself in a form that is ready to be linked to your project binaries. This relation is shown in the following image:

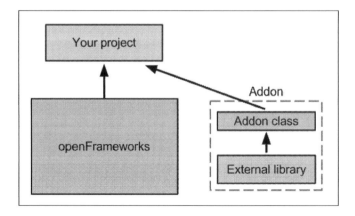

The term **wrapper** here means that it lets your project and a library communicate in some way. openFrameworks' addon mission is to simplify such a communication and do it in a standardized way (in "the openFrameworks's style"). Hence, you do not need to learn about a library interface and its usage but just learn how to use an addon, and that would be enough for most situations. So using addons accelerates project development a lot. Furthermore, when you need deeper capabilities of the library, not included in the addon, you can always access them by reaching the library objects and functions directly or through the addon's class members.

Remember, an addon is just an openFrameworks extension; it only links to a project, which is using it, but does not affect the other projects and openFrameworks itself.

Sometimes an addon is not a wrapper, but just a class that adds some new functionality without linking any new library to the project. See the following image:

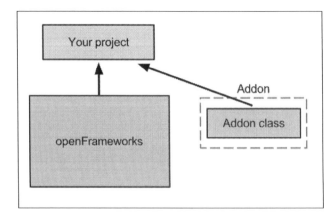

Addons in openFrameworks

Every openFrameworks's addon class name begins with `ofx`. This is an acronym for *openFrameworks extension*. For example, `ofxXmlSettings` is a class for writing and reading settings in XML files.

Addons are located in the `addons` folder of openFrameworks. The examples of addons' usage are located in the `examples/addons` folder of openFrameworks.

There are two classes of addons. The first class of addons is called **core addons** and is distributed with openFrameworks. You have the addons of this class in the `addons` folder right after installing openFrameworks. They are stable and useful addons that are needed in many interactive projects.

The second class of addons is called **non-core addons** and are available for download at `http://ofxaddons.com`. There are both mature addons as well as the ones currently in development. Please test them carefully before using them in your installations or performances. Fortunately, all the addons have open code, and you can always check and modify them. Nevertheless, sometimes addons have binary `.lib` or `.a` files; it is very difficult to find and correct errors in such addons rapidly, so again, test addons before using them.

Installing a non-core addon

To install a non-core addon into openFrameworks, perform the following steps:

1. Go to `http://ofxaddons.com`, find the desired addon and click on its name.
2. The addon's page will be opened. The page contains addon's description and downloading button. Currently download button is named **Download ZIP** and is located in the right part of the page. Press it to download the addon's archive.
3. Unpack it into the openFrameworks' `addons` folder.
4. If the name of the unpacked folder containing an addon does not match the addon's name, for example, `ofxOpenNI-master.zip`, rename the folder to the addon's name, `ofxOpenNI`.
5. If the addon's folder contains examples of its usage, it is a good idea to move the examples to the `examples/addons` folder.

The world of addons is rapidly evolving. New addons appear and are renamed regularly. The most useful non-core addons eventually become core addons. And some core addons migrate into openFrameworks core. (Then the `ofx` prefix in the class name turns into `of`). So, it would not make much sense to discuss all the existing addons because next year, the list could be totally outdated. Nevertheless, we will discuss the current core and some non-core addons in the *List of selected addons* section.

Adding new capabilities to your projects using addons is very easy and comfortable. But there are many libraries and algorithms that have not been implemented in addons yet. So if your project needs some functionality, and if there are no addons for this, don't be upset and solve the problem without addons. For example, if you need to control a new device from your project, then find its SDK, the library or example of its usage, and use it in your C++ project directly without addons.

Once you succeed in doing this, you can package your code as an addon and publish it for the openFrameworks' community by following the recommendations at `http://www.ofxaddons.com/howto/`.

Now we will talk about linking addons to your project.

Linking addons to a new project

All the core addons and most of the non-core addons have examples of their usage. So if you are starting a new project and need to use just one particular addon, the simplest way to do it is to just copy the folder containing the example of the addon into a new folder, rename the folder, and start to change the project's code for your needs.

For example, if you plan to make a project that will use XML files to store the settings in the project, then copy the folder `xmlSettingsExample` from `examples/addons` to `apps/myApps` and rename the copied `xmlSettingsExample` to `myProjectXml`. Finally, open the project inside `myProjectXml` folder and continue developing it there. The `ofxXmlSettings` class is included in the project, so you can use it.

If you need to link several addons to the new project, it is a good idea to generate an empty project with linked addons using the **Project Generator** wizard application, included in openFrameworks.

Using Project Generator

To create a new project with Project Generator, perform the following steps:

1. Run the Project Generator application. Depending on your OS, it is located in the folder `projectGenerator` or in `apps/projectGenerator`. You will see its main screen with a number of buttons as shown in the following screenshot:

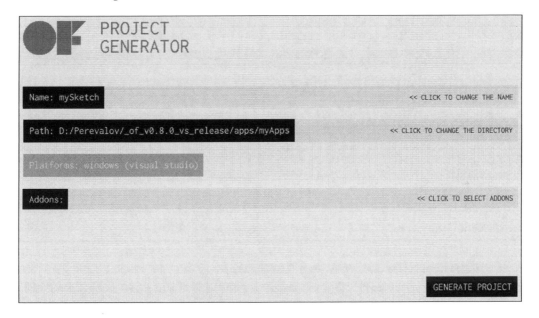

2. Click on the **Name: mySketch** button, the text input window appears. Enter the desired name for your project here, for example `myProject1`, and click on the **OK** button.

3. If you want, click on the **Path: ...** button and select a folder for your project.

4. Now, click on the **Addons:** button. You will see a window with the list of addons currently installed in the `addons` folder:

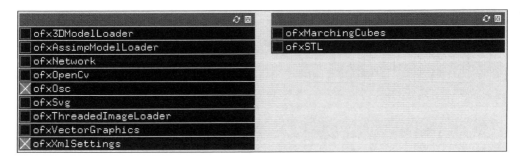

5. On the left-hand side, you will see the list of core addons, and on the right-hand side, you will see the list of non-core addons. Note that if you have not installed any addons by yourself yet, the list to the right will be empty.

6. Select the addons you need for your project by checking the corresponding checkboxes. For example, if we want to use the OSC protocol and xml files, check the **ofxOSC** and **ofxXmlSettings** boxes:

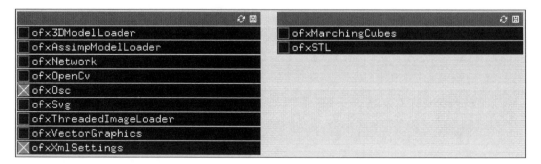

7. Click on the **<< Back** button and you will return to the generator's main screen.

8. Click on the **GENERATE PROJECT** button to generate a new project. Once generated, at the bottom of the generator's screen, you will see the text, **generated: [path to our project]**.

9. By now, the project is generated and the addons are linked to the project but to use addons, we should add the #include directives of these header files. So the next step is to open the generated project and add the corresponding #include directives for the addons. Normally, the name of the included file for the addon is exactly the addon's name with the .h suffix. In our example, we should add the following lines after the line #include "ofMain.h" in the testApp.h file:

```
#include "ofxOsc.h"
#include "ofxXmlSettings.h"
```

10. Now, you can continue developing and using all the addons you linked to the project.

There is one tricky thing regarding the linking of non-core addons; there is a dependence between the addons. That is, some addons may require other addons for their work. So if you link such an addon and try to compile the project without the required addons, you will get compiler errors. Fortunately, you can discover which addons you are missing by reading the compiler error message. For example, an error text such as **Cannot open include file: 'ofxSTL.h': No such file or directory** means that you are missing the ofxSTL addon. To resolve the problem, you need to install all the missing addons, restart Project Generator, select all the needed addons, and generate the project again.

Linking an addon to an existing project

If you are working on the project and suddenly realize that you need to link an addon, don't worry. You can do it at any time by performing the following steps:

1. If the addon is not installed in the `addons` folder yet, download and install it by following instructions from the *Installing a non-core addon* section.

2. Add all the `.h`, `.cpp`, and `.lib` or `.a` files from the `src` and `lib` folders of the addon to your development environment's project.

3. If necessary, add paths to the addon's folder and all its subfolders into the project's settings.

 Most addons contain the file `install.xml` in their folders. This file describes the exact information about linking an addon for each platform. By the way, Project Generator uses this information to link an addon. You can read this file and follow its information to link the addon yourself.

Note, for adding paths to addon's folder in openFrameworks's project for Linux, you need to just add line with the addon's name in `addons.make` file in the project's folder. See details at `http://www.openframeworks.cc/setup/linux-codeblocks/`.

List of selected addons

Here we will list some of the most useful addons (selected just by our opinion). Remember, there are many more great addons adding functionality in the various areas of multimedia and interactivity, so search and explore them.

Some of the core addons are:

- **ofxXmlSettings**: It reads and writes data from and to XML files. It's very useful for storing project settings such as screen size, frame rate, number of camera, and physics constants.

- **ofxGui**: It contains a number of interface elements for creating a number of buttons and sliders on the screen.

- **ofxOsc**: It lets you send and receive short amount of data with **OSC** protocol messages via the network. It is a way of communicating with other applications written in openFrameworks, Processing, Max/MSP, and other software such as VDMX and TouchOSC. See details of it in *Chapter 11, Networking*.

- **ofxNetwork**: It lets you send and receive TCP protocol messages, and it can send huge amount of data such as images via the network. See details of it in *Chapter 11, Networking*.

- **ofxOpenCv**: It is the wrapper for the computer vision library, OpenCV. See details of it in *Chapter 9, Computer Vision with OpenCV*.

- **ofxKinect**: It is addon for working with Microsoft Kinect depth camera. See its details in *Chapter 10, Using Depth Cameras*.

- **ofxSvg**: It loads and renders vector graphics from the SVG file format. This addon is useful when you need to draw vector-based graphics.

- **ofxVectorGraphics**: It creates PS files with your drawings. These are vector files used for high-quality printing.

- **ofx3DModelLoader**: It loads and renders 3D models in the 3DS file format. It is an easy way to work with static 3D objects in your project. However, the addon is too simple for serious use so for advanced 3D models rendering, you need other addons such as ofxAssimpModelLoader.

- **ofxAssimpModelLoader**: It loads and renders 3D models, including animated models.

- **ofxThreadedImageLoader**: It loads and renders images from files or the Web in a separate thread so your application will not pause while the image is loading.

Some of the non-core addons are:

- **ofxOpenNI**: It is the wrapper for the OpenNI library, working with depth cameras. See its details in *Chapter 10, Using Depth Cameras*.

- **ofxMarchingCubes**: It implements the Marching Cubes algorithm for rendering isosurfaces in 3D. This addon needs the ofxSTL addon to work.

- **ofxSyphon**: Currently this addon is only for Mac OS X. It is a wrapper on the **Syphon** protocol for interchanging images among applications on the same computer. We often use this addon by sending screen from openFrameworks project to VDMX.

Summary

In this chapter, we learned what addons are, how to install them in openFrameworks, and how to link them to your project. A shortlist of the most useful addons was also given.

There are lots of interesting and useful addons, so take some time to install addons, play with their examples, and read their source code. In this way, you will get ideas for new projects, develop ideas on how to improve existing projects, and learn something new about libraries and the technology of programming in general.

B

Perlin Noise

Perlin noise is the algorithm for generating a series of slowly changing random values that behave just like the parameters of live motion of a living creature. It is one of the most used algorithms in computer graphics. It is used for random object movement, texture generation, and so on. Many examples in the book are essentially based on using Perlin noise. In this appendix, we will find out what Perlin noise is and how to use it in openFrameworks projects; we will cover the following topics:

- Perlin noise basics
- Using the ofNoise() function
- Space-coherent noise

Perlin noise basics

Perlin noise is the algorithm used for computing values of a pseudo-random function, smoothly depending on its parameters. It was originally developed in 1982 by Ken Perlin and named after him. Today, it's called **classical noise**. In 2001, Ken Perlin developed a modification of the algorithm and called it **simplex noise**. Simplex noise works faster than classical noise, but the results differ a little.

Nowadays both noises are widely used. Often it is not very important which algorithm is used in a given case; that's why we will refer to both of them as just **Perlin noise**.

For a developer, the Perlin noise function `ofNoise( t )` just takes values in the range [0, 1] and depends on the parameter t. The dependence is smooth; that is, a small change in the value of the input parameter t leads to a small change in the output result. But, unlike any other mathematical function such as `sin( t )` or `exp( t )`, Perlin noise is not periodic and is not constantly increasing. It has complex and non-repetitive behavior, which is called **pseudo-random behavior**. That is, on one hand it is a function that seems random, and on the other hand it is fixed. No matter how many times you compute `ofNoise( t )` for the given t, you will obtain exactly the same result.

The main advantage of Perlin noise compared to an ordinary pseudo-random number generator, `ofRandom( a, b )`, is the controllable smoothness. Indeed, if we will consider float values `A0 = ofNoise( t )`, `A1 = ofNoise( t+0.01 )`, and `A2 = ofNoise( t+0.1 )` for different values of t, we will find that often A1 is closer to A0 than A2. Hence we can control the resultant smoothness of the graph of `ofNoise( t )`, built for discrete set of values t, by controlling the step of incrementing these values. Contradictorily, two calls of `ofRandom( 0, 1 )` generate two **uncorrelated** numbers, and there is no way to control their proximity.

Now let's see how to use Perlin noise in openFrameworks projects.

Using the ofNoise() function

openFrameworks has a built-in implementation of simplex noise, implemented in the `ofNoise( t )` function. For example, the following code draws the Perlin noise function, `ofNoise( t )`, for t ranging from 0 to 10 on the screen:

```
ofSetColor( 0, 0, 0 );
for (int x=0; x<1000; x++) {
  float t = x * 0.01;
  float y = ofNoise( t );
  ofLine( x, 300, x, 300 - y * 300 );
}
```

 This is the example `13-PerlinNoise/01-PerlinGraph`.

Run the code and you will see the following graph:

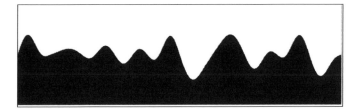

Now replace the line `float y = ofNoise( t );` with the following line:

```
float y = ofNoise( t + 493.0 );
```

This code renders the noise function in the range [443, 453].

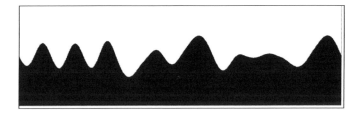

Considering the preceding graphs, you can note the following properties:

- The function values are from 0 to 1, and the mean value is clearly about 0.5. Hence you can think about the noise function as describing the fluctuation of some random parameter near its center value, equal to 0.5.

- These two graphs depict different ranges of t – [0, 10] and [443, 493]. They look different but the scales of fluctuations in t are roughly the same for both these (and actually, any other) ranges of the same width. This property is called **statistical homogeneity** and means that the statistical properties of the function in the range [t, t+Q] for any fixed and big constant Q does not depend on any particular value of t. So you can get as many random functions as you want by just considering the noise function shifted by some constant in t. For example, `ofNoise( t + 293.4 )` and `ofNoise( t + 3996.4 )` will generate two distinct and uncorrelated random values for a given t.

 An interesting feature of this noise is that its value, `ofNoise( t )`, is equal to `0.5` for all the integer values of t. So do not wonder when you obtain a constant output from `ofNoise( t )` —just check, maybe you are accidentally using integer values for t.

You can use this function for randomly changing some parameters of the objects in your project; for example, position, size, or angle. Normally, we don't use the pure ofNoise(t) function, but a more complex formula.

```
float value = amplitude * ofNoise( timePosition + position0 );
```

Here, amplitude defines the output range of the value, namely [0, amplitude]; position0 is a constant (for example, random); and timePosition is a value that increases with time.

See a simple example of the implementation of this idea for controlling sound volumes in *The singing voices example* section in *Chapter 6, Working with Sounds*. Using Perlin noise for creating a knot curve and changing its color is shown in *The twisting knot example* section in *Chapter 7, Drawing in 3D*.

Another interesting example is drawing a cloud of a hundred randomly flying points. It can be done with the following code:

```
ofSetColor( 0, 0, 0 );
float time = ofGetElapsedTimef();
for (int i=0; i<100; i++) {
  float ampX = ofGetWidth();
  float ampY = ofGetHeight();
  float speed = 0.1;
  float posX0 = i * 104.3 + 14.6;
  float posY0 = i * 53.3 + 35.2;
  float x = ampX * ofNoise( time * speed + posX0 );
  float y = ampY * ofNoise( time * speed + posY0 );
  ofCircle( x, y, 10 );
}
```

 This is example 13-PerlinNoise/02-PerlinPoints.

Here, constants 104.3, 14.6, 53.3, and 35.2 were chosen quite arbitrarily—just to obtain distinct values for posX0 and posY0. On running this, you will see a cloud of slowly flying points:

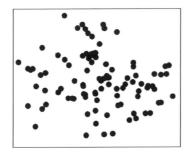

See the further evolution of this example in the *Dancing cloud example* section in *Chapter 6*, *Working with Sounds*.

By summing up several Perlin noises with different scales, it is possible to obtain more interesting noises. See the openFrameworks example in the openFrameworks' folder `examples/math/noise1dOctaveExample`. It sums up several noises and you can see the resultant function.

> There is a signed version of the `ofNoise( t )` function. It's a function called `ofSignedNoise( t )` that returns a noise value in the range [-1, 1]. The mean value of the function is zero. Actually, `ofSignedNoise( t )` is just equal to `2.0*ofNoise( t ) - 1.0`.

Now we will see how to use multidimensional Perlin noise for generating textures and other fields.

Space-coherent noise

There are a number of overloaded `ofNoise()` functions that depend on two, three, or four parameters: `ofNoise( x, y )`, `ofNoise( x, y, z )`, and `ofNoise( x, y, z, t )`. They have behavior like `ofNoise( t )` but use several input parameters. Their coordinates may be scaled as 2D or 3D space coordinates of some point and may even include time. So such functions give a way for generating 2D, 3D, and 4D fields with coherently changing values that are static or evolving with time. For example, the `ofNoise( x, y )` function can be used for drawing a smooth random texture in the following way:

```
float scaleX = 0.007;    //1.0 / scaleX is coherence in x
float scaleY = 0.008;    //1.0 / scaleY is coherence in y
```

```
float posX0 = 593.2;
float posY0 = 43.7;
for (int y=0; y<500; y++) {
  for (int x=0; x<500; x++) {
    float value = ofNoise( x*scaleX+posX0, y*scaleY+posY0 );
    ofSetColor( value*255, value*255, value*255 );
    ofRect( x, y, 1, 1 );
  }
}
```

 This is example `13-PerlinNoise/03-PerlinTexture`.

On running the code, you will see the following texture:

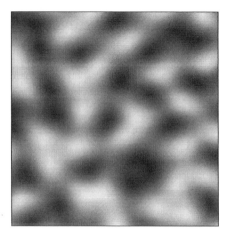

Now add the third parameter in the calling function `ofNoise()`, which increases with time, and you will obtain a texture that slowly evolves with time.

```
float value = ofNoise( x*scaleX+posX0, y*scaleY+posY0,
                       time*0.1 + 445.6 );
```

This code is simple and great for demonstrating the idea. But it works extremely slowly because we render each texture's pixel as a separate rectangle with size 1 × 1. To obtain real-time performance, prepare the texture colors in the `ofImage image` object and draw it in one step using `image.draw()` (see the *Creating images* section in *Chapter 4, Images and Textures*).

The fastest way of generating textures is by using shaders; see the *A liquify distortion example* section in *Chapter 8, Using Shaders*. Though the example is about texture distortion with Perlin noise, it is simple to change it for generating textures. Using shaders is especially useful while generating really big textures in real time.

A similar technique can be used for generating values for evolving height maps of 3D surfaces (see *The oscillating plane example* section in *Chapter 7, Drawing in 3D*).

Summary

In this appendix we learned the basic principles of using Perlin noise. We have seen examples of creating smooth random motion of objects and generating smooth random textures that evolve with time.

Index

Symbols

W

warpPerspective() 263
warpPerspective(A, B, C, D) function 262
WAV 146
webgl-noise library
  URL 226
windowResized(w, h) function 24
wireframe drawing 197
Wireless LAN. *See* WLAN
WLAN 301

wrapper 312

X

Xcode
  Mac OS, installing with 13, 14

Z

z-buffer 185
ZigBee 301

Thank you for buying
Mastering openFrameworks:
Creative Coding Demystified

About Packt Publishing

Packt, pronounced 'packed', published its first book "*Mastering phpMyAdmin for Effective MySQL Management*" in April 2004 and subsequently continued to specialize in publishing highly focused books on specific technologies and solutions.

Our books and publications share the experiences of your fellow IT professionals in adapting and customizing today's systems, applications, and frameworks. Our solution based books give you the knowledge and power to customize the software and technologies you're using to get the job done. Packt books are more specific and less general than the IT books you have seen in the past. Our unique business model allows us to bring you more focused information, giving you more of what you need to know, and less of what you don't.

Packt is a modern, yet unique publishing company, which focuses on producing quality, cutting-edge books for communities of developers, administrators, and newbies alike. For more information, please visit our website: www.packtpub.com.

About Packt Open Source

In 2010, Packt launched two new brands, Packt Open Source and Packt Enterprise, in order to continue its focus on specialization. This book is part of the Packt Open Source brand, home to books published on software built around Open Source licenses, and offering information to anybody from advanced developers to budding web designers. The Open Source brand also runs Packt's Open Source Royalty Scheme, by which Packt gives a royalty to each Open Source project about whose software a book is sold.

Writing for Packt

We welcome all inquiries from people who are interested in authoring. Book proposals should be sent to author@packtpub.com. If your book idea is still at an early stage and you would like to discuss it first before writing a formal book proposal, contact us; one of our commissioning editors will get in touch with you.

We're not just looking for published authors; if you have strong technical skills but no writing experience, our experienced editors can help you develop a writing career, or simply get some additional reward for your expertise.

Cinder – Begin Creative Coding

ISBN: 978-1-84951-956-4   Paperback: 146 pages

A quick introduction into the world of creative coding with Cinder through basic tutorials and a couple of advanced examples

1. More power – Cinder is one of the most powerful creative coding engines out there and it will be hard to find a better one for your professional grade project

2. Do it fast – each section should not take longer than one hour to complete

3. We give you the tools and it is up to you what you do with them – we won't go into complicated algorithms, but rather give you the brushes and paints so you can paint the way you already know

Cinder Creative Coding Cookbook

ISBN: 978-1-84951-870-3   Paperback: 352 pages

Create compelling animations and graphics with Kinect and camera input, using one of the most powerful C++ frameworks available

1. Learn powerful techniques for building creative applications using motion sensing and tracking

2. Create applications using multimedia content including video, audio, images, and text

3. Draw and animate in 2D and 3D using fast performance techniques

Please check **www.PacktPub.com** for information on our titles

Processing 2: Creative Coding Hotshot

ISBN: 978-1-78216-672-6   Paperback: 266 pages

Learn Processing with exciting and engaging projects to make your computer talk, see, hear, express emotions, and even design physical objects

1. Teach your computer to create physical objects, visualize data, and program a custom hardware controller

2. Create projects that can be run on a variety of platforms, ranging from desktop computers to Android smartphones

3. Each chapter presents a complete project and guides you through the implementation using easy-to-follow, step-by-step instructions

Processing 2: Creative Programming Cookbook

ISBN: 978-1-84951-794-2   Paperback: 306 pages

Over 90 highly-effective recipes to unleash your creativity with interactive art, graphics, computer vision, 3D, and more

1. Explore the Processing language with a broad range of practical recipes for computational art and graphics

2. Wide coverage of topics including interactive art, computer vision, visualization, drawing in 3D, and much more with Processing

3. Create interactive art installations and learn to export your artwork for print, screen, Internet, and mobile devices

Please check **www.PacktPub.com** for information on our titles

33090270R00205

Made in the USA
Lexington, KY
12 June 2014